Preface

Dear Student,

Your journey to achieve success has begun. The CL Educate team brings to you an offering, which incorporates a **theme based learning** that revolves around different concepts with **diverse applications**. The outcome is an enriching learning experience.

Our integrated thematic methodology is driven by latest research, undertaken to enhance learning. Numerous practice exercises and tests have been incorporated to reinforce the conviction in one's ability. Our teaching experience coupled with extensive research has lent credence to our conviction that learning is at its very best when concept based understanding and applications go hand in hand.

To enhance your learning and assimilation of relevant concepts, our attempt has been to identify the basic concepts (or themes) that are required to solve different questions in MBA entrance examinations. Our class exercises integrate the different types of questions which require application of these concepts. Each set of concepts along with relevant question types therefore, forms a module. At the end of each module, we expect the students to:

1) Clearly understand a concept through its repeated application via different question types.
2) Quickly and effectively apply relevant concepts to different question types in a time-bound examination scenario.
3) Develop long-lasting skills by imbibing each concept that is clearly covered through a module.

Armed with the latest tools for success, along with your diligence and positive attitude, you have begun your march towards success. Have faith in yourself!

The woods are lovely, dark and deep,
But I have promises to keep,
And **miles to go before I sleep**,
And **miles to go before I sleep**

(Robert Frost)

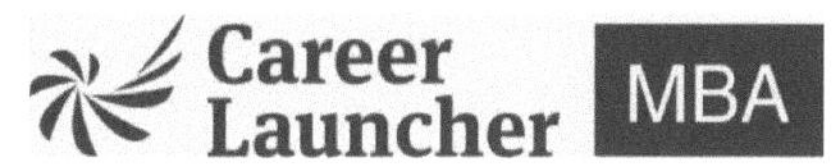

CL MEDIA (P) LTD.

Edition : 2019

© *PUBLISHER*

Typeset by : *CL Media DTP Unit*

Administrative and Production Offices

Published by : **CL Media (P) Ltd.**

A-45, Mohan Cooperative Industrial Area, Near Mohan Estate Metro Station, New Delhi - 110044

Marketed by : **G.K. Publications (P) Ltd.**

A-45, Mohan Cooperative Industrial Area, Near Mohan Estate Metro Station, New Delhi - 110044

For product information :

Visit *www.gkpublications.com* or email to *gkp@gkpublications.com*

How to use this book

1. Before you enter the class read the topics that are to be covered beforehand. This will help you immensely in understanding the concepts when they are taught in the class.

2. After each class, once again go through the relevant topics very carefully, in order to understand the concepts and relate them to what was taught in the class.

3. Do not directly jump to the practice problems but go through the solved examples first as they will enhance your problem solving skills and help in further clarifying concepts.

4. After you are through with the fundamentals and the solved examples, move on to the unsolved problems given at the end of the book and the practice exercises.

5. Start with the Level - I problems as they are easier. Move to Level - II problems, if and only if you have completely understood the concept used in every problem in Level - I. Similarly, move to the Level - III problems after you have completed all the problems in Level - II.

6. Start with Number System, followed by Modern Math. In each exam this sub-category comprises 10-15% of the questions, from the QA section. Being adept in this sub-section can help you maximize your score. Therefore, it is important that you invest sufficient time preparing for it.

Contents

Number System

Learning Objectives

By the end of the chapter, you should be able to
- To understand the classification of numbers.
- Convert recurring numbers to p/q form
- Ascertain if a given number is divisible by any other number
- Explain the meaning and relevance of Factors, Multiples, Factorisation, HCF and LCM and should be able to find the HCF & LCM of given set of numbers
- Application of HCF and LCM.
- Find the number of factors of any given natural number.
- Calculate the remainder when any expression is divided by any natural number.
- Calculate the largest power of a number that divides any given factorial or a number.
- Identify the unit's digit of x^y.
- Understanding the base system.

Did You Know : India's contribution to number system

Not all ancient civilizations based their numbers on a ten base system. In ancient Babylon, a sexagesimal (base 60) system was in use. In India a decimal system was already in place during the Harappan period.
It is generally acknowledged that the concept of zero, crucial to the development of science, is India's contribution to the world, which was given to Europe through the Arabs. The ancient India astronomer Brahmagupta is credited with having put forth the concept of zero for the first time.
Aryabhatta gave the value of π as 3.1416 (circa 500 AD) claiming, for the first time, that it was an approximation.

Number System

What do you mean by the term 'number'?
Number is a symbol representing quantity.
In this chapter of Number System, we are going to learn about various types of numbers.

1. **Real Numbers:** Real numbers are those numbers which you can commonly identify and quantify.
   For example, $-10, -8.33, -1, -0, 1, 2, 5.77$ etc.
   What is a number line?
   Number line is a line on which all the positive and negative numbers can be marked in a sequence. It stretches from negative infinity to positive infinity.

All the numbers which can be represented on the number line are called real numbers.

2. **Imaginary numbers:** Imaginary numbers are those numbers which cannot be represented on the number line. Imaginary numbers are those numbers about which we can just imagine but cannot physically perceive.
   For example: $\sqrt{-1}, \sqrt{-2}$, etc. Square roots of all negative numbers are imaginary.

   $\sqrt{-1}$ is represented by the letter 'i'.
   Combination of Real and Imaginary Numbers are called complex numbers.
   For example, $(2 + 3i)$ is a complex number.
   In this chapter, we will discuss only about the Real Numbers, because imaginary numbers are outside the preview of most management entrance examinations.

Types of Real Numbers

All the real numbers can be divided into two parts. They are Rational numbers and Irrational numbers.

Rational numbers: All the numbers that can be expressed in the form of $\dfrac{p}{q}$, where p & q are integers and $q \neq 0$, are called rational numbers.

For example, -1, 2, $-\dfrac{2}{5}$, 0, 1, 1.7 etc.

We can illustrate the examples mentioned above, in $\dfrac{p}{q}$ form in the following manner:

$$-1 = \dfrac{-1}{1} = \dfrac{p}{q}(q \neq 0)$$

$$\dfrac{2}{5} = \dfrac{p}{q}(q \neq 0), \ 0 = \dfrac{0}{1} = \dfrac{p}{q}(q \neq 0),$$

$$1.7 = \dfrac{17}{10} = \dfrac{p}{q}(q \neq 0)$$

Irrational Numbers: All the numbers that cannot be expressed in the form of $\dfrac{p}{q}$ are called irrational numbers.

For example, $\pi, \sqrt{2}, \left(\sqrt{3}+1\right)$ etc.

Typically they are having non-terminating and non-recurring decimal part.

Rational numbers can also be classified as integers and fractions.

Integers: All the rational numbers which do not have any decimal or fractional part are called integers.
For example, $-3, -2, -1, 0, 1, 2, 3$ etc.
Fractions: All the rational numbers which are in the form $\dfrac{p}{q}$, where $p, q \neq 0$ and p is not a multiple of q are called fractions. The number on the bottom of the fraction is called the denominator and the number on the top of the fraction is called the numerator.

For example, $1.2, \dfrac{5}{2}, \dfrac{4}{3}, 1.7, 0.2$ etc.

In the fraction $\dfrac{5}{2}$, 5 is the numerator and 2 is the denominator.

Fractions are of three types — proper, improper and mixed.

A proper fraction is a fraction whose numerator is smaller than its denominator.

For example, $\dfrac{2}{5}, \dfrac{3}{11}$ are proper fractions.

An improper fraction is a fraction whose numerator is greater than its denominator.

For example, $\dfrac{5}{2}$ and $\dfrac{8}{3}$ are improper fractions.

A mixed fraction is an integer plus a fraction.

For example, $3\dfrac{1}{5}$ or $7\dfrac{1}{3}$. Mixed fraction are sometimes called mixed numbers.

Types of integers

Whole numbers: All the non-negative integers are whole numbers. The set of whole number contains 0, 1, 2, 3, 4 etc.

Natural Numbers: Whole numbers except zero are called natural numbers. Natural numbers start from 1.

Natural Numbers can be classified into different categories based on their property as follows:

a. **On the basis of divisor:**
   Even numbers: All the natural numbers which are multiple of 2 or in other words divisible by 2 are called even numbers such numbers are denoted by 2k (where 'k' is a natural number).
   For example, 2, 4, 6, 8, ……

   Odd Numbers: All the natural numbers which are not a multiple of 2 or in other words which are not divisible by 2 are called odd numbers.
   Such numbers are denoted by $2k \pm 1$. (where 'k' is a natural number)

Facts about odd and even numbers:

odd	$\pm$ odd	= even
odd	$\pm$ even	= odd
even	$\pm$ even	= even
odd	$\times$ odd	= odd
odd	$\times$ even	= even
even	$\times$ even	= even

b. **On the basis of their origin:**
   Prime numbers: All the natural numbers greater than 1 which are only divisible by 1 and the number itself are called Prime Numbers. In others words we can say that each Prime Number is divisible by only two numbers.
   For example, 2, 3, 5, 7, 11, 13, 17, etc.

Career Launcher MBA

Prime numbers are randomly distributed in the set of natural numbers. Interestingly all the prime numbers (greater than 3) can be expressed as $6k \pm 1$, the where 'k' is a natural number.

Composite Numbers: All the natural numbers greater than 1 which are divisible by at least one more number, other than 1 and the number itself are called composite numbers. In other words the natural numbers (except 1) which are not prime are composite numbers. Please note that '1' is neither prime nor composite. Can we say that a composite number is always divisible by 3 or more different natural numbers?

How to find whether a number is prime or not?

For small numbers, we could find by checking, if that number is divisible by any other prime number till that number itself.

But for the larger numbers like, say 631, there is an alternative method.

Step 1: Find the approximate square root of the given number, i.e. 25.

Step 2: Check if any prime number from 2 to 25 divides 631.

The prime numbers from 2 to 25 are 2, 3, 5, 7, 11, 13, 17, 19 and 23. Since, none of these numbers divides 631 exactly, 631 must be a prime number.

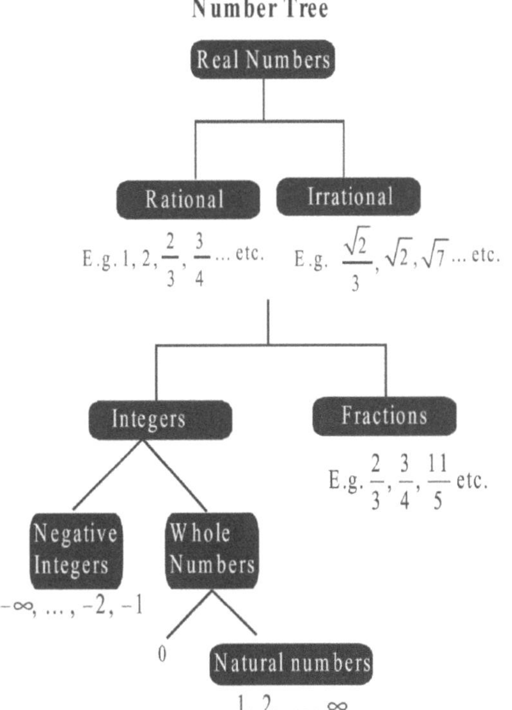

Conversion of recurring decimal into fractions:

What is the $\frac{p}{q}$ form of 0.5555... (also represented as $0.\overline{5}$)?

Let, $x = 0.55555... \Rightarrow 10x = 5.55555...$

$\therefore 9x = 10x - x = (5.5555...) - (0.55555...)$

$\therefore x = \dfrac{5}{9}$

If $x = 0.232323...$

$\Rightarrow 100x = 23.232323...$

$99x = 100x - x$

$= (23.232323...) - (0.232323...) = 23$

$\therefore x = \dfrac{23}{99}$

For a purely recurring number (all digits after decimal point recur) we can identify the procedure as:

The $\frac{p}{q}$ form of a purely recurring number

$$= \frac{\text{The recurring part written once}}{\text{As many 9's as the number of digits in the recurring part}}$$

In the number like 0.14333... i.e. $0.14\overline{3}$

Let, $x = 0.143333...$

$\Rightarrow 100x = 14.3333...$

$\Rightarrow 1000x = 143.3333...$

$\Rightarrow 900x = 1000x - 100x = (143.3333...) = 129$

$\therefore x = \dfrac{129}{900}$

Thus, for any recurring number we can identify the procedure as:

The $\frac{p}{q}$ form of any recurring number

$$= \frac{(\text{The non – recurring and recurring part written once}) - (\text{The non – recurring part})}{\text{As many 9's as the number of digits in the recurring part followed by as many 0's as digits in the non – recurring part.}}$$

 **Example 1**

Express $0.\overline{643}$ as a fraction.

Let x = $0.\overline{643}$

$\Rightarrow 1000x = 643.\overline{643}$ or

$\Rightarrow 1000\,x - x = 643.\overline{643} - 0.\overline{643}$

$\Rightarrow 999x = 643$

$\therefore x = \dfrac{643}{999}$

? Example 2

Arrange the following rational numbers in ascending order: $-\dfrac{7}{10}, -\dfrac{5}{8}, -\dfrac{2}{3}$

✓ Solution

$-\dfrac{7}{10} = -0.7, -\dfrac{5}{8} = -0.625$ and $-\dfrac{2}{3} = -0.666$

Clearly, $-0.7 < -0.666 < -0.625$.

So, $-\dfrac{7}{10} < -\dfrac{2}{3} < -\dfrac{5}{8}$

Operations on Numbers

BODMAS — Order of simplification of expression of numbers

B $\rightarrow$ Bracket
O $\rightarrow$ Of
D $\rightarrow$ Division
M $\rightarrow$ Multiplication
A $\rightarrow$ Addition
S $\rightarrow$ Subtraction

In a given expression of numbers, the above order of operations has to be strictly followed.

For example,

$$\dfrac{3}{5} \text{ of } \dfrac{5}{9} \div \dfrac{1}{5} + \left(1 + \dfrac{1}{3}\right) - \left(\dfrac{29}{7} - \dfrac{8}{7}\right)$$

$$= \dfrac{3}{9} \div \dfrac{1}{5} + \dfrac{4}{3} - \dfrac{21}{7} = 0$$

Quotient and Remainder:
Suppose, we want to divide 57 by 9 we can do it in the following manner:

$$9\,)\,\overline{57}\,(\,6$$
$$\underline{54}$$
$$3$$

$\Rightarrow$ Divisor $)$ Dividend $($ Quotient

$$\overline{\qquad\qquad}$$
Remainder

In the example, given above, 9 is the divisor, 57 is the dividend, 6 is the quotient and 3 is the remainder

Therefore,
Dividend = (Divisor × Quotient) + Remainder.

Note: A number having remainder 'r' when divided by 'd' can be represented as (d × n) + r, where 'n' is a natural number.

? Example 3

If dividend is 15968, quotient is 89 and the remainder is 37, then what is the divisor ?

✓ Solution

$$\text{Divisor} = \left(\dfrac{\text{Dividend} - \text{Remainder}}{\text{Quotient}}\right)$$

$$= \left(\dfrac{15968 - 37}{89}\right) = 179$$

Indices

When a quantity is multiplied by itself a certain number of times, the product thus obtained is called a power of that quantity.

Thus, a^m means 'a' is multiplied 'm' times consecutively and 'm' is called the exponent or the index.

Rules of indices

1. $a^m \times a^n = a^{m+n}$
2. $\dfrac{a^m}{a^n} = a^{m-n}$
3. $(a^m)^n = a^{mn}$
4. $a^{-m} = \dfrac{1}{a^m}$
5. $a^0 = 1$
6. $(ab)^m = a^m b^m$
7. $\sqrt[m]{a} = a^{\frac{1}{m}}$
8. $a^{\frac{p}{q}} = \sqrt[q]{a^p}$

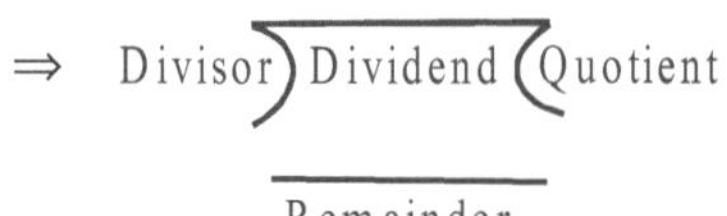

$$\left(x^a\right)^b \neq x^{a^b}$$

$$\left(2^3\right)^2 = 2^{3\times 2} = 2^6 = 64$$

$$2^{3^2} = 2^9 = 512$$

Which would be greater a^b or b^a, given $b > a$? (a and b are both greater than 3)

Surds

Surds are those numbers which are written as the square root or cube root of the numbers. For example $\sqrt{2}, \sqrt{3}$. Please note that $\sqrt{4}$ is not a surd.

General form of the surd is $\sqrt[n]{a}$, where a is called radicand and it must be a positive rational number. n is called the order of the surd and it must be a natural number.

If $\sqrt[n]{a}$ is an integer then it is not a surd.

Properties of Surds:

Addition:

$\sqrt{x} + \sqrt{y}$ cannot be written as a single surd.

However, $\sqrt{x} + \sqrt{x} = 2\sqrt{x}$

For example, $\sqrt{5} + 3\sqrt{5} + 6\sqrt{5} = 10\sqrt{5}$

Multiplication:

$\sqrt{x} \times \sqrt{y} = \sqrt{xy}$

For example, $\sqrt{3} \times \sqrt{27} = \sqrt{81} = 9$

Sometimes multiplication of surds can give rational numbers $\sqrt{3}$ and $\sqrt{27}$ are surds whereas $\sqrt{81}$ is a rational number.

Conjugate surd: To find conjugate of any surd, for example $\sqrt{2} + \sqrt{5}$, write down the same two terms but replace the sign in between.

For example conjugate surd of

$\sqrt{2} + \sqrt{5} = \sqrt{2} - \sqrt{5}$.

Conjugate surds are used to rationalise the denominators of surds.

Rationalisation of surds:

Rationalising is a process where the surd is written in a different form. In which denominator finally contains only rational numbers. Here, in this process we multiply the numerator and denominator by the conjugate surd of denominator.

For example:

$$\frac{2+\sqrt{2}}{2-\sqrt{2}} = \frac{2+\sqrt{2}}{2-\sqrt{2}} \times \frac{2+\sqrt{2}}{2+\sqrt{2}}$$

$$= \frac{4+4\sqrt{2}+2}{2} = \frac{6+4\sqrt{2}}{2}$$

$$= 3+2\sqrt{2}$$

If one is not comfortable and fluent with indices, it would be fruitful to work on the following examples before proceeding ahead:

1. Find the value of $\dfrac{1}{(216)^{-\frac{2}{3}}} + \dfrac{1}{(256)^{-\frac{3}{4}}} + \dfrac{1}{(243)^{-\frac{1}{5}}}$.

2. Simplify: $\left[\dfrac{a^{-1}b^2}{a^2b^{-4}}\right]^7 \div \left[\dfrac{a^3b^{-5}}{a^{-2}b^3}\right]^{-5}$.

3. If $a^x = b$, $b^y = c$, $c^z = a$, then find the value of xyz.

4. Which of the following is equal to $3^{-5} + \dfrac{1}{3^5} + \dfrac{3^{-4}}{3}$?

   (a) 3^{-2} (b) 3^2 (c) 3^{-4}
   (d) 3^4 (e) 3^{-3}

5. Which of the following is equal to $\sqrt{\sqrt[3]{0.000729}}$?

   (a) 0.03   (b) 0.3   (c) 3.0
   (d) 0.003   (e) 0.0003

6. If $a = 2^{44}$ and $b = 2^{22^2}$, then which of the following is true?

   (a) $a > b$ (b) $a < b$ (c) $a = b$

7. If $(6)^{15} \times (10)^5 \times (15)^6 = 2^x \times 3^y \times 5^z$, then find the value of $x + y + z$.

   (a) 26   (b) 52   (c) 42
   (d) 48   (e) 45

8. If $(9)^{3x-5} = (3)^{2x-2}$, then find the value of x.

   (a) 1   (b) 2   (c) 3
   (d) 4   (e) 5

9. Ram was supposed to take the cube root of A and then square of that. Instead of that he took the square of A first and then took the cube root. The answer obtained is
   (a) smaller than expected answer
   (b) larger than expected answer
   (c) same as expected answer
   (d) depends on value of A
   (e) None of these

Divisibility Rules

1. **Divisibility Rule for 2:** If the last digit (units place) of a number is 0, 2, 4, 6, or 8. E.g. 742 is divisible by 2 but 743 is not.

2. **Divisibility Rule for 3:** If the sum of all the digits is divisible by 3, the number is divisible by 3.
   E.g. 1452 (Sum of digits = 12) is divisible by 3 but 763 (Sum of digits = 16) is not divisible by 3. Infact, the remainder when 16 is divided by 3 i.e. 1 will also be the remainder when 763 is divided by 3.

3. **Divisibility Rule for 4 :** If the last two digits of a number are divisible by 4 or are 00, the number is also divisible by 4.
   E.g. 67432 is divisible by 4 (as 32 is divisible by 4) whereas 2146 is not divisible by 4 (as 46 is not divisible by 4). In fact, the remainder when 46 is divided by 4 i.e. 2 will also be the remainder when 2146 is divided by 4. Also note 700 is divisible by 4 as the last two digits are 00.

4. **Divisibility Rule for 5:** If the last digit (unit's digit) is 0 or 5, the number is divisible by 5.
   E.g. 13265 is divisible by 5 whereas 9864 is not.

5. **Divisibility Rule for 6:** A number is divisible by 6 if the number is divisible by both 2 and 3 simultaneously. E.g. 5424 is divisible both by 2 and by 3 (sum of digits = 15) and thus also divisible by 6. However 3332 is not divisible by 6 as it is not divisible by 3.

6. **Divisibility Rule for 8:** If the last three digits of a number are divisible by 8 or are 000, the number is also divisible by 8.
   E.g. 67432 is divisible by 8 (as 432 is divisible by 8) whereas 2148 is not divisible by 8 (as 148 is not divisible by 8). In fact, the remainder when 148 is divided by 8 i.e. 4 will also be the remainder when 2148 is divided by 8. Also note 13000 is divisible by 8 as the last three digits are 000.

7. **Divisibility Rule for 9 :** If the sum of all the digits is divisible by 9, the number is divisible by 9.
   E.g. 658215 (Sum of digits = 27) is divisible by 9 but 763 (Sum of digits = 16) is not divisible by 9.

In fact, the remainder when 16 is divided by 9 i.e. 7 will also be the remainder when 763 is divided by 9.

8. **Divisibility Rule for 11 :** A number is divisible by 11, if the difference between the sum of the digits in the even places and the sum of the digits in the odd places is either 0 or is divisible by 11.
   E.g. 6595149 is divisible by 11 as the difference of $6 + 9 + 1 + 9 = 25$ and $5 + 5 + 4 = 14$ is 11.
   However 27813 is not divisible because sum of digits in the odd places = 13 and the sum of digits in the even places = 8. their difference is neither 0 nor divisible by 11.

If number is divisible by 2 and also by 3, then it is divisible by $2 \times 3 = 6$. Does this mean that if a number is divisible by 4 and also by 6, then the number is divisible by $4 \times 6 = 24$? 12, 36 are divisible by 4 and by 6 but not by 24. Why does the rule hold in case of 2 and 3 but not in case of 4 and 6?

If one is not comfortable with divisibility rules, it would be fruitful to work on the following examples before proceeding ahead:

1. If abc4d is divisible by 4, then what is/are the value/s of d?

2. A number 344ab5 is divisible by both 9 and 25. Find the number. [Given (a + b) < 8]

3. A number 1568X35Y is divisible by 88. What are the values of X and Y?

4. If 'n' is a positive integer greater than 1, then $n(n^2 - 1)$ is always divisible by
   (a) 6   (b) 12   (c) 24
   (d) 48   (e) 96

5. Which of the following numbers is divisible by 99?
   (a) 32373   (b) 37332   (c) 32337
   (d) 23337   (e) None of these

6. What is the remainder when 9876532123 is divisible by 9?
   (a) 1   (b) 2   (c) 3
   (d) 4   (e) 5

7. The number aaaaaa, where a is a single digit natural number, is divisible by
   (a) 11   (b) 13   (c) 143
   (d) 7   (e) All of these

8. How many numbers between 300 and 500 are divisible by both 8 and 5?
   (a) 3   (b) 4   (c) 5
   (d) 6   (e) 7

9. What is the remainder when 78X85Y868 is divided by 8?
   (a) 1   (b) 3   (c) 4
   (d) 7   (e) 5

10. If the number 786P86Q is divisible by 8 and 9 both, then values of P and Q are
    (a) 4, 9   (b) 6, 4   (c) 8, 6
    (d) 6, 8   (e) None of these

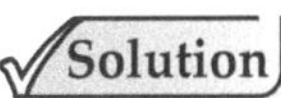 **Example 1**

What is the least number that must be subtracted from 2000 to get a number which is exactly divisible by 17?

Solution

On dividing 2000 by 17, we get 11 as remainder.
∴ Required number to be subtracted = 11.

Example 2

What is the least number that must be added to 3000 to obtain a number exactly divisible by 19?

Solution

On dividing 3000 by 19, we get 17 as remainder.
∴ Number to be added = (19 − 17) = 2.

Example 3

Find the number which is nearest to 3105 and exactly divisible by 21.

Solution

On dividing 3105 by 21, we get 18 as remainder.
∴ Number to be added to 3105 is (21 − 18) = 3.
∴ 3108 is the required number.

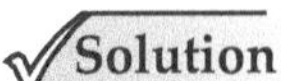 **Example 4**

A number when divided by 342 gives a remainder 47. When the same number is divided by 19, what would be the remainder?

Solution

On dividing the given number by 342, let k be the quotient and 47 the remainder.
Then, number = 342k + 47
= [(19 × 18k) + (19 × 2 + 9)]
= [19 (18k + 2) + 9]
∴ The given number when divided by 19 gives (18k + 2) as quotient and 9 as remainder.

Alternative method:

342 is a multiple of 19, divide the remainder by the second dividend to get the remainder. 47 when divided by 19 gives 9 as remainder.

Factorial
The continued product of first n natural number is called 'n factorial' and is denoted by n! or ⌊n
n! = 1 × 2 × 3 × … × (n − 1) × n
E.g. 6! = 1 × 2 × 3 × 4 × 5 × 6 = 720
By definition 0! = 1.

Cyclicity

Unit's place digit of a Number:
The digit at the unit's place of any number is the remainder when the number is divided by 10.

For example, lets consider the number 364. The remainder when 364 is divided by 10 is 4. Hence, '4' is the unit's digit of the number 364.

To find the unit's digit of a number which is the product of two or more numbers, multiply the unit's digit of the numbers and find the unit's digit of the resultant number.

For example, 19 × 64, the product of the units digit of 19 and 64 is 36 and the unit's digit of 36 is 6, hence the unit's digit of 19 × 64 is 6.

Unit's digit of higher powers of any Number:

$2^1 = 2$	$2^2 = 4$	$2^3 = 8$	$2^4 = 16$
$2^5 = 32$	$2^6 = 64$	$2^7 = 128$	$2^8 = 256$
$2^9 = 512$	$2^{10} = 1024$	$2^{11} = 2048$	$2^{12} = 4096$

We can see that the unit's digit of 2^1, 2^5, 2^9 is 2, units digit of 2^2, 2^6, 2^{10} is 4, units digit of 2^3, 2^7, 2^{11} is 8 and units digit of 2^4, 2^8, 2^{12} is 6.
Therefore, after every four powers of 2, the units digit of the number starts repeating. Thus we say that cyclicity of unit's digit of higher powers of 2 is 4.

Similarly the digits whose cyclicity is 4 are 2, 3, 7 and 8. The digits whose cyclicity is 2 are 4 and 9.

Any power of numbers whose units digit 1, 5 or 6 always ends in 1, 5 and 6 respectively.

For example,
$$11^2 = 121, 25^2 = 625 \text{ and } 16^2 = 256.$$

 *Remainders are cyclic but ideally avoid finding remainder using their cyclic property. It can be very cumbersome.*

The cyclicity of the digits are as follows:

Digit	Cyclicity
0, 1, 5 and 6	1
2, 3, 7 and 8	4
4 and 9	2

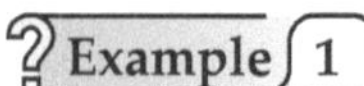 **Example 1**

Find the unit's digit of a. 3^{57} and b. 13^{59}.

 **Solution**

a. The cyclicity of 3 is 4. Hence, $\dfrac{57}{4}$ gives the remainder 1. So the last digit of 3^{57} is same as the last digit of 3^1, i.e. 3.

b. The number of digits in the base will not make a difference to the last digit. It is the last digit of the base which decides the last digit of the number itself. For 13^{59}, we find $\dfrac{59}{4}$ which gives a remainder 3.

So the last digit of 13^{59} is same as the last digit of 3^3, i.e. 7.

Example 2

Find the unit's digit of the product $7^{23} \times 8^{13}$.

Solution

Both 7 and 8 exhibit a cyclicity of 4.
7^{23} ends with the same last digit as 7^3, i.e. 3.
8^{13} ends with the same last digit as 8^1, i.e. 8.
Hence, the product of the two numbers would end with the same last digit as that of 3×8, i.e. 4.
The unit's digit of any number N is also the remainder when N is divided by 10.

For example, the unit's digit of the number 1176 is 6. Remainder when 1176 is divided by 10 is also 6.

Ten's place digit of a number:
The tens place digit of a number can be found out by dividing the number by 100.

For example, consider the number 11872.
When 11872 is divided by 100, the quotient is 118 and the remainder is 72.

Finding the last two digits of a number

We are going to discuss the way to calculate the last two digits of any power of a natural number. Given below are the cases in which these problems will fall:

I. For a number A^k, where A ends in 0 and k is a natural number

II. For a number A^k, where A ends in 5 and k is a natural number

III. For a number of the form $(2 \times m)^{40k+1}$, where m is an odd natural number not ending in 5 and k is a natural number

IV. For all the remaining cases

I. **For a number Ak, where A ends in 0 and k is a natural number**
When a natural number A ends in 0, A^k will always end in 00 where k is a natural number greater than 1.

II. **For a number Ak, where A ends in 5 and k is a natural number**
When a natural number A ends in 5, A^k will always end in 25 where k is a natural number greater than 1.

III. **For a number of the form $(2 \times m)^{40k+1}$, where m is an odd natural number not ending in 5 and k is a natural number**
When the condition given above is satisfied, the last two digits of $(2 \times m)^{40k+1}$
= the last two digits of $(2 \times m + 50)$.

Example 1

Find the last two digits of 26^{81}.

Solution

$26 = 2 \times 13$, which is of the form $2 \times$ odd number. Also, the exponent is $40 \times 2 + 1$, which is of the form $40k + 1$. Hence, the last two digits of 26^{81} = the last two digits of $(26 + 50) = 76$.

Example 2

Find the last two digits of 94^{561}.

Solution

$94 = 2 \times 47$, which is of the form $2 \times$ odd number. Also, the exponent is $40 \times 14 + 1$, which is of the form $40k + 1$. Hence, the last two digits of 94^{561} = the last two digits of $(94 + 50) = 44$.

IV. For all the remaining cases

For all the remaining cases, the last two digits of $A^{40k + r}$ will be equal to the last two digits of A^r.

Example 3

Find the last two digits of 72^{842}.

Solution

$72^{842} = 72^{40 \times 21 + 2}$. Now we can say that the last two digits of 72^{842} will be equal to the last two digits of 72^2. Hence, the last two digits of 72^{842} are 84.

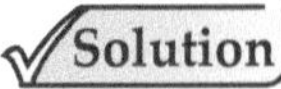

Example 4

Find the last two digits of 47^{900}.

Solution

$47^{900} = 47^{40 \times 22 + 20}$. So the last two digits of 47^{900} will be same as the last two digits of 47^{20}.

The table on the right shows the last two digits of a few powers of 47. Using them,

$$47^{20} = 47^{16} \times 47^4$$
$$= 21 \times 81 = 01.$$

$47^1 = 47$
$47^2 = 09$
$47^4 = (09)^2 = 81$
$47^8 = (81)^2 = 61$
$47^{16} = (61)^2 = 21$

Hence, the last two digits of 47^{900} are 01.

Example 5

Find the last two digits of 52^{873}.

Solution

$52^{873} = 52^{40 \times 21 + 33}$. So its last two digits will be same as the last two digits of 52^{33}.

The table on the right shows the last two digits of a few powers of 52. Using the table,

$$52^{33} = 52^{32} \times 52^1$$
$$= 96 \times 52 = 92.$$

Hence, the last two digits of 52^{873} are 92.

$52^1 = 52$
$52^2 = 04$
$52^4 = (04)^2 = 16$
$52^8 = (16)^2 = 56$
$52^{16} = (56)^2 = 36$
$52^{32} = (36)^2 = 96$

How to make the table of powers of a two-digit natural number

We just need to remember the squares of the first 25 natural numbers to make the table of powers of a number. What we need to look at is the absolute difference of the number from either 50 or 100, whichever is closer.

Study the following examples to understand the process:

Last two digits of 47^2.
The absolute difference of 47 from 50 is 3 and last two digits of 3^2 are 09. So the last two digits of 47^2 are also 09.

Last two digits of 81^2.
The absolute difference of 81 from 100 is 19 and last two digits of 19^2 are 61. So the last two digits of 81^2 are also 61.

Last two digits of 61^2.
The absolute difference of 61 from 50 is 11 and last two digits of 11^2 are 21. So the last two digits of 61^2 are also 21.

Last two digits of 52^2.
The absolute difference of 52 from 50 is 2 and last two digits of 2^2 are 04. So the last two digits of 52^2 are also 04.

Last two digits of 56^2.
The absolute difference of 56 from 50 is 6 and the last two digits of 6^2 are 36. So the last two digits of 56^2 are also 36.

Last two digits of 36^2.
The absolute difference of 36 from 50 is 14 and the last two digits of 14^2 are 96. So the last two digits of 36^2 are also 96.

Last two digits of 88^2.
The absolute difference of 88 from 100 is 12 and the last two digits of 12^2 are 44. So the last two digits of 88^2 are also 44.

Factors, Multiples and Factorisation

For any relation of the type $x \times n = y$ (x, y, n are all natural numbers), x is called a factor of y and y is called a multiple of x. E.g. Since $4 \times 9 = 36$, 4 is a factor of 36 and 36 is a multiple of 4. But since there does not exist any natural number n such that $4 \times n = 38$, 4 is not a factor of 38 and 38 is not a multiple of 4.

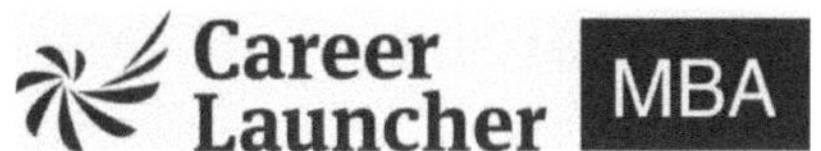

Factors :

a is a factor of b if there exists a relation such that a × n = b, where n is any natural number. Basically it means that a is a factor of b if a can completely divide b.

Thus factors of a number are all those numbers that completely divide the given number.

Needless to say, 1 is a factor of all numbers as 1 × b = b. Also it would be obvious that factor of a number cannot be greater than the number (infact the largest factor will be the number itself). Thus the factors of any number will lie between 1 and the number itself (both inclusive) and thus are limited.

If number of factors of a number are limited, is there a way to find the number of factors of a given number ? Yes indeed there is a process and we will see it shortly.

Multiples :

a is a multiple of b if there exists a relation of the type b × n = a. Thus the multiples of 6 are 6 × 1 = 6, 6 × 2 = 12, 6 × 3 = 18, 6 × 4 = 24, and so on.

We can easily deduce that the smallest multiple will be the number itself and the number of multiples would be infinite.

To understand what multiples are, let's just take an example of multiples of 3.

The multiples are 3, 6, 9, 12, ... so on. We find that every successive multiple appears as the third number after the previous.

So if one wishes to find the number of multiples of 6 less than 255, we could arrive at the number through $\dfrac{255}{6} = 42$

(and the remainder 3).

The remainder is of no consequence to us. So in all there are 42 multiples.

If one wishes to find the multiples of 36, find $\dfrac{255}{36} = 7$

(and the remainder is 3).
Hence, there are 7 multiples of 36.

Factorisation :

It is the process of splitting any number into the form, where it is expressed only in terms of the most basic prime factors.

For example, $12 = 2^2 \times 3^1$. 12 is expressed in the factorised form in terms of its basic prime factors. This is the factorised form of 12.

 *If any number x does not have a factor between 2 and $\sqrt{x}$, it is a prime number. Why do we check for factors just till $\sqrt{x}$ and why not beyond that till x?*

It is possible to find the number of factors of a composite number without listing all those factors, from its factorised form.

Take 12 for instance, it can be expressed as $12 = 2^2 \times 3^1$.

The factors of 12 are:
$(2^0 \times 3^0), (2^0 \times 3^1), (2^1 \times 3^0), (2^1 \times 3^1), (2^2 \times 3^0), (2^2 \times 3^1), .$

Here the powers of 2 can be one of (0, 1, 2) and the powers of 3 can be one of (0, 1). So the total possibilities if you take the two as combination is 3 × 2 = 6. Each combination of the powers of 2 and 3 gives a distinctly different factor. Hence, since there are 6 different combinations of the powers of 2 and 3, there are 6 distinctly different factors of 12.

In general, for any composite number, C, which can be expressed as $C = a^m \times b^n \times c^p \times \ldots$, where a, b, c, … are all prime factors and m, n, p are positive integers, the number of factors is equal to $(m + 1)(n + 1)(p + 1) \ldots$

 *The factors of 12, in increasing order are 1, 2, 3, 4, 6, 12 i.e. a total of 6 factors We see that,*

product of 1st and 6th = 12
product of 2nd and 5th = 12
product of 3rd and 4th = 12.
Same is the case with factors of any number, e.g. factors of 24 are 1, 2, 3, 4, 6, 8, 12, 24
What happens if the number of factors is odd?
Can you extend this logic to determine which numbers will have odd number of factors.

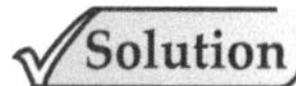

Example 1

Find the total number of factors of 576.

Solution

The factorised form of 576 is (24 × 24)
$= (2^3 \times 3)(2^3 \times 3) = (2^6 \times 3^2)$.
So the total number of factors is $(6 + 1)(2 + 1) = 21$.

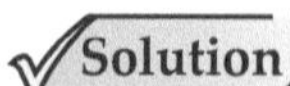

Example 2

If $N = 12^3 \times 3^4 \times 5^2$ then find the total number of even factors of N.

Solution

The factorised form of N is $(2^2 \times 3^1)^3 \times 3^4 \times 5^2$
$\Rightarrow 2^6 \times 3^7 \times 5^2$.

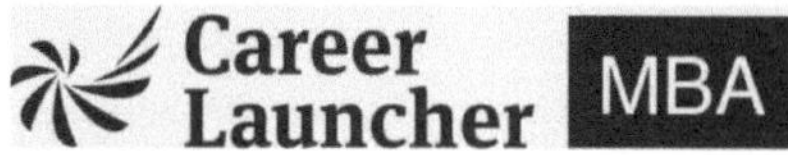

Hence, the total number of factors of N is $(6 + 1)(7 + 1)(2 + 1) = 7 \times 8 \times 3 = 168$.

Some of these are odd multiples and some are even. The odd multiples are formed only with the combination of 3s and 5s. So, the total number of odd multiples is $(7 + 1)(2 + 1) = 24$.

Therefore, the number of even multiples $= 168 - 24 = 144$.

 **Example 3**

A number N when factorised can be written as $N = p_1^4 \times p_2^3 \times p_3^7$. Find the number of perfect squares which are factors of N.

(The three prime numbers p_1, p_2, $p_3 > 2$.)

Solution

In order that the perfect square divides N, the powers of p_1 can be 0, 2, or 4, i.e. 3.

Powers of p_2 can be 0, 2, i.e. 2.

Powers of p_3 can be 0, 2, 4 or 6, i.e. 4.

Hence, a combination of these powers gives $3 \times 2 \times 4$, i.e. 24 numbers.

So there are 24 perfect squares that divide N.

Example 4

In how many ways can 36 be written as a product of two natural numbers.

Solution

$36 = 2^2 \times 3^2$ and will have $3 \times 3 = 9$ factors. The factors in increasing order are 1, 2, 3, 4, 6, 9, 12, 18, 36. Product of factors equidistant form the centre will be 36. Thus there are $4 + 1 = 5$ ways of writing 36 as a product of 2 natural numbers viz 1×36, 2×18, 3×12, 4×9 and 6×6.

 *We all know that prime numbers have just two factors. Can you identify which numbers will have exactly 3 factors?*

 *x, a & b are natural numbers. If x is divisible by a & b each then find a condition for which x is definitely divisible by a × b?*

 *Along a long corridor there are 100 doors marked as 1, 2, 3, ... 100. As you know the doors can be in two states - open or close. Initially all doors are closed. Person number 1 changes the state of all doors that are a multiple of 1 i.e. basically all doors. Person number 2 then changes the state of all doors that are a multiple of 2. Person number 3 then changes the*

state of all doors that are multiple of 3 and so on till the person number 100 changes state of door number 100. Now how many doors are closed.

Hint: *Try to find for a particular door, how many persons will change the state?*

 *How many multiples of x exists from a to b (both inclusive) when*
a.   neither a nor b is a multiple of x
b.   one of a and b is a multiple of x.
c.   both a and b are multiples of x.

HCF and LCM

HCF and LCM are one of the basic concepts of mathematics which have variety of applications in our daily life.

Understanding HCF:

Let us take two numbers 15 and 20

Factors of 15 are = 15, 5, 3, 1

Factors of 20 are = 20, 10, 5, 1

To find the HCF, check what is the highest factor common to both the numbers. We can see that it is 5.

Understanding LCM:

Let us take two numbers 15 and 20

Multiples of 15 = 15, 30, 45, 60, 75, 90, 105, 120, 135, etc.

Multiples of 20 = 20, 40, 60, 80, 100, 120, 140, etc.

To find the LCM of these two numbers, check what is the lowest number common to the sets of multiples of both the numbers. We can find that it is 60.

How to find HCF of two numbers?

There are two methods:

    a.   Division method.

    b.   Prime factorisation method.

a.   **Division method:**

In this method Divisor becomes dividend and remainder becomes

Divisor and this process continues till one can divide. The last divisor is your answer.

Now, try to understand the following illustrative examples.

To find to HCF of 15 & 20

$$15\overline{)\,20\,}(1$$
$$\underline{-15}$$
$$5\overline{)\,15\,}(3$$
$$\underline{-15}$$
$$0$$

So HCF of 15 and 20 is 5.

To find the HCF of 20 & 28.

$$\begin{array}{r} 20\overline{)28}(1 \\ \underline{-20} \\ 8\overline{)20}(2 \\ \underline{-16} \\ 4\overline{)8}(2 \\ \underline{-8} \\ 0 \end{array}$$

So the HCF of 20 and 28 is 4.
To find the HCF of 20, 28 & 45
We have seen that HCF of 20 & 28 is 4.
So, we will take HCF of 4 & 45.

$$\begin{array}{r} 4\overline{)45}(11 \\ \underline{-44} \\ 1\overline{)4}(4 \\ \underline{-4} \\ 0 \end{array}$$

So, HCF of 20, 28 & 45 is 1.

b. **Prime factorization method:**
    Write the number in terms of prime factors.
    $20 = 2^2 \times 5^1 \times 3^0$
    $45 = 2^0 \times 3^2 \times 5^1$

    For finding out their, HCF, take the lowest power of all prime numbers. The HCF of 20 and 45 is $2^0 \times 3^0 \times 5^1$ i.e. 5.

How to find LCM of two or more numbers?

There are two methods
   i. **Division method**
   ii. **Prime factorisation method**

i. **Division method**
    LCM of 18, 27 and 30.

$$\begin{array}{r|rrr} 3 & 18, & 27, & 30 \\ \hline 3 & 6, & 9, & 10 \\ \hline 2 & 2, & 3, & 10 \\ \hline & 1, & 3, & 5 \end{array}$$

LCM $= 3 \times 3 \times 3 \times 2 \times 5 = 270$

ii. **Prime factorisation method**
    Take two numbers 20 and 45.
    Write the numbers in terms of prime factors.
    $20 = 2^2 \times 5^1 \times 3^0$
    $45 = 2^0 \times 3^2 \times 5^1$

    For finding out their LCM, take the highest power of all prime numbers. The LCM of 20 and 45 is $2^2 \times 3^2 \times 5^1$ i.e. 180.

 *If the LCM of a, b, c is x and that of d, e is y, would the LCM of x, y be the LCM of a, b, c, d, e.*

If the HCF of a, b, c is x and that of d, e is y, would the HCF of x, y be the HCF of a, b, c, d, e.

Example 1

Find the HCF of 24 and 72.

Solution

$24 = 2 \times 2 \times 2 \times 3$
$72 = 2 \times 2 \times 2 \times 3 \times 3$
HCF $= 2 \times 2 \times 2 \times 3 = 24$
Similarly, you can find the HCF of sets containing more than 2 numbers.

Example 2

Find the largest number that can exactly divide 513, 783 and 1107.

Solution

Required number = HCF of 513, 783 and 1107.
Now, $513 = 3^3 \times 19$, $783 = 3^3 \times 29$, $1107 = 3^3 \times 41$
$\therefore$ HCF $= 3^3 = 27$. Hence, the required number is 27.

Example 3

Find the least number exactly divisible by 12, 15, 20 and 27.

Solution

Required number = LCM of 12, 15, 20, 27
$\therefore$ LCM $= 3 \times 4 \times 5 \times 9 = 540$

Example 4

Find the least number which when divided by 6, 7, 8, 9 and 12 leave the same remainder 1 in each case.

Solution

Required number = (LCM of 6, 7, 8, 9, 12) + 1
$\therefore$ LCM $= 3 \times 2 \times 2 \times 7 \times 2 \times 3 = 504$
Hence, required number = (504 + 1) = 505

Example 5

The traffic lights at three different road-crossings, change after every 24 sec, 72 sec and 120 sec respectively. If they all change simultaneously at 10 : 54 : 00 hr, then at what time will they change next simultaneously?

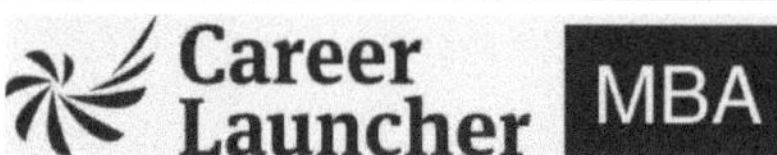

Solution

Interval of change = LCM of (24, 72, 120) sec = 360 sec. The lights will change simultaneously after every 360s, i.e., 6 min 00 sec. So, they will change next simultaneously at 11 : 00 : 00 hrs.

Example 6

How many three-digit numbers are divisible by 6?

Solution

There are 16 numbers before 100 which are divisible by 6.

There are 166 numbers before 999 which are divisible by 6. Total three-digit numbers divisible by 6 are 166 − 16 =150.

Important results

If two numbers a and b are given, and their LCM and HCF are L and H respectively, then L × H = a × b.

LCM and HCF of fractions

$$\text{LCM of fractions} = \frac{\text{LCM of numerators}}{\text{HCF of denominators}}$$

$$\text{HCF of fractions} = \frac{\text{HCF of numerators}}{\text{LCM of denominators}}$$

Example:

Find the LCM and HCF of $\dfrac{25}{12}$ and $\dfrac{35}{18}$.

$$\text{LCM} = \frac{\text{LCM of 25 and 35}}{\text{HCF of 12 and 18}} = \frac{175}{6}$$

$$\text{HCF} = \frac{\text{HCF of 25 and 35}}{\text{LCM of 12 and 18}} = \frac{5}{36}$$

Note: Do not directly apply the formula if the fractions are not in their simplest form.

Example 7

The HCF of two numbers is 11 and their LCM is 693. If one of the numbers is 77, then find the other number.

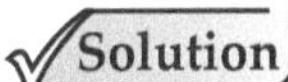

Solution

The other number $= \dfrac{11 \times 693}{77} = 99$

Application of HCF and LCM

I. **Of the type when would clocks strike together simultaneously**

Example 1

Two cyclists were preparing for the Olympics in the Yamuna Velodrome. The first cyclist takes 10 min to cover one full round, whereas the second takes 9 min (no wonder, India has never won an Olympics medal in cycling!!). Assuming that they have enough stamina to last as long as your answer, find when would they both be together again at the starting block if they both started simultaneously?

Solution

This might seem to be a problem on time, speed and distance. Yes, but the logic is based on LCM concept. The first cyclist would be at the starting point at every multiple of 10 min. The second would be at the starting point at every multiple of 9 min. If both of them have to be together at the starting block again, then a multiple of 10 min must be equal to a multiple of 9 min. So they would be together at the starting block for the first time after LCM(10, 9) = 90 min.

II. **Least number leaving remainder 'r' in each case when divided by 'x', 'y' and 'z'.**

Example 2

There is a number greater than 3 which when divided by 4, 5 and 6 always leaves the same remainder 3. Find the following such numbers which satisfy the given condition.
a. Smallest
b. Second smallest
c. Largest number less than 1000

Solution

a. The smallest number which, when divided by 4, 5 and 6, leaves the remainder 3 in each case is LCM(4, 5, 6) + 3 = 63.
b. All numbers which are of the form {LCM(4, 5, 6)} N + 3 always satisfy the property that when divided by 4, 5 or 6, it leaves a remainder 3.
   [N is any natural number.]
   The numbers that satisfy this property are 63, 123, 183, ..., so on.
   Hence, the second smallest number is 123.

c. To solve the problem, we have to find the largest number of the form $60N + 3$, that is less than 1000. The largest such number is 963.

> Thus least number leaving remainder 'r' in each case when divided by 'x', 'y' and 'z' = (LCM of x, y, z) + r. The series of such numbers will be (LCM of x, y, z) × n + r.

III. **Least number leaving remainder (x – a), (y – a) and (z – a) when divided by x, y and z respectively.**

Find the smallest number which when divided by 5, 6, and 8 leaves remainder 2, 3, and 5?

Here we see that the (divisor - remainder) is same for all divisors, in this case 3. The following number line will make the solution to this problem very transparent.

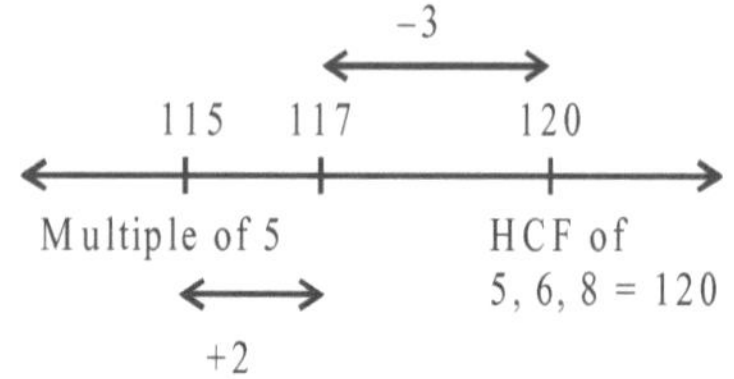

Hence, the smallest number is
LCM (5, 6, 8) – 3 = 117.

> Thus least number leaving remainder (x – a), (y – a) and (z – a) when divided by x, y, z respectively = (LCM of x, y, z) – a.
> The series of such numbers will be (LCM of x, y, z) × n – a.

10 thieves steal x gold coins and escape. While all are asleep, 2 thieves wake up and divide the coins between them and find 1 coin extra. Just then a 3rd thief wakes up. So the 3 thieves divide all the coins among them and find 2 coins extra. Again just then a 4th thief wakes up. Again on dividing the coins among them, 3 coins are extra. This continues till the 10th thief wakes up and on dividing the coins among them 9 coins are extra. What is the least value of x?

In the above problem, if on each division, 1 coin was left, what would have been the least value of x?

If the HCF of A, B and C is x, is the HCF of A —B, B —C and A —C also x? If not always, under what condition will it be equal to x?

IV. **Of the type largest measure that measures x, y and z exactly.**

? **Example** 3

A rectangular piece of cloth has dimensions 16m × 6m. What is the least number of equal squares that can be cut out of this cloth such that no cloth is wasted?

✓ **Solution**

We want to find out the length of the edge of the square piece (largest) to be cut out of this cloth in such a way that no piece of cloth is left over. In other words, we have to find the largest number which completely divides the dimensions 16m and 6m (i.e. the HCF of 16 and 6). This would give the side of the largest squares that satisfy the given conditions.
HCF(16m, 6m) = 2m.
There will be $16 \div 2 = 8$ divisions along the length and $6 \div 2 = 3$ divisions along the breadth. Therefore, total number of square pieces = $8 \times 3 = 24$.
This is the minimum number of squares that can be cut out of this piece of cloth without wasting any part of the cloth.

? **Example** 4

In a school 437 boys and 342 girls have been divided into classes, so that each class has the same number of students and no class has boys and girls mixed. What is the least number of classes needed?

✓ **Solution**

We should have the maximum number of students in a class.
So we have to find HCF(437, 342) = 19.
HCF is also the factor of difference of the numbers.

$$\therefore \text{Number of classes} = \frac{437}{19} + \frac{342}{19} = 23 + 18$$

$$= 41 \text{ classes.}$$

What is the smallest number which when divided by 7, 8, 9 leaves a remainder of 2, 4, 6 respectively?

A set of number with HCF x can be assumed to be $x \times a$, $x \times b$, $x \times c$ ... where a, b and c are co-prime number.

V. Miscellaneous

Example 5

Manas and his girlfriend met at Nehru Place after a long time. Manas stays at Vivek Vihar and his girlfriend stays in Gurgaon. Both of them commute by bus. They reached the bus stop, and got to know that a bus had left just then for each of their destinations. Neither wanted to leave the other alone at the bus stop. If the frequency of buses to Gurgaon was 7 min and that to Vivek Vihar was 11 min, then
a. how long would they wait at the bus stop?
b. how many buses going to their destinations would each one decide not to board?

Solution

a. Since both the buses had left for the two destinations just then, their respective buses would be at the bus stop simultaneously after LCM(7, 11) = 77 min.
b. In 77 min, the total number of buses for Gurgaon

that would have come to the bus stop is $\dfrac{77}{7} = 11$.

Similarly, the total number of buses to Vivek Vihar

that would have arrived at the bus stop is $\dfrac{77}{11} = 7$.

Hence, Manas and his girlfriend decided not to board 6 and 10 buses respectively.

Example 6

Mr Tamatar buys some apples at 5 per rupee from one trader, and a similar quantity at 7 per rupee from another trader. He mixes both the varieties, and sells the whole at 6 per rupee. What is the profit or loss percentage that he makes?

Solution

Assume that Mr Tamatar buys LCM(5, 6, 7) = 210 apples of each variety. Amount spent on the first

variety = $\dfrac{210}{5}$ = ₹42.

Amount spent on the second variety = $\dfrac{210}{7}$

= ₹30.
Total amount spent = ₹42 + ₹30 = ₹72.
Now the total (210 + 210) = 420 apples are sold at 6 per rupee.

The total revenue = $\dfrac{420}{6}$ = ₹70.

Hence, the loss = ₹72 – ₹70 = ₹2.

Loss percentage = $\dfrac{2}{72} \times 100 = 2\dfrac{7}{9}\%$.

 *A difficult one but good for clarity.*
How many sets of two numbers will have the LCM as
$p_1^a \times p_2^b$ *where p_1 and p_2 are prime numbers and a and b are natural numbers.*

Highest power dividing a factorial

Example 1

What is the highest power of 2 that divides 20! completely?

Solution

$20! = 1 \times 2 \times 3 \times 4 \times ... \times 18 \times 19 \times 20 = 1 \times (2^1) \times 3 \times (2^2) \times 5 \times (2^1 \times 3^1) \times 7 \times (2^3) \times ...$ so on.
In order to find the highest power of 2 that divides the above product, we need to find the sum of the powers of all 2s in this expansion.

All numbers that are divisible by 2^1 will contribute

1 to the exponent of 2 in the product $\dfrac{20}{2^1} = 10$.

Hence, 10 numbers contribute 2^1 to the product. Similarly, all numbers that are divisible by 2^2 will contribute an extra 1 to the exponent of 2 in the

product, i.e. $\dfrac{20}{2^2} = 5$.

Hence, 5 numbers contribute an extra 1 to exponents. Similarly, there are 2 numbers that are divisible by 2^3 and 1 number that is divisible by 2^4.

Hence, the total 1's contributed to the exponent of 2 in 20! is the sum of $(10 + 5 + 2 + 1) = 18$.
Hence, group of all 2s in 20! gives $2^{18} \times (N)$, where N is not divisible by 2.
If 20! is divided by 2^x, the maximum value of x = 18.

Example 2

What is the highest power of 5 that divides 100!?

Solution

Calculating contributions of the different powers of

5, we have $\dfrac{100}{5^1} = 20$, $\dfrac{100}{5^2} = 4$.

Hence, the total contribution to the power of 5 is 24. Or the number 100! is divisible by 5^{24}.

Thus the approach to find the highest power of x dividing y! is $\left[\dfrac{y}{x}\right]+\left[\dfrac{y}{x^2}\right]+\left[\dfrac{y}{x^3}\right]......$, where $[\ ]$ represents just the integral part of the answer ignoring the fractional part and x is a prime number.

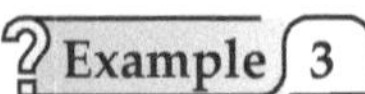 **Example 3**

What is the highest power of 6 that divides 9!?

 **Solution**

If we go by the above process, then we will get the answer as $\dfrac{9}{6}=1$ and $\dfrac{9}{6^2}=0$.

Thus answer we get is 1 which is wrong. True there is just one multiple of 6 from 1 to 9 but the product $2 \times 3 = 6$ and also $4 \times 9 = 36$, can further be divided by 6. Thus, when the divisor is a composite number find the highest power of its prime factors and then proceed. In this case 9! can be divided by 2^7 and 3^4 and thus by 6^4 (In this case we need not have checked power of 2 as it would definitely be greater then that of 3).

 *What is the least value of x such that $\dfrac{60!}{x}$ will be a odd number?*

 *Factorials of 0 to 4 have no trailing zeros (at the end) Factorials of 10 to 14 have 2 trailing zero and 15 to 19 have 3 and so on...*
While factorials of 20 to 24 have 4 trailing zeros, those of 25 to 29 have 6 (and not 5) trailing zeros. Similarly while factorial of 45 to 49 have 10 trailing zeros, factorials of 50 to 54 have 12 trailing zeros. How many more trailing zeros would 625! have compared to 624!

Remainders

Consider two numbers x and y which when divided by 6 leave remainder 3 and 2 respectively. What will be the remainder when each of the following is divided by 6 :

a. x + y   b. x − y   c. x × y   d. y − x   e. y^5

a.   x can be written as 6m + 3 and y can be written as 6n + 2. Thus, x + y = 6(m + n) + 5, i.e. (x + y) is a multiple of 6 plus 5 and hence when divided by 6 will leave remainder of 5 (basically 3 + 2).

b.   Similarly x − y = 6(m − n) + 1, i.e. when (x − y) is divided by 6, the remainder is 1(basically 3 − 2)

c.   x × y = (6m + 3)(6n + 2) = 36mn + 12m + 18n + 6 = 6(6mn + 2m + 3n + 1) i.e. it is a multiple of 6 and remainder is 0.

By now it will be clear that whatever is the operation that is performed on the divisors, the same operation has to be performed on the remainders of respective divisors to get the remainder.

d.   However when we try to do the same for y − x, the remainder will be 2 − 3 = −1.

What does this mean? Basically it means that the expression y − x will boil down to 6p − 1 = 6(p − 1) + 5 i.e. the remainder is 5. Visually it can be understood from the following number line.

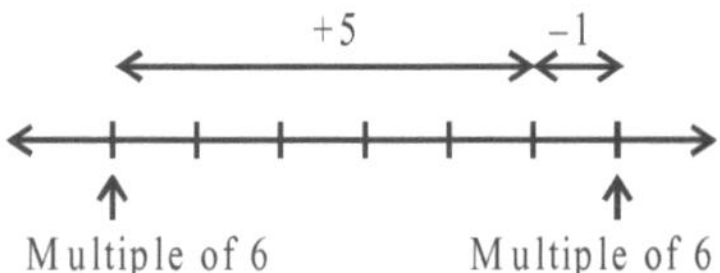

Thus, if remainder, calculated by performing the same operation on respective remainders as that performed on divisors, is negative, all one needs is to reduce the divisor by this negative value to get the effective remainder.

e.   In this case the expression is y × y × y × y × y and the remainder will be $2 \times 2 \times 2 \times 2 \times 2 = 32$.

But we know the remainder when a number is divided by 6 has to lie between 0 to 5 (both inclusive). This can be understood as the expression would evaluate to 6p + 32 which is nothing but 6(p + 5) + 2 i.e. the remainder is 2.

Thus, if one gets a remainder higher than the divisor, just divide this value with the divisor again and find the remainder.

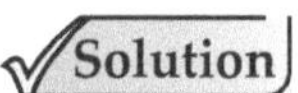 **Example 1**

What is the remainder if 7^{25} is divided by 6?

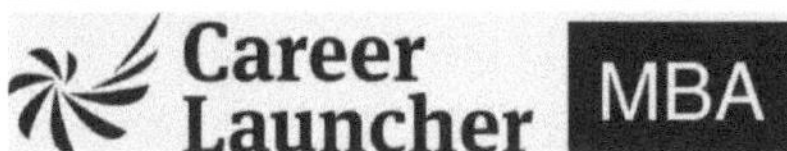 **Solution**

$$\frac{7^{25}}{6} = \frac{7 \times 7 \times 7 ...7(25\text{ times})}{6}$$

7 divided by 6 leaves remainder 1.
Thus, 7^{25} when divided by 6 will leave remainder $1 \times 1 \times 1 ... (25\text{ times}) = 1$.

Method 2: Using binomial expansion
$(7)^{25}$ can be written $(6 + 1)^{25}$.
Using binomial theorem, $(a + b)^n$ can be written as $aN + b^n$ i.e. a multiple of a plus b^n .
Thus, $(6 + 1)^{25} = 6N + 1^{25} = 6N + 1$.
Thus, this number when divided by 6 will leave remainder 1.

Career Launcher MBA

Using binomial expansion, if we have to find the remainder when y^n is divided by x, express y^n as $(ax + b)^n$ where a is any natural number and b should ideally be −1, 0, 1.

$(ax + b)^n = Nx + b^n$

Thus, if b is −1, 0, 1, b^n can easily be evaluated irrespective of the value of n and the remainder can be found out.

Example 2

What is the remainder if 7^{25} is divided by 4?

Solution

7^{25} can be written $(8 - 1)^{25}$.

There are 26 terms in all. All the first 25 terms are divisible by 8, hence also by 4. The last term is $(-1)^{25}$.

Hence, $(8 - 1)^{25}$ can be written as $8X - 1$ or $4Y - 1$ (where $Y = 2X$). So $4Y - 1$ when divided by 4 leaves the remainder 3.

Example 3

What is the remainder if 3^{45} is divided by 8?

Solution

3^{45} can be written as $9^{22} \times 3$. 9 can be written as $(8 + 1)$. Hence, any power of 9 can be written $8N + 1$. In other words, any power of 9 is 1 more than a multiple of 8. Hence, $(8N + 1) \times 3$ leaves the remainder 3 when divided by 8.

Example 4

What is the remainder when $14^{15^{16}}$ is divided by 5?

Solution

$14^{15^{16}} = (15 - 1)^{odd} = 15n + (-1)^{odd}$, i.e. a (multiple of 5) − 1. Thus when divided by 5 the remainder will be −1, i.e. 4.

144 divided by 60 leaves a reminder of 24. But 144 and 60 have common factor. Lets remove the common factor and see how it affects the remainder. If we divide 144 and 60 by 2, we have 72 divided by 30 and remainder is 12 (original remainder 24 divided by 2)

If we divide 144 and 60 by 3, we have 48 divided by 20 and remainder is 8 (original remainder 24 divides by 3) If we divide 144 and 60 by 4 we have 36 divided by 15 and remainder is 6 (again 24 divided by 4)

Euler's Totient function and the Fermat-Euler theorem

If N is a natural number such that $N = a^p b^q c^r ...$ where a, b, c etc are prime numbers, then Euler's Totient function is given by

$$\phi(N) = N\left(1 - \frac{1}{a}\right)\left(1 - \frac{1}{b}\right)\left(1 - \frac{1}{c}\right) ...$$ Here $\phi(N)$ is the number of numbers less than and prime to N. If P is some other natural number which is prime to N, then the remainder when $P^{\phi(N)}$ is divided by N is 1.

E.g. since $45 = 3^2 \times 5$, $\phi(45) = 45\left(1 - \frac{1}{3}\right)\left(1 - \frac{1}{5}\right) = 24$.

It means that there are 24 numbers which are less than and prime to 45. As 11 is prime to 45, the remainder when 11^{24} is divided by 45 is 1.

If N is prime in the theorem given above, then $\phi(N) = N\left(1 - \frac{1}{N}\right) = N - 1$. So we can say that if N is a prime number and P is some other number which is prime to N, then the remainder when P^{N-1} is divided by N is 1.

Wilson's Theorem

If P is a prime number, then the remainder when $(P - 1)!$ is divided by P is $P - 1$.

E.g. the remainder when 46! is divided by 47 is 46.

Further, since $46! = 45! \times 46$, the remainder when 45! is divided by 47 should be 1.

Base System

The number system that we work in is called the 'decimal system'. This is because there are 10 digits in the system 0-9. There can be alternative systems that can be used for arithmetic operations. Some of the most commonly used systems are: binary, octal and hexadecimal.

These systems find applications in computing.

Binary system has 2 digits: 0, 1.

Octal has 8 digits: 0, 1, 2, ..., 7.

Hexadecimal has 16 digits: 0, 1, 2, ..., 9, A, B, C, D, E, F.

After 9, we use the letters to indicate digits. For instance, A has a value 10, B has a value 11, C has a value 12, ... so on in all base systems.

The counting sequences in each of the systems would be different though they follow the same principle.

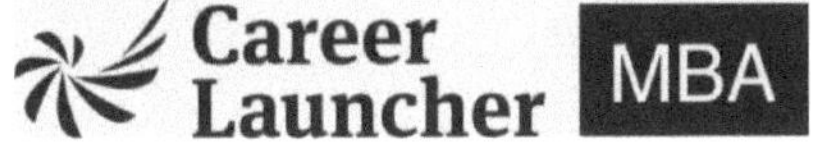

For instance, the sequence of the first few numbers on the number line starting with 0 is:

Decimal	Binary	Octal	Hexadecimal
0	0	0	0
1	1	1	1
2	10	2	2
3	11	3	3
4	100	4	4
5	101	5	5
6	110	6	6
7	111	7	7
8	1000	10	8
9	1001	11	9
10	1010	12	A
11	1011	13	B
15	1111	17	F
16	10000	20	10
17	10001	21	11
18	10010	22	12

(a)   Conversions of numbers from:
   (1) base 10 (decimal system) to some other base system,
   (2) some other base system to decimal system (base 10).
(b)   Arithmetic operations like
   (1) addition
   (2) subtraction

Base System works like a odometer of your vechicle. (that which record cumulative mileage) Whenever a wheel starts repeating the cycle, it increases the wheel on the left by 1.

a.   Conversion

12 in decimal system coincides with 14 in the octal system. How do we identify this equivalence?

1.   Conversion from base 10 to any other base

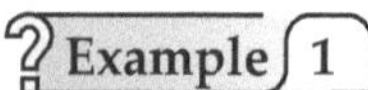

Convert $(122)_{10}$ to base 8 system.

Solution

$$8 \mid 122$$
$$8 \mid 15 \text{ - } 2$$
$$8 \mid 1 \text{ - } 7$$
$$0 \text{ - } 1$$

The number in decimal is consecutively divided by the number of the base to which we are converting the decimal number. Then list down all the remainders in the reverse sequence to get the number in that base.

So here $(122)_{10} = (172)_8$.

Example 2

Convert $(270)_{10}$ to hexadecimal system.

Solution

$$16 \mid 270$$
$$16 \mid 16 \text{ - } (14)\ E$$
$$16 \mid 1 \text{ - } 0$$
$$0 \text{ - } 1$$

The solution is not 1014. It is 10E, where E = 14 in the hexadecimal system.

Example 3

Convert $(1987.725)_{10} \rightarrow (\ )_8$

Solution

First convert non-decimal part into base 8.

$$8 \mid 1987$$
$$8 \mid 248 \quad 3$$
$$8 \mid 31 \quad 0$$
$$8 \mid 3 \quad 7$$
$$3$$

$\therefore (1987)_{10} = (3703)_8$
$(0.725)_{10} \rightarrow (\ )_8$
Multiply $0.725 \times 8 = 5.8 \qquad 5$
$0.8 \times 8 = 6.4 \qquad 6$
$0.4 \times 8 = 3.2 \qquad 3$
$0.2 \times 8 = 1.6 \qquad 1$
$0.6 \times 8 = 4.8 \qquad 4$
Keep on accomplishing integral parts after multiplication with decimal part till the decimal part is zero.
$\therefore (.725)_{10} = (.56314 ...)$
$\therefore (1987.725)_{10} = (3703.56314...)$

2.   Conversion from any other base to decimal system

Example 4

Convert $(231)_8$ into decimal system.

In $(231)_8$, the value of the position of each of the numbers (as in decimal system) is:

$1 = 8^0 \times 1$

$3 = 8^1 \times 3$

$2 = 8^2 \times 2$

[This is equivalent to 10^0 (unit's); 10^1 (ten's); 10^2 (hundred's) places in the decimal system.

Hence, $(231)_8 = (8^0 \times 1 + 8^1 \times 3 + 8^2 \times 2)_{10}$

$= (1 + 24 + 128)_{10} = (153)_{10}$

Example 5

Convert $(761.56)_8 \rightarrow (\quad)_{16}$

Solution

In such conversion which are standard form conversions, it is easier to convert in this manner. $(761.56)_8 \rightarrow (\quad)_2 \rightarrow (\quad)_{16}$ Converting every digit in base 8 to base 2, $(111110001.101110)_2 \rightarrow (1F1.B8)_{16}$

Example 6

Convert $(1AB)_{16}$ into decimal system.

Solution

$(1AB)_{16} = 16^2(1) + 16^1(A) + 16^0(B)$

$= 16^2(1) + 16^1(10) + 16^0(11)$

$= 256 + 160 + 11 \Rightarrow 427$

Hence, $(1AB)_{16} = (427)_{10}$

In order to convert from one base x to any other base y (x, y $\neq$ 10), we can convert using the intermediate step of decimal system.

Example 7

What is the value of the following sum if both the numbers are in octal system?

```
  2 4 7
+ 3 4 5
-------
```

Solution

There are two methods.

a. Convert both the numbers into decimal numbers. Add the decimal numbers, and convert back this sum into octal system.

b. Direct addition:

Step 1: $7 + 5 = 12$ in decimal.

It is equal to 14 in octal.

Hence, keep back 4 and carry over 1 as in decimal addition.

Step 2: $4 + 4 + 1 = (9)_{10} = (11)_8$

Keep back 1 and carry over 1.

So on final sum =

```
    2 4 7
  + 3 4 5
  -------
  (6 1 4)₈
```

Example 8

Subtract $(247)_8$ from $(345)_8$.

```
  3 4 5
− 2 4 7
-------
```

Solution

Step 1: 5 is less than 7. So borrow 1 from the previous digit. Since we are working in octal system, if we borrow 1, then 5 become $5 + 8 = 13$. Subtract 7 from 13, i.e. 6.

```
  3 4 5
− 2 4 7
-------
      6
```

Step 2: Since we borrow 1, the 4 in the first row has now become 3. Borrow 1 from 3. So it now becomes $3 + 8 = 11$.

Subtracting 4 from it, we get 7.

Hence,
```
  3 4 5
− 2 4 7
-------
  0 7 6
```

For multiplication and division of numbers in other base systems, convert them into decimal system; and after doing the arithmetic operation, convert the result back into the respective base system.

Perfect square:

A number is said to be a perfect square if and only if the square root of that number is an integer.

Some important facts about perfect squares

1. The square of an even number is always even.
2. The square of an odd number is always odd.
3. Square of an integer cannot end in 2, 3, 7 or 8.
4. The square of a real number (negative or positive) is always positive.

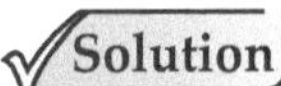

Some important formulae used in simplification:

1. $(a + b)^2 = a^2 + b^2 + 2ab$
2. $(a - b)^2 = a^2 + b^2 - 2ab$
3. $(a + b)^2 = (a - b)^2 + 4ab$
4. $a^2 - b^2 = (a - b)(a + b)$
5. $a^3 + b^3 = (a + b)(a^2 - ab + b^2)$
6. $a^3 - b^3 = (a - b)(a^2 + ab + b^2)$
7. $a^2 + b^2 = \dfrac{1}{2}[(a + b)^2 + (a - b)^2]$

Example 1

Simplify $\dfrac{527 \times 527 \times 527 + 183 \times 183 \times 183}{527 \times 527 - 527 \times 183 + 183 \times 183}$.

Solution

The given expression is equivalent to

$$\frac{(527)^3 + (183)^3}{(527)^2 - 527 \times 183 + (183)^2}$$

We know that, $\dfrac{a^3 + b^3}{a^2 - ab + b^2} = a + b$

In the above example a = 527 and b = 183

∴ The expression is equal to $(527 + 183) = 710$

Example 2

Simplify $\left(\dfrac{(614 + 168)^2 - (614 - 168)^2}{614 \times 168} \right)$.

Solution

Expression $\dfrac{(a + b)^2 - (a - b)^2}{ab} = \dfrac{4ab}{ab} = 4$

Example 3

Find the square of (1605).

Solution

$(1605)^2 = (1600 + 5)^2$
$= (1600)^2 + 2 \times 1600 \times 5 + (5)^2$
$= 2560000 + 16000 + 25 = 2576025$

Example 4

Find the value of $896 \times 896 - 204 \times 204$.

Solution

$a^2 - b^2 = (a + b)(a - b)$ (where a = 896 and b = 204)
$= (896 + 204)(896 - 204)$
$= 1100 \times 692 = 761200$

Example 5

Evaluate $(57)^2 + (43)^2 + 2 \times 57 \times 43$.

Solution

$(a^2 + b^2 + 2ab) = (a + b)^2 = (57 + 43)^2 = 100^2$
$= 10000$

Example 6

Simplify $(81)^2 + (68)^2 - 2 \times 81 \times 68$.

Solution

$(81 - 68)^2 = 13^2 = 169$

Example 7

Evaluate $(313 \times 313 + 287 \times 287)$.

Solution

$a^2 + b^2 = \dfrac{1}{2}\left[(a + b)^2 + (a - b)^2\right]$

(where a = 313 and b = 287)

$= \dfrac{1}{2}\left[(313 + 287)^2 + (313 - 287)^2\right]$

$= \dfrac{1}{2}\left[(600)^2 + (26)^2\right] = 180338$

Rules of counting numbers

1. Sum of first n natural numbers $= \dfrac{n(n+1)}{2}$
2. Sum of first n odd numbers $= n^2$
3. Sum of first n even numbers $= n(n + 1)$
4. Sum of the squares of first n natural numbers $= \dfrac{n(n+1)(2n+1)}{6}$
5. Sum of the cubes of first n natural numbers $= \left[\dfrac{n(n+1)}{2}\right]^2$

Career Launcher MBA

Fundamentals of Numbers

If square root of 15 = 3.88, then find the square root of $\dfrac{5}{3}$.

Solution

$$\sqrt{\dfrac{5}{3}} = \sqrt{\dfrac{5 \times 3}{3 \times 3}} = \dfrac{\sqrt{15}}{3} = \dfrac{3.88}{3} = 1.29$$

Example 9

A four-digit number divisible by 7 becomes divisible by 3, when 10 is added to it. Find the largest such number.

Solution

Largest four-digit number is 9999. On dividing 9999 by 7, we get 3 as remainder. Largest four-digit number divisible by 7 is 9996.
Let $9996 - x + 10$ be divisible by 3.
By trial and error, we find that $x = 7$
Required number $= (9996 - 7) = 9989$

Example 10

A three-digit number 4a3 is added to another three-digit number 984 to give the four-digit number 13b7 which is divisible by 11. Find the value of $(a + b)$.

Solution

$$\begin{array}{r} 4\,a\,3 \\ +\,9\,8\,4 \\ \hline 1\,3\,b\,7 \\ \hline \end{array}$$

Here $a + 8 = b$, if 13b7 is divisible by 11 then $(7 + 3) - (b + 1) = 0$; $b = 9$ and $a + 8 = b$ or $a = 1$.
Hence, $a + b = 9 + 1 = 10$.

Example 11

Of the three numbers, the sum of the first two is 45; the sum of the second and the third is 55; and the sum of the third and thrice the first is 90. Find the third number.

Solution

Let the numbers be x, y and z. Then, $x + y = 45$; $y + z = 55$ and $3x + z = 90$.
$y = 45 - x$ and $z = 55 - y = 55 - (45 - x) = 10 + x$

$\therefore 3x + 10 + x = 90$ or $x = 20$
$y = (45 - 20) = 25$ and $z = (10 + 20) = 30$
$\therefore$ Third number $= 30$

Miscellaneous

Example 1

There is a two-digit number ab in decimal system. Both a and b are natural numbers. What is the value of ab?

Solution

From the basic counting rules, we know that a is in ten's place and b is in unit's place. Hence, the value of ab is $10(a) + b$.

Example 2

A two-digit number ab is added to the number formed by reversing the original digits. If their sum is divisible by 11, 9 and 2, find the number of pairs of (a, b).

Solution

The value of the number $= 10a + b$.

The number formed by reversing the digits $= ba$.

Value of this number $= 10b + a$.

Sum of the two numbers $= 11a + 11b$
$$= 11(a + b).$$

Now if the sum is divisible by 11, 9, 2, it means that $(a + b)$ must be divisible by both 9 and 2.

Hence, $a + b = 18$. So it means $a = b = 9$.

The original number is 99.

So there is only one pair of (a, b).

Example 3

In a two-digit prime number, if 18 is added, we get another prime number with reversed digits. How many such numbers are possible?

Solution

Let a two-digit number be ab.
$10a + b + 18 = 10b + a$
or $-9a + 9b = 18$
or $b - a = 2$
Only two numbers '13' and '79' satisfy the given condition.

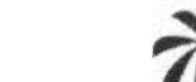

Example 4

If a a and a − b = 2, then find a, b.

    +b b
    ─────
    c c 0

Solution

These problems involve basic number theory rules.
a. aa + bb = 11(a + b)
b. aa, bb are two-digit numbers.
    Hence, their sum cannot exceed 198.
    So c must be 1.
c. Hence, cc0 = 110.
    This implies a + b = 10 or a = 6 and
    b = 4.

Such problems are part of a category of problems called alphanumerics.

Example 5

If   a 3 b , then find a, b, c if each one of them is

  (−)   a c
  ─────────
      a a 9

distinctly different digit.

Solution

a. Since the first digit of (a 3 b) is written as it is after subtracting ac from it. It means that there is no carry over from a to 3.
b. There must be a carry over from 3 to b, because if no carry over is there, it means 3 − a = a

$$\Rightarrow 2a = 3 \Rightarrow a = \frac{3}{2}$$

which is not possible because a is a digit. For a carry over 1, 2 − a = a

$$\Rightarrow a = 1$$

c. Now 10 + b − c = 9

$$\Rightarrow b - c = -1$$

It means b and c are consecutive digits (2, 3), (3, 4), ..., (8, 9).

Example 6

    1 a 4   Find S, T, b.
    x 3 b
    ─────────
    8 C 8
   S 7 2
  ───────────
  T 5 d 8

Solution

Let us consider 1a4 × 3 = S72.

a × 3 results in a number ending in 6.
As 16 and 26 is ruled out, a is 2.
Thus, S = 3, T = 4.
Now 1 a 4 × b = 8C8; b = 2 or 7
Again 2 is ruled out because in that case, product would be much less than 800.
∴ b = 7.

Example 7

How many numbers from 100 to 300 are divisible by
a. 5 and 6?   b. 5 or 6?   c. 5 or 6 or 10?

Solution

a. All numbers that are divisible by both 5 and 6 are multiples of LCM (5, 6) = 30.

From 0 to 300, there are $\dfrac{300}{30} = 10$

numbers that are divisible by 30.

From 0 to 99, there are $\dfrac{99}{30} = 3$

numbers that are divisible by 30.

Hence, from 100 to 300, there are (10 − 3) = 7 numbers that are divisible by both 5 and 6.

b. NM (5 or 6) = NM (5)+ NM (6) − NM (5 and 6)
    [Note: NM is the number of multiples.]
    So number of multiples of 5 or 6 from 100 to 300

is $\left\{\left[\dfrac{300}{5}\right]-\left[\dfrac{99}{5}\right]\right\}+\left\{\left[\dfrac{300}{6}\right]-\left[\dfrac{99}{6}\right]\right\}-$

$\left\{\left[\dfrac{300}{30}\right]-\left[\dfrac{99}{30}\right]\right\} = 41+34-7 = 68$

c. The number of multiples of 5 or 6 or 10 would remain the same, since all the multiples of 10 have already been included as multiples of 5.

Example 8

How many times would 3 appear in all the numbers from 255 to 432 (both inclusive)?

Let's take from 255 to 454, and then deduct the relevant number of 3s?

Unit's place: Every tenth number will have a 3 appearing once. So from 255 to 454, out of the 200 numbers there would be 20 3s.

Ten's place: Every hundred numbers would have 10 3s in the ten's place. So from 255 to 454, there would be twenty 3's.

Hundred's place: There are hundred numbers in 300s which have a 3 in the hundred's place. So total number of 3s = 20 + 20 + 100 = 140.

From 433 to 454, there are 10 3s.

Hence, there are in all 140 − 10 = 130 3s from 255 to 432.

Example 9

What is the sum of all digits that appear from 1 to 100?

There are 100 numbers in all. 1 to 9 would appear in the unit's place 10 times. 1 to 9 would appear in the ten's place 10 times. 1 would appear in the hundred's place once.

Hence, the sum of all the digits = $(1 + 2 + 3 + ... + 9)(20) + 1 = 45 \times 20 + 1 = 901$.

Example 10

The value of a number is five times the sum of its digits. Find the number.

The number can only be a two-digit number.

Let the number be XY.

Then the value of the number = $10X + Y$

$= 5(X + Y)$. So $5X = 4Y$.

Since X and Y are integers, the only possible values are $X = 4$ and $Y = 5$.

[Why cannot it be a three-digit number?]

{Explanation: Sum of three-digits does not exceed 27. So the three-digit number cannot be greater than 135. Hence, the first digit has to be 1. Also five times the sum of the digits cannot exceed 95, which itself is a two-digit number.}

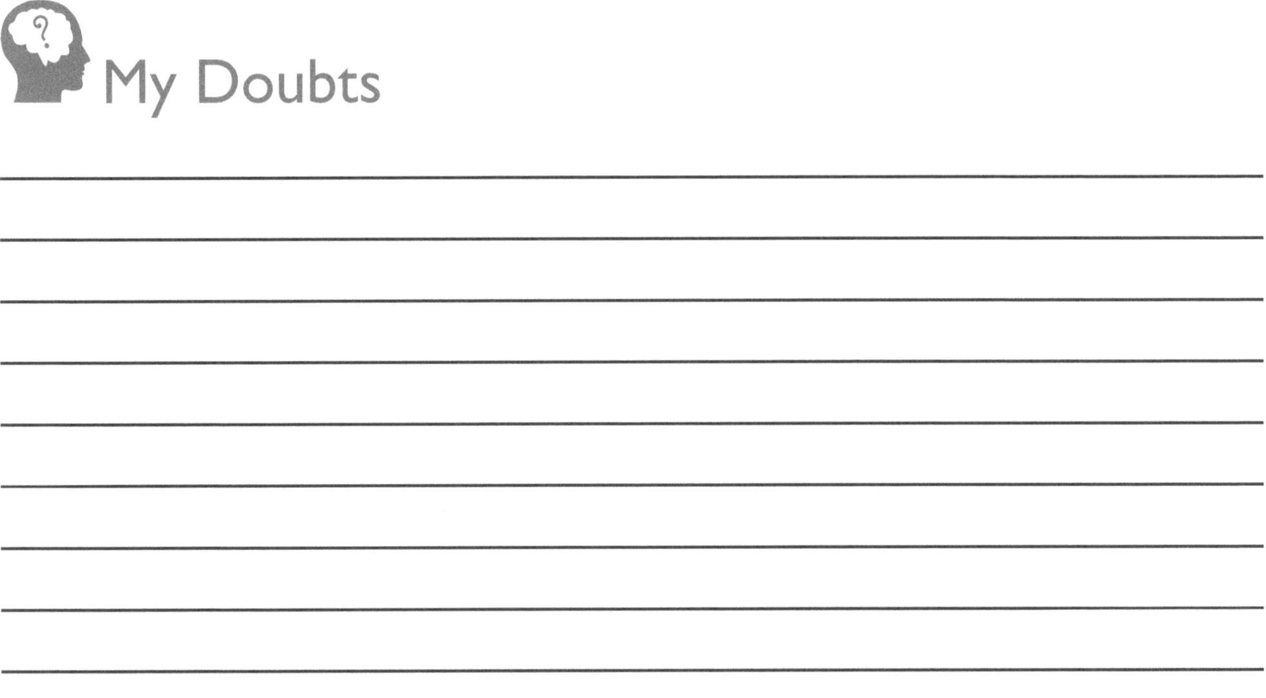

My Doubts

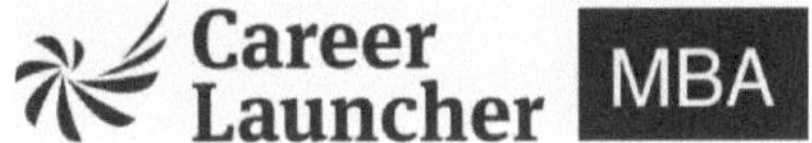

2 Practice Exercises

Introduction

There are 7 practice exercises out of which 2 are of level-1, 3 are of level-2 and 2 are of level 3 apart from Non MCQ Questions to Strengthen you fundamentals. While solving the exercises make sure that each and every concept is understood properly.

Problems for Practice (Non MCQ)

Level 1

1. Convert 4.32323232... into a $\dfrac{p}{q}$ form.

2. What least number must be added to 8961 to make it exactly divisible by 84?

3. Find the nearest integer to 1834 which is exactly divisible by both 12 and 16.

4. Which is larger, 5^7 or 7^5?

5. If the HCF of 2 numbers is 48, and the HCF of 2 other numbers is 36, what is the HCF of all the four numbers?

6. If there are 8 numbers whose HCF has to be found by the division method, how many steps would be needed in order to find it?

7. What is the smallest number less than 10,000 which when increased by 3 is divisible by 21, 25, 27 and 35?

8. Two athletes were making rounds in a stadium. The first one takes 7 min to complete one full round and the second one takes 4 min to complete one full round. When will they meet for the first time at the start if both of them started simultaneously?

9. What is the remainder when 732^{732} is divided by 27?

10. A number when divided by 5 and 7 successively, leaves the remainders 2 and 4 respectively. Find the remainder when   the same number is divided by 35.

11. What is the last digit of the number $(729)^{59}$?

12. What is the last digit of the number $(123)^7$?

13. How many prime factors are there of the number $(12)^{43} \times (34)^{48} \times (2)^{57}$?

14. A gardner planted saplings in such a way that every row had as many saplings as every column. If in all there were 729 trees, then how many saplings were there in each row?

15. In the previous problem, if he decides to plant one new sapling between every two saplings, how many new saplings would he have to plant?

16. A wealthy businessman gave away $\dfrac{1}{2}$ of his wealth to the first son; $\dfrac{1}{3}$ of the remaining to his second son; $\dfrac{1}{2}$ of the remaining to his third son; and the rest to his

---

  Career Launcher MBA **Fundamentals of Numbers**

youngest son. If the youngest son got ₹6x lakh, where x is an integer, then what is the minimum wealth that the businessman had?

17. The product of 3 positive integers is 36. If one knows the sum of the 3 numbers, but is not able to uniquely identify the numbers, what is the sum of the 3 numbers?

18. Find the largest number that can be formed using four 3's.

19. Convert from decimal into base 12.
    (a) $(54)_{10}$ (b) $(142)_{10}$

20. Convert into decimal from some other base.
    (a) $(110011)_2$ (b) $(ABCD)_{16}$

21. Find the following.
    (a) $(457)_{12} - (249)_{12}$ (b) $(347)_8 - (734)_8$

Level 2

22. The sum of 2 integers X and Y is 19. If $4X + 6Y = 9$, then what are the values of X and Y?

23. The ratio between a two-digit number and the sum of the digits of that number is 4 : 1. If the digit in the unit's place is 3 more than the digit in the ten's place then, find the number.

24. Which is the largest three-digit number which when divided by 6 leaves the remainder 5, and when divided by 5 leaves the remainder 3?

25. What is the largest four-digit number that if added to 2748, makes the sum divisible by 15, 20, 21, 23, 35?

26. Three people A, B and C can finish a job in 6, 7, 8 days respectively. If all the three work on the job simultaneously, how long will it take to complete the job?

27. A number N when divided by 5 leaves the remainder 1, and when divided by 6 leaves the remainder 5. Find the smallest positive N.

28. A number when divided by 145 leaves the remainder 58. What is the remainder, if it is divided by 29?

29. What will be the remainder when $86 \times 293 \times 4919$ is divided by 17?

30. Find the remainder when $7^{13} + 1$ is divided by 6.

31. What is the remainder when 10^{200} is divided by 8?

32. Find the remainder if 30^{40} is divided by 17.

33. On dividing a certain number by 5, 7 and 8 successively, the remainders are 2, 3 and 4 respectively. What would be the remainders if the order of the division is reversed?

34. Find the number of factors of a number $N = 2^3 \times 3^2 \times 5^3$.

35. How many factors are there of the expression $6^{10} \times 7^{17} \times 11^{27}$? How many of them are prime?

36. The factorised form of a number $N = 2^4 \times 3^2 \times 5^4$. Find the number of unique sets of a and b such that $ab = N$.

37. If PQRS = (PQR) ×(QS), where P, Q, R, S stand for distinct decimal digits, then find the value of Q.

38. What is the value of $\sqrt{12345678987654321}$?

39. Simplify:
$$\sqrt{5+\sqrt{5}+\sqrt{3+\sqrt{5}+\sqrt{14+\sqrt{180}}}}$$

40. x, y are two different digits. If the sum of the two-digit numbers formed by using both the digits is a perfect square, then find the value of x + y.

Level 3

41. The sum of the digits of a two-digit number is 8. If the digits are reversed, then the number is decreased by 54. Find the number.

42. How many numbers are there between 2000 and 3000, which are divisible by 3 or 4?

43. What is the value of (X + Y) if 789432X64Y is divisible by both 8 as well as 9? X and Y being single digit numbers.

44. The sum of 2 numbers is 144. Their HCF is 24. Find the numbers.

45. What is the remainder in $\dfrac{2^{643}}{96}$?

46. Prove that $(244)^{1500} - 1$ is divisible by 1001. (1001 can be written in factorised form as $7 \times 11 \times 13$.)

47. Find the last digit of the number $7^{11^{22^{33}}}$.

48. Find the number of zeroes at the end of the product
(a) of first 100 multiples of 10.
(b) $5 \times 10 \times 15 \times 20 \times 25 \times 30 \times 35 \times 40 \times 45$.

49. Which is the greatest power of
(a) 6 that divides the number 34! exactly?
(b) 12 that divides the number 34! exactly?

50. What is the total number of positive integer solutions that satisfy the equation $4x + 3y = 120$?

51. A man is climbing a staircase in either steps of 5 or 3. If the flight of the stairs has 100 steps in all, then how many times did he take steps of 5?

52. A boy multiplied 423 by a certain number and obtained 65589 as his answer. If only the 5s are wrong, what is the correct product?

53. The letters in the alphanumatic addition are all different. Find the numbers indicated in codes. All the letters are digits from 0 to 9.

```
    F O R T Y
(+)   T E N
(+)   T E N
  ---------
  S I X T Y
```

54. You choose any 17 numbers from the set of all successive natural numbers $A = \{1, 2, 3, ..., 32\}$. If you find the sum of any pair of numbers from these 17 numbers, there would always be one pair that adds up to P. Find P.

55. Starting with 1, if all positive integers are written one after the another, what is the 10,000th digit that will be written?

56. There are 5 numbers: 20, 22, 23, 25 and 27. How many distinctly different sums would you get taking 2 at a time?

57. Convert:
(a) $(13.421)_{10} = (\ )_8$
(b) $(13.421)_8 = (\ )_{10}$
(c) $(1100011010)_2 = (\ )_8$
(d) $(3221301)_4 = (\ )_{16}$

58. Meera offers her prayers to Lord Krishna in a temple everyday. She offers $\frac{1}{4}$ of the number of flowers she has in the first temple, $\frac{1}{4}$ of the remaining in the second temple, $\frac{1}{4}$ of the rest in the third temple and $\frac{1}{2}$ of the rest in the fourth temple. One day, she was left with flowers that were less than 60 and more than 20.
(a) What is the minimum number of flowers she carried to the first temple?
(b) What is the maximum number of flowers that she carried to the first temple?

 My Doubts

____

____

____

____

1. The LCM of two numbers is 5200 and their HCF is 40. If one of the numbers is 520, then the other number is
   (a) 240   (b) 560   (c) 400
   (d) 320   (e) 520

2. The value of factorial zero (i.e. 0!) is
   (a) 0   (b) $\dfrac{1}{2}$ (c) 8
   (d) 1   (e) Not definied

3. Zero is counted as
   (a) Whole number
   (b) Positive Integer
   (c) Natural number
   (d) Both a positive integer and a negative integer
   (e) Both (a) and (d)

4. Which of the following options contains all irrational numbers only?
   (a) $\sqrt{4}, 8$

   (b) $\dfrac{3}{2}, \sqrt{4}, -7, -\dfrac{9}{8}$

   (c) $\pi, (\pi - 1), \left(3 + \sqrt{2}\right), -\sqrt{3}$

   (d) $\dfrac{3}{2}, \sqrt{4}, -\dfrac{7}{\sqrt{2}}, -\dfrac{9}{8}$

   (e) All of these

5. Find the digit in the units place in the product $254 \times 361 \times 159 \times 18$.
   (a) 1   (b) 6   (c) 4
   (d) 8   (e) 2

6. The value of $\sqrt[3]{32} \times \sqrt[3]{250}$ is
   (a) 50   (b) 0.031   (c) 20
   (d) 0.001   (e) 2

7. Find the value of $3125 \div (25 \times 25) - \sqrt[3]{125}$
   (a) 5   (b) 0   (c) 25
   (d) 100   (e) 20

8. Solve: $18.18 \div 9 + 2.7 \times 3$
   (a) 101.2   (b) 27.32   (c) 10.12
   (d) 10.13   (e) 101.3

9. Solve: $8127 - 5422 + 1614 - 808$
   (a) 3580   (b) 3058   (c) 3503
   (d) 3511   (e) 3501

10. The unit's digit of the product $(247 \times 318 \times 577 \times 313)$ is
    (a) 2   (b) 1   (c) 4
    (d) 9   (e) 6

11. What least value must be assigned to * so that the number 451 * 603 becomes exactly divisible by 9?
    (a) 2   (b) 7   (c) 8
    (d) 5   (e) 1

12. What least value must be assigned to * so that the number 63576 * 2 is divisible by 8?
    (a) 1   (b) 2   (c) 3
    (d) 4   (e) 7

13. Simplify: 8756×99999
    (a) 815491244   (b) 796491244   (c) 875991244
    (d) 875591244   (e) 875951244

14. Evaluate: 1399×1399
    (a) 1687401   (b) 1901541   (c) 1943211
    (d) 1957201   (e) 1975102

15. Find the value of $397 \times 397 + 104 \times 104 + 2 \times 397 \times 104$.
    (a) 250001   (b) 251001   (c) 260101
    (d) 261001   (e) 270101

16. Two rational numbers lying between $\dfrac{4}{5}$ and $\dfrac{6}{7}$ are
    (a) $\dfrac{65}{84}, \dfrac{5}{6}$ (b) $\dfrac{29}{35}, \dfrac{5}{6}$ (c) $\dfrac{29}{35}, \dfrac{62}{70}$
    (d) $\dfrac{28}{34}, \dfrac{35}{39}$ (e) $\dfrac{31}{35}, \dfrac{7}{8}$

17. If $x = \left(6 - \sqrt{35}\right)$, then the reciprocal of x is
    (a) $\dfrac{1}{(6 + \sqrt{35})}$ (b) $(6 + \sqrt{35})$
    (c) $\sqrt{35}$ (d) 12
    (e) $2\sqrt{35}$

18. Which of the following is exactly divisible by 99?
(a) 114345   (b) 135792   (c) 3572404
(d) 913464   (e) 143098

19. The difference between two numbers is 1365. When larger number is divided by the smaller one, the quotient is 6 and the remainder is 15. The smaller number is
(a) 270   (b) 360   (c) 240
(d) 295   (e) 380

20. There are four prime numbers written in ascending order of magnitude. The product of first three is 385 and that of last three is 1001. Find the first number.
(a) 5   (b) 7   (c) 11
(d) 17   (e) 19

21. The number nearest to 99547 which is exactly divisible by 687 is
(a) 100166   (b) 99615   (c) 99579
(d) 98928   (e) 100302

22. Which is the largest five-digit number that divisible by 99?
(a) 99999   (b) 99981   (c) 99909
(d) 99990   (e) 99792

23. Which is the smallest six-digit number that is divisible by 111?
(a) 111111   (b) 110011   (c) 100011
(d) 100001   (e) 100455

24. When n is divided by 4, the remainder is 3. What is the remainder when 2n is divided by 4?
(a) 1   (b) 6   (c) 3
(d) 2   (e) 0

25. Find the value of $\left(\dfrac{2^n + 2^{n-1}}{2^{n+1} - 2^n}\right)$.
(a) $\dfrac{1}{2}$ (b) $\dfrac{2}{3}$ (c) $\dfrac{1}{2^n}$
(d) $\dfrac{3}{2}$ (e) $\dfrac{1}{2^{n+1}}$

26. Let D be a rational number of the form D = 0. abcd abcd abcd ... , where digits a, b, c and d are integers lying between 0 and 9. At most three of these digits are zero. By what minimum number D be multiplied so that the result is a natural number?
(a) 999   (b) 9990   (c) 9999
(d) 49995   (e) None of these

27. $N = 144^3 + 22^3 - 166^3$, then N is necessarily divisible by
(a) both 11 and 13
(b) both 12 and 83
(c) both 7 and 19
(d) both 13 and 83
(e) None of these

28. Dividing by $\dfrac{3}{8}$ and then multiplying by $\dfrac{5}{6}$ is equivalent to dividing by what number?
(a) $\dfrac{5}{16}$ (b) $\dfrac{16}{40}$ (c) $\dfrac{9}{20}$
(d) $\dfrac{40}{18}$ (e) $\dfrac{9}{10}$

29. The LCM of two numbers is 72 and their HCF is 12. If one of the numbers is 24, what is the other number?
(a) 38   (b) 26   (c) 36
(d) 42   (e) 27

 My Doubts

____

____

____

____

____

____

Career Launcher MBA

1. $P = 441 \times 484 \times 529 \times 576 \times 625$. The total number of factors of P is
   (a) 607   (b) 5706   (c) 1024
   (d) 6075   (e) 2025

2. There are four numbers in a sequence. The average of first three is 6, the average of the last three is 7, and the last number is 3 more than the first. The average of the second and the third numbers is
   (a) 6   (b) 6.5   (c) 5.75
   (d) 7   (e) Cannot be determined

3. A number is divided in a way such that the divisor is 12 times the quotient. If the remainder is 48, then find what could be dividend, given that the divisor is 5 times the remainder.
   (a) 4803   (b) 3684   (c) 3648
   (d) 4848   (e) 3848

4. $2! + 4! + 6! + 8! + 10! + \cdots 100!$ when divided by 5, would leave remainder
   (a) 0   (b) 1   (c) 2
   (d) 3   (e) 4

5. The average of three consecutive prime numbers is $\dfrac{223}{3}$. What is the difference between the greatest and the smallest number that can be a part of such a set?
   (a) 8   (b) 14   (c) 16
   (d) 10   (e) None of these

6. What is the sum of the greatest and the least fraction in the set of following fractions?
   $$\frac{2}{3}, \frac{13}{21}, \frac{11}{18}, \frac{8}{13}$$
   (a) $1\dfrac{29}{126}$ (b) $1\dfrac{5}{18}$ (c) $1\dfrac{11}{39}$
   (d) $1\dfrac{64}{273}$ (e) $1\dfrac{6}{21}$

7. The sum of the digits of a two-digit number is $\dfrac{1}{11}$ of the sum of the number and the number obtained by interchanging its digits. What is the difference between the digits of the number?
   (a) 3   (b) 0   (c) 1
   (d) 2   (e) Data is insufficient

8. The average of four consecutive even numbers is 27. The largest of these numbers is
   (a) 24   (b) 30   (c) 26
   (d) 28   (e) 32

9. Convert 1153 from base 10 to base 15.
   (a) 51D   (b) 61E   (c) 51C
   (d) 61C   (e) None of these

10. If $x = 17^4$ and $y = 14 \times 16 \times 18 \times 20$, then
    (a) $x - y > 10000$
    (b) $y - x > 100$
    (c) $x - y > 1000$
    (d) $y - x > 10000$
    (e) None of these

11. What is the last digit of the number 23457^{194321}?
    (a) 9   (b) 1   (c) 3
    (d) 7   (e) 4

12. In how many ways can a number 6084 be written as a product of two different factors?
    (a) 27   (b) 26   (c) 13
    (d) 14   (e) None of these

13. A number system has 100 as base. How many digits do we need to write 100 in that system?
    (a) 1   (b) 2   (c) 4
    (d) 100   (e) None of these

14. What will be the remainder when $25^{625} + 26$ is divided by 24?
    (a) 1   (b) 2   (c) 3
    (d) 0   (e) None of these

15. If $N = 2^3 \times 3^4$, $M = 2^2 \times 3^5$, then find the number of factors of N that are common with the factors of M.
    (a) 8   (b) 15   (c) 18
    (d) 24   (e) 20

16. $N = (11111111)^2$. What is the sum of the digits of N?
    (a) 72   (b) 62   (c) 64
    (d) 68   (e) None of these

17. What is the value of $\dfrac{\left(1+\frac{1}{3}\right)^{4}+\left(1+\frac{1}{3}\right)^{-4}+1}{\left(1+\frac{1}{3}\right)^{2}+\left(1+\frac{1}{3}\right)^{-2}+1}$?

(a) $\dfrac{193}{144}$ (b) $\dfrac{293}{144}$ (c) $\dfrac{191}{144}$

(d) $\dfrac{291}{144}$ (e) None of these

18. Find the value of N, where

$$N=\left(\frac{2\times8+8\times32+18\times72\ ...\ \text{upto}\ \text{n terms}}{1+16+81+...\ \text{up to n terms}}\right)^{\frac{1}{4}}$$

(a) 2n   (b) 2^{n} (c) 2
(d) 4   (e) None of these

19. The average of 2, 7, 6 and x is 5, and average of 18, 1, 6, x and y is 10. Find the value of y.
(a) 10   (b) 15   (c) 20
(d) 30   (e) 25

20. P + Q + R + S is odd. At least how many of these (is / are) odd?
(a) 0   (b) 1   (c) 2
(d) 3   (e) Cannot be determined

21. Find the value of

$$\left(28+10\sqrt{3}\right)^{\frac{1}{2}}-\left(7-4\sqrt{3}\right)^{-\frac{1}{2}}.$$

(a) 3   (b) 5   (c) 7
(d) 14   (e) 9

22. What will be the remainder when 13^{36} is divided by 2196?
(a) 0   (b) 1   (c) 12
(d) 2195   (e) None of these

23. Which of the following statements is not correct about $19^{n}+1$?
(a) It is never divisible by 18.
(b) When n is odd it is divisible by 20.
(c) When n is even it is not divisible by 20.
(d) When n is odd it is divisible by 18.
(e) None of these

24. How many numbers are there between 200 and 400 which are divisible by 11 and 3 but not by 2?
(a) 5   (b) 6   (c) 4
(d) 3   (e) None of these

25. Suppose P is a prime number greater than 3, then P can always be written in the form
(a) 6k + 1, where k is a natural number
(b) 6k – 1, where k is a natural number
(c) 13k + 1
(d) 13k –1
(e) Nothing can be said with certainty about prime numbers

26. A box contains 4 small boxes. Each of the 4 boxes contains 3 smaller boxes, in each of which there are 2 boxes. How many boxes are there altogether?
(a) 24   (b) 40   (c) 41
(d) 42   (e) 28

27. If m < n, where m and n are real numbers, then which of the following is definitely true?
(a) $m^{2}<n^{2}$ (b) $m^{2}>n^{2}$ (c) $m<n^{2}$
(d) $m^{3}<n^{3}$ (e) $m=n$

28. Ravi and Gopal are playing mathematical puzzles. Ravi asks Gopal, "Which whole numbers, greater than one, can divide all of the nine three-digit numbers 111, 222, 333, 444, 555, 666, 777, 888 and 999?" Gopal immediately gave the desired answer. It was
(a) 3, 37 and 119
(b) 3, 37 and 111
(c) 9, 37 and 111
(d) 9, 36 and 1124
(e) 3, 9, 37

29. Which of the following statements is false?
(a) The product of three consecutive even numbers must be divisible by 48.
(b) The numbers $(100)_{2}$, $(100)_{3}$, $(100)_{4}$, $(100)_{5}$ ... so on, when converted to decimal system are all in an arithmetic progression.
(c) The factorial of any natural number greater than 1 cannot be a perfect square.
(d) x% of y% of z is same as z% of x% of y.
(e) b and c

30. The product of n consecutive positive integers is always divisible by
(a) $n^{2}-1$ (b) $(n+1)!$ (c) $2n+1$
(d) $n^{2}+1$ (e) $n!$

31. When a two-digit number is divided by the sum of its digits, the quotient is 4. If the digits are reversed, the new number is 6 less than twice the original. The number is
(a) 12   (b) 21   (c) 42
(d) 24   (e) 27

32. Which of the following statements is true?
    I. $a^{2n} - b^{2n}$ is divisible by a + b but not
         by a – b when n is an integer.
    II. $a^{n+1} + b^{n+1}$ is always divisible by a + b, n being
         an integer.
    III. 2485035 is the perfect square of an integer.
    IV. If A is the AM of 2 positive numbers and M is the
         GM of the same 2 numbers, then A ≥ M.

    (a) I   (b) II   (c) III
    (d) IV   (e) I & II

33. Let 'p' be a prime number greater than 3. Find the
    remainder when $p^2 + 17$ is divided by 12.
    (a) 6   (b) 1   (c) 0
    (d) 8   (e) 7

34. How many zeroes will be there at the end of the
    number N, if N = 100! + 200!?
    (a) 73   (b) 49   (c) 20
    (d) 48   (e) 24

35. Between 100 and 200, how many numbers are there
    in which one digit is the average of the other two?
    (a) 11   (b) 12   (c) 10
    (d) 8   (e) 9

My Doubts

1. The sum of the squares of first ten natural numbers is
   (a) 281   (b) 385   (c) 402
   (d) 502   (e) 770

2. The largest number among the following is
   (a) $(2 + 2 \times 2)^3$ (b) $[(2+2)^3]^{1/2}$ (c) 2^5
   (d) $(2 \times 2 - 2)^7$ (e) $(2 \times 7 - 2)^2$

3. The smallest number among the following is
   (a) $(7)^3$ (b) $(8.5)^3$ (c) $(4)^4$
   (d) $(6^5)^{3/5}$ (e) $(3^{4/5})^5$

4. Find the sum of the first 50 even numbers.
   (a) 1275   (b) 2650   (c) 5100
   (d) 2550   (e) 1550

5. Evaluate: $11^2 + 11^4 \div 11^3 - 11 + (0.5)\,11^2$
   (a) 302.5   (b) 181.5   (c) 484.0
   (d) 121   (e) 162.5

6. Which one of the following is incorrect?
   (a) Square root of 5184 is 72.
   (b) Square root of 15625 is 125.
   (c) Square root of 1444 is 38.
   (d) Square root of 1296 is 34.
   (e) Square root of 1369 is 37

7. The sum of first 45 natural numbers is
   (a) 2070   (b) 975   (c) 1280
   (d) 1035   (e) 1575

8. The greatest fraction among $\dfrac{2}{5}, \dfrac{3}{5}, \dfrac{1}{5}, \dfrac{7}{15}$ and $\dfrac{4}{5}$ is
   (a) $\dfrac{4}{5}$ (b) $\dfrac{3}{5}$ (c) $\dfrac{2}{5}$
   (d) $\dfrac{7}{15}$ (e) $\dfrac{1}{5}$

9. The lowest four-digit number which is exactly divisible by 2, 3, 4, 5, 6 and 7 is
   (a) 1400   (b) 1300   (c) 1250
   (d) 1260   (e) 1464

10. The sum of the two numbers is twice their difference. If their product is 27, then the numbers are
    (a) 5, 15   (b) 10, 30   (c) 9, 6
    (d) 9, 3   (e) 5, 7

11. The largest fraction among the following is
    (a) $\dfrac{17}{21}$ (b) $\dfrac{11}{14}$ (c) $\dfrac{12}{15}$
    (d) $\dfrac{5}{6}$ (e) $\dfrac{3}{5}$

12. If the product of three consecutive integers is 720, then their sum is
    (a) 54   (b) 45   (c) 18
    (d) 27   (e) 37

13. How many numbers between 200 and 600 are divisible by 4, 5 and 6?
    (a) 5   (b) 6   (c) 7
    (d) 8   (e) 4

14. The number $(10^n - 1)$ is divisible by 11 for
    (a) even values of n
    (b) odd values of n
    (c) all values of n
    (d) n = multiples of 11
    (e) No general rule exists

15. Solve: $3 + \dfrac{3}{3 + \dfrac{1}{3 + \dfrac{1}{3}}}$
    (a) 1   (b) 3   (c) $\dfrac{43}{11}$
    (d) $\dfrac{63}{19}$ (e) $\dfrac{41}{10}$

16. How many numbers are there between 500 and 600 in which 9 occurs only once?
    (a) 19   (b) 20   (c) 21
    (d) 18   (e) 17

17. How many zeros are there at the end of the product $33 \times 175 \times 180 \times 12 \times 44 \times 80 \times 66$?
    (a) 2   (b) 4   (c) 5
    (d) 6   (e) 3

18. $N = 56^{56} + 56$. What would be the remainder when N is divided by 57?
    (a) 0   (b) 56   (c) 55
    (d) 1   (e) None of these

Fundamentals of Numbers

19. The largest number that always divides the product of 3 consecutive multiples of 2 is
   (a) 8   (b) 16   (c) 24
   (d) 48   (e) 36

20. The sum of two natural numbers is 85 and their LCM is 102. Find the numbers.
   (a) 51 and 34   (b) 50 and 35   (c) 60 and 25
   (d) 45 and 40   (e) 17 and 68

21. By what smallest number, 21600 must be multiplied or divided in order to make it a perfect square?
   (a) 6   (b) 5   (c) 8
   (d) 10   (e) 12

22. If we write down all the natural numbers from 259 to 492 side by side we shall get a very large natural number 259260261262 $\cdots$ 490491492. How many 8's will be used to write this large natural number?
   (a) 52   (b) 53   (c) 32
   (d) 43   (e) None of these

23. $n^3 + 2n$ for any natural number n is always a multiple of
   (a) 3   (b) 4   (c) 5
   (d) 6   (e) 8

24. A number when divided by 238 leaves a remainder 79. What will be the remainder when that number is divided by 17?
   (a) 8   (b) 9   (c) 10
   (d) 11   (e) 12

25. What is the remainder when 17^{23} is divided by 16?
   (a) 0   (b) 1   (c) 2
   (d) 3   (e) 15

26. $9^6 + 1$ when divided by 8, would leave a remainder
   (a) 0   (b) 1   (c) 2
   (d) 3   (e) 4

27. $N = 2 \times 4 \times 6 \times 8 \times 10 \times \cdots 100$. How many zeros are there at the end of N?
   (a) 24   (b) 13   (c) 12
   (d) 15   (e) None of these

28. It is given that $2^{32} + 1$ is exactly divisible by a certain number. Which one of the following is also divisible by the same number?
   (a) $2^{96} + 1$ (b) $2^{16} - 1$ (c) $2^{16} + 1$
   (d) 7×2^{33} (e) $2^{64} + 1$

29. $4^{61} + 4^{62} + 4^{63} + 4^{64} + 4^{65}$ is divisible by
   (a) 3   (b) 5   (c) 11
   (d) 17   (e) 13

30. What is the smallest perfect square that is divisible by 8, 9 and 10?
   (a) 4000   (b) 6400   (c) 3600
   (d) 14641   (e) 900

 My Doubts

____

____

____

____

____

____

____

____

____

1. What is the least number which must be subtracted from 2024, so that the resultant number when divided by 7, 10 and 15 will leave in each case the same remainder 3?
   (a) 224   (b) 131   (c) 24
   (d) 225   (e) 141

2. The product of two numbers is 16200. If their LCM is 216, then find their HCF.
   (a) 75   (b) 70   (c) 80
   (d) 60   (e) Data inconsistent

3. 4a56 is a four-digit number divisible by 33. What is the value of a?
   (a) 3   (b) 4   (c) 5
   (d) 6   (e) 2

4. A two-digit number is such that cube of its 24th part is the same as the number obtained by interchanging the digit of the number. What is the number?
   (a) 24   (b) 72   (c) 48
   (d) 96   (e) None of these

5. A number formed by writing any digit 6 times (say as 444444 or 999999) is always divisible by
   (a) 1001   (b) 7   (c) 13
   (d) 11   (e) All of these

6. The positive integer which is nearest to 1000 and divisible by 2, 3, 4, 5 and 6 is
   (a) 1020   (b) 1040   (c) 960
   (d) 1030   (e) 1050

7. The difference of the greatest and the least five-digit numbers that can be formed by using the digits 0, 2, 3, 4 and 5 is (Repetition is not allowed)
   (a) 25694   (b) 33975   (c) 30870
   (d) 36246   (e) 33946

8. An amount of ₹417 is divided among A, B, C, and D in such a way that A gets ₹13 more than B, B gets ₹9 more than C, and C gets ₹6 more than D. Find A's share.
   (a) ₹121   (b) ₹116   (c) ₹120
   (d) ₹124   (e) ₹92

9. Convert 1234 from base 6 to base 10.
   (a) 3100   (b) 3010   (c) 301
   (d) 310   (e) None of these

10. N = 148 × 293 × 581 × 874. What will be the remainder when N is divided by 29?
    (a) 7   (b) 6   (c) 5
    (d) 9   (e) None of these

11. What is the highest power of 31 in 1000!?
    (a) 31   (b) 32   (c) 33
    (d) 35   (e) None of these

12. For any natural number n, $n^4 + n^2 + 1$ is always
    (a) odd
    (b) even
    (c) odd multiple of 3
    (d) even multiple of 3
    (e) Cannot be determined

13. Which among the following is greatest:
    $\sqrt{5}, \sqrt[3]{11}, \sqrt[6]{123}, \sqrt[4]{1331}$?
    (a) $\sqrt{5}$ (b) $\sqrt[3]{11}$ (c) $\sqrt[6]{123}$
    (d) $\sqrt[4]{36}$ (e) $\sqrt[12]{27}$

14. Convert 1556 from base 10 to base 16.
    (a) 641   (b) 64A   (c) 6A4
    (d) 614   (e) 6B4

15. Convert 413 from base 7 to base 8.
    (a) 613   (b) 362   (c) 316
    (d) 216   (e) None of these

16. Which among the following is greatest:
    $\sqrt{7}+\sqrt{3}, \sqrt{5}+\sqrt{5}, \sqrt{6}+2, \sqrt{2}+\sqrt{8}$?
    (a) $\sqrt{7}+\sqrt{3}$ (b) $\sqrt{5}+\sqrt{5}$ (c) $\sqrt{6}+2$
    (d) $\sqrt{2}+\sqrt{8}$ (e) All are equal

17. When 75% of a two-digit number is added to it, the digits of the number are reversed. Find the ratio of the unit's digit to the ten's digit in the original number.
    (a) 1 : 2   (b) 1 : 3   (c) 1 : 4
    (d) 2 : 1   (e) 2 : 3

18. If $N = \dfrac{1}{2} + \dfrac{1}{6} + \dfrac{1}{12} + \dfrac{1}{20} + \dfrac{1}{30} + \cdots + \dfrac{1}{156}$,

then the value of N is

(a) $\dfrac{12}{13}$ (b) $\dfrac{13}{12}$ (c) $\dfrac{1}{13}$

(d) $\dfrac{1}{12}$ (e) None of these

19. How many two-digit natural numbers are there so that ten's digit is never less than the unit's digit?
(a) 44   (b) 55   (c) 54
(d) 49   (e) None of these

20. What is the last digit of the number $3^{5^{7^9}} + 1$?
(a) 1   (b) 7   (c) 4
(d) 3   (e) None of these

21. What will be the last digit of $2^{3^{4^5}} - 2^{3^{5^4}}$?
(a) 0   (b) 2   (c) 4
(d) 6   (e) None of these

22. Simplify:

$$\dfrac{1}{\sqrt{1}+\sqrt{3}} + \dfrac{1}{\sqrt{3}+\sqrt{5}} + \dfrac{1}{\sqrt{5}+\sqrt{7}} + \ldots \text{up to 50 teams.}$$

(a) $\dfrac{\sqrt{101}-1}{2}$ (b) $\sqrt{109} - \sqrt{99}$

(c) $1 - \dfrac{1}{\sqrt{101}}$ (d) $\dfrac{1}{\sqrt{99}} - \dfrac{1}{\sqrt{101}}$

(e) None of these

23. If $1 + 2 + 3 + 4 + 5 + 6 + 7 + 8 + 9 + 10 = 100$, then atleast in how many places you need to change '+' with '×' to make the equality hold good?
(a) 2   (b) 4   (c) 3
(d) 1   (e) Cannot be determined

24. Find the value of

$$\sqrt{\dfrac{(12.12)^2 - (8.12)^2}{(0.25)^2 + (0.25)(19.99)}} + \dfrac{\left[(8^{\frac{-3}{4}})^{\frac{5}{2}}\right]^{\frac{8}{15}} \times 16^{\frac{3}{4}}}{\sqrt[3]{\left[\left((128)^{-5}\right)^{\frac{3}{7}}\right]^{\frac{-1}{5}}}}$$

(You have to take positive square roots only.)

(a) 0   (b) 1   (c) $\dfrac{9}{2}$

(d) $\dfrac{3}{2}$ (e) None of these

25. For a set of 5 unique integers a, b, c, d, e (in the ascending order), which of the following is always true?
(a) $d \times e > c \times b$

(b) $\dfrac{e}{a} > \dfrac{d}{b}$

(c) $c >$ Average of (a, b, c, d, e)
(d) $c + d > a + b$
(e) None of these

26. Mrs Doubtfire wrote all the numbers from 100 to 200. Then she started counting the number of one's that has been used while writing all these numbers. What is the number that she got?
(a) 119   (b) 120   (c) 121
(d) 111   (e) None of these

 My Doubts

____

____

____

____

____

Direction for questions 1 and 2: Answer the questions based on the following information.

59292564P61Q is divisible by 99, but not by 22. Q is greater than P, then

1. P is
   (a) 5   (b) 2   (c) 0
   (d) 4   (e) None of these

2. Q is
   (a) 5   (b) 3   (c) 7
   (d) 9   (e) None of these

3. M is the smallest natural number in such a way that when multiplied by 7 it gives a number made up of 6's only. Sum of the digits of M is N. The last digit of N^{36} is
   (a) 6   (b) 7   (c) 1
   (d) 9   (e) None of these

4. What is the remainder when 7^{187} is divided by 800?
   (a) 143   (b) 343   (c) 243
   (d) 743   (e) 127

5. The number 'a' is exactly divisible by 5. The remainder after the division of the number 'b' by 5 is equal to 1 and the remainder after the division of the number 'c' by 5 is equal to 2. What is the remainder when the number $(2a + 3b – 4c)$ is divided by 5 ?
   (a) 0   (b) 1   (c) 2
   (d) 3   (e) 4

6. Let P and Q represent non-zero digits. Let PP represents a two-digit number with identical digits. If Q times the cube of PP is a four-digit number whose ten's digit is 1, then find the numeric value of Q.
   (a) 8   (b) 7   (c) 6
   (d) 10   (e) 9

7. When a particular positive number is divided by 5, the remainder is 2. If the same number is divided by 6, the remainder is 1. If the difference between the quotients of division is 3, then find the number.
   (a) 37   (b) 97   (c) 67
   (d) 127   (e) 87

8. Seven bells ring at intervals of 2, 3, 4, 6, 8, 9 and 12 min respectively. They started ringing simultaneously at 6 a.m. How many more times would all seven bells ring simultaneously till 5 p.m. on the same day?
   (a) 8   (b) 9   (c) 10
   (d) 12   (e) 7

9. How many times does the digit 6 appear when you count from 11 to 100?
   (a) 9   (b) 18   (c) 17
   (d) 20   (e) 19

Directions for questions 10 and 11: Answer the questions based on the following information.

The first 25 natural numbers are randomly arranged in the form of a square $[(5 \times 5)$ grid].

10. If from each row the smallest number is selected and the smallest of these numbers is called A, then A =
    (a) 5   (b) 1   (c) 4
    (d) 6   (e) Cannot be determined

11. If B is the largest of the largest numbers from each column, then B – A = (Use the data from previous question)
    (a) 0   (b) 1   (c) 24
    (d) 2   (e) Cannot be determined

12. Which of these is true?
    I. $3\sqrt{3}$ is not a rational number.
    II. If a is rational and n is an integer greater than 1, then a^n is rational.
    III. 7 is not the cube of a rational number.

    (a) I and II   (b) I and III   (c) II and III
    (d) II   (e) All three

13. A teacher was trying to form groups of students such that every group has equal number of students and that number should be a prime number. She tried for first 5 prime numbers, but on each occasion exactly one student was left behind. How many different possible solutions are there for the total number of students, if the total number of students is in 4 digits.
    (a) 0   (b) 2   (c) 3
    (d) 4   (e) 5

14. Juhi and Bhagyashree were playing a simple mathematical game. Juhi wrote a two-digit number and asked Bhagyashree to guess it. Juhi also indicated that the number is exactly thrice the product of its digits. What was the number that Juhi wrote?
    (a) 36   (b) 24   (c) 12
    (d) 48   (e) 30

15. $(AA)^2 = DCBA$, where A, B, C and D are distinct digits with B being odd. Find the value of D.
    (a) 1   (b) 6   (c) 4
    (d) 1 or 4   (e) 4 or 6

16. $V = 798630 \times 10^{24}$ and $A = 18 \times 10^{24}$. What is the remainder when V is divided by A?
    (a) 3×10^{24} (b) 6×10^{24} (c) 12×10^{24}
    (d) 6   (e) 8×10^{24}

17. Four bells begin to toll together. After that, they toll at the intervals of 6 s, 7 s, 8 s and 9 s respectively. The maximum number of times they will toll together in any interval of 2 hrs is
    (a) 14 times   (b) 15 times   (c) 13 times
    (d) 11 times   (e) 9 times

18. If x, y and z are distinct non-zero whole numbers such that y > x and xy = z, then which of the following can be true?
    (a) $y > z$ (b) $y = z$ (c) $z > x^3$
    (d) $x > z$ (e) $x = z$

19. If $a_1, a_2, a_3, a_4, ..., a_n$ are the terms of a series defined by $a_n = a_{n-1} + a_{n-2}$, (here a_n is a positive real number). What can be the value of a_1 if $a_3^2 - a_2^2 = 57$?
    (a) 19   (b) 8   (c) 3
    (d) 0   (e) 11

20. Which of the following statements is true?
    I. Perfect squares always end in one of {1, 4, 5, 6, 8, 9}.
    II. Number of digits in the square of a natural number having n digits is always equal to either 2n or 2n + 1.
    III. If a perfect square ends in 9, the second last digit is never even.

    (a) I   (b) II   (c) III
    (d) I and II   (e) None of these

21. A number 'n' is decreased by 4 and the result is multiplied by 4, the operation being repeated four times. The answer after the fourth operation is 4. What is the initial value of 'n'?
    (a) $\dfrac{341}{64}$ (b) 1   (c) $\dfrac{341}{256}$
    (d) $\dfrac{89}{64}$ (e) $\dfrac{89}{256}$

22. Find the largest number, smaller than the smallest four-digit number, which when divided by 4, 5, 6 and 7 leaves a remainder 2 in each case.
    (a) 422   (b) 656   (c) 12723
    (d) 748   (e) 842

23. The numerator and the denominator of a positive fraction are in the ratio 1 : 5. A new fraction is formed by subtracting 2 from the numerator and adding 5 to the denominator. The difference between the original fraction and the new fraction is $\dfrac{1}{10}$. What is the numerator of the original fraction?
    (a) 4   (b) 5   (c) 25
    (d) 20   (e) 15

24. What is the tens digit of $(51)^{51}$?
    (a) 0   (b) 1   (c) 5
    (d) 4   (e) 3

Directions for questions 25 and 26: Answer the questions on the basis of the following information.

25. Among the following find a whole number such that when one of its digit is erased, the resulting number is equal to one-ninth of the original number. The resulting number is also a multiple of 9.
    (a) 90   (b) 83438   (c) 10125
    (d) 70847   (e) 62423

26. In the above question, the digit erased must be
    (a) 9   (b) 0   (c) 7
    (d) Any of these   (e) None of these

27. How many five-digit numbers can be formed using only odd digits such that the number is divisible by 125?
    (a) 13   (b) 100   (c) 125
    (d) 25   (e) 50

28. What is the smallest number of ducks that could swim in this formation:
   Two ducks in front of a duck, two ducks behind a duck and a duck between two ducks.
   (a) 4   (b) 5   (c) 3
   (d) 6   (e) 7

29. A 3 digit number is such that its hundredth digit is equal to the product of the other 2 digits which are prime. Also, the difference between the number & its reverse is 297. Then tens digit of the number is
   (a) 2   (b) 3   (c) 7
   (d) 5   (e) 6

30. Ten bags contain 10 coins each. All the coins look alike but the coins in one bag weigh 1 g less than that in other bags. What is the least number of weighings using a spring balance needed to identify the bag containing 9 g coins?
   (a) 1   (b) 2   (c) 3
   (d) 4   (e) 5

31. What is the highest power of 5 that divides $90 \times 80 \times 70 \times 60 \times 50 \times 40 \times 30 \times 20 \times 10$?
   (a) 15   (b) 12   (c) 9
   (d) 14   (e) 10

32. Shekhar suddenly got angry and started tearing pages from a new copy of his 500-page textbook. On calming down, he realized that the first page he had torn was numbered 123. Further, he had torn successive pages till the page number formed using the same digits as 123. How many pages had Shekhar torn away? (Pages are numbered on both sides)
   (a) 10 or 199
   (b) 10 or 190
   (c) 199 or 190
   (d) 99 or 10
   (e) Cannot be determined

33. A certain number when divided by 222 leaves a remainder 35; another number when divided by 407 leaves a remainder 47. What is the remainder when the sum of these 2 numbers is divided by 37?
   (a) 47   (b) 9   (c) 17
   (d) 12   (e) 8

34. Between 100 and 300, how many numbers begin or end with 2?
   (a) 120   (b) 20   (c) 110
   (d) 119   (e) 88

My Doubts

1. The least number which on division by 35 leaves the remainder 25 and on division by 45 leaves the remainder 35 and on division by 55 leaves the remainder 45 is
   (a) 2515   (b) 3455   (c) 2875
   (d) 2785   (e) 3655

2. A heap of coconuts is divided into groups of 2, 3 and 5, and each time one coconut is left out. The least number of coconuts in the heap is
   (a) 31   (b) 41   (c) 51
   (d) 61   (e) 21

3. If $x = 5 - \sqrt{7}$, then find the value of $x + \dfrac{1}{x}$.
   (a) $\dfrac{95 + 17\sqrt{7}}{18}$ (b) $\dfrac{95 - 17\sqrt{7}}{18}$ (c) $\dfrac{85 - 17\sqrt{7}}{18}$
   (d) $\dfrac{85 + 17\sqrt{7}}{18}$ (e) $\dfrac{90 + 17\sqrt{7}}{18}$

4. 243 has been divided into three parts such that half of the first part, one-third of the second part and one-fourth of the third part are equal. The largest part is
   (a) 108   (b) 86   (c) 92
   (d) 74   (e) 96

5. If n is positive integer, then $(3^{4n} - 4^{3n})$ is always divisible by
   (a) 145   (b) 17   (c) 112
   (d) 7   (e) 19

6. Six bells commence tolling together and toll at intervals of 3, 6, 9, 12, 15 and 18 s respectively. In 30 min, how many times do they toll together?
   (a) 4   (b) 11   (c) 10
   (d) 15   (e) 9

7. When 'n' is divided by 5 the remainder is 2. What is the remainder when n^2 is divided by 5?
   (a) 2   (b) 1   (c) 3
   (d) 4   (e) 0

8. The expression
   $$\frac{1}{1.2} + \frac{1}{2.3} + \frac{1}{3.4} + \ldots + \frac{1}{n(n+1)}$$
   for any natural number n, is
   (a) always less than 1
   (b) always greater than 2
   (c) always equal to 1
   (d) alway lies between 1 and 2
   (e) None of these

9. If $y = \sqrt{2} + 1$, then value of $y + \dfrac{1}{y}$ is
   (a) $\sqrt{\dfrac{3}{2}}$ (b) $\dfrac{\sqrt{3}}{2}$ (c) $\dfrac{1}{\sqrt{2}}$
   (d) $2\sqrt{2}$ (e) $\sqrt{3}$

10. The ratio between a two-digit number and the sum of the digits of that number is 4 : 1. If the digit in the unit place is 3 more than the digit in the ten's place, what is that number?
    (a) 25   (b) 14   (c) 36
    (d) 69   (e) 47

11. If $32^{x-2} = \dfrac{64}{8^x}$, then find the value of x.
    (a) −2   (b) 3   (c) 2
    (d) −3   (e) −4

12. What is the greatest positive power of 5 that divides 30! exactly?
    (a) 5   (b) 6   (c) 7
    (d) 8   (e) 9

13. If the sum of two natural numbers is multiplied by each number separately, the products so obtained are 2418 and 3666. What is the difference between the numbers?
    (a) 16   (b) 22   (c) 26
    (d) 35   (e) 27

14. How many even numbers from 20 to 2000 are not perfect squares?
    (a) 1941   (b) 1940   (c) 970
    (d) 1171   (e) None of these

15. Product of two positive integers is 15210 and their HCF is 39. How many such pairs are possible?
    (a) 1   (b) 2   (c) 3
    (d) 4   (e) None of these

16. If the last 2 digits of a four-digit number are interchanged, the new number obtained is greater than the original number by 54. What is the difference between the last two digits of the number?
(a) 9   (b) 12   (c) 6
(d) 3   (e) Data Inadequate

17. LCM of two numbers x and y is 161. Find the value of $(4x - 3y)$, given that $y > x$, $x > 1$.
(a) -25 (b) -16 (c) -41
(d) -455 (e) Cannot be determined

18.
$$\begin{array}{ll} AA & A > 0 \\ \underline{+\,BB} & B > 0 \\ CDC & \end{array}$$
All A, B, C are integers. Find the value of D.
(a) 4   (b) 3   (c) 2
(d) 1   (e) 5

19. The sum of the digits of a two-digit number is 5. If we put the digits of the number in reverse order, the new number is 41 less than twice the original number. Find 40% of the number.
(a) 11.8   (b) 12.8   (c) 20.8
(d) 18.8   (e) None of these

20. The HCF and LCM of two numbers are 13 and 455 respectively. If one of the numbers lies between 75 and 125, then that number is
(a) 91   (b) 78   (c) 117
(d) 104   (e) 65

21. Three consecutive whole numbers are such that the square of the middle number is greater than the product of the other two by 1. Find the middle number.
(a) 6   (b) 18   (c) 12
(d) 31   (e) All of these

22. $A = 1^1 \times 2^2 \times 3^3 \times 4^4 \times \cdots 100^{100}$. How many zeroes will be there at the end of A?
(a) 1300   (b) 1320   (c) 1325
(d) 1050   (e) None of these

23. If x is a prime such that $(x^2 + 3)$ is also a prime, then x can have
(a) two values
(b) one value
(c) more than 3 values
(d) more than 2 values
(e) None of these

24. If $f(x)$ = sum of all the digits of x, where x is a natural number, then what is the value of $f(101) + f(102) + f(103) + \cdots + f(200)$?
(a) 1000   (b) 901   (c) 999
(d) 1001   (e) 1111

25. What is the highest power of 54 that divides 31! completely?
(a) 2   (b) 6   (c) 4
(d) 5   (e) None of these

 My Doubts

____

____

____

____

____

____

____

____

Career Launcher MBA   Fundamentals of Numbers

1. Convert 1101.011 from base 2 to base 10.
   (a) 13.357   (b) 12.375   (c) 13.375
   (d) 133.75   (e) None of these

2. The value of
$$\frac{3}{4} + \frac{5}{36} + \frac{7}{144} + \cdots + \frac{17}{5184} + \frac{19}{8100} \text{ is}$$
   (a) 0.99   (b) 0.98   (c) 0.95
   (d) 0.90   (e) None of these

3. If the number 3402 is converted from base 10 to base x, it becomes 12630. What is the value of x?
   (a) 6   (b) 8   (c) 9
   (d) 7   (e) None of these

4. In a basket, there are some apples. Sanjay takes half of them but returns one of them. Preeti takes one-third of the remaining and returns two of them. Dharam takes one-fourth of the remaining and returns three of them. No apple is cut. The minimum number of apples left in the basket at the end is
   (a) 9   (b) 28   (c) 12
   (d) 15   (e) Cannot be determined

5. abc is a three-digit natural number so that $abc = a! + b! + c!$. What is the value of $(b + c)^a$?
   (a) 1296   (b) 3125   (c) 19683
   (d) 9   (e) None of these

6. abc is a three-digit whole number so that $abc = a^3 + b^3 + c^3$. $[300 < abc < 400]$
   What is the value of $a + b + c$?
   (a) 10   (b) 11   (c) 12
   (d) 9   (e) Cannot be determined

7. a and b are two distinct whole numbers less than 10.
   $N = a \times b$
   $N! = a! \times b!$
   How many pairs of a and b are possible?
   (a) 8   (b) 9   (c) 10
   (d) 2   (e) None of these

8. Two different numbers when divided by a certain divisor leave remainders 547 and 349 respectively. When the sum of those two numbers is divided by the same divisor, the remainder is 211. Find the divisor.
   (a) 896   (b) 586   (c) 685
   (d) 698   (e) Cannot be determined

9. If G(x) = Total number of factors of x, where x is a perfect square, then G(x) is always
   (a) an even number
   (b) an odd number
   (c) a prime number
   (d) non-prime number
   (e) Cannot be determined

10. Pawan writes all the numbers from 100 to 999. The number of zeroes that he uses is m, the number of 5's that he uses is n and the number of 8's that he uses is p. What is the value of n + p – m?
    (a) 280   (b) 380   (c) 180
    (d) 80   (e) None of these

11. A is the smallest integer which when multiplied with 3 gives a number made of 5's only. Sum of the digits of A is B. Sum of the digits of B is C. What is the value of C^3?
    (a) 125   (b) 64   (c) 216
    (d) 27   (e) None of these

12. P is an integer. P > 883. If P – 7 is a multiple of 11, then the largest number that will always divide (P + 4) (P + 15) is
    (a) 11   (b) 121   (c) 242
    (d) 22   (e) None of these

13. If p^q is a perfect square as well as a perfect cube, where p and q are natural numbers, then q must be a multiple of
    (a) 2   (b) 3   (c) 6
    (d) 9   (e) Cannot be determined

14. What is the highest power of 82 contained in $(83! – 82!)$?
    (a) 3   (b) 2   (c) 164
    (d) 1   (e) None of these

15. What is the remainder when $1923^{1924^{1925}}$ is divided by 1924?
    (a) 1922   (b) 1923   (c) 1
    (d) 2   (e) None of these

16. If a five-digit natural number is added to a number made by putting the digits of the original number in reverse order, the sum will always be divisible by
    (a) 11   (b) 11111   (c) 101
    (d) 1001   (e) None of these

17. If an n-digit natural number is added to a number made by putting the digits of the original number in reverse order, the sum is always divisible by k where n is an even number, then k must be a multiple of
(a) 22   (b) 111   (c) 11
(d) 1001   (e) None of these

18. ab and cd are two 2-digit natural numbers. $4b + a = 13k_1$ and $5d - c = 17k_2$ where k_1 and k_2 are natural numbers. The largest number that will always divide the product of ab and cd is
(a) 13   (b) 17   (c) 221
(d) 663   (e) None of these

19. Let $A = \{a_1, a_2, a_3 \cdots a_n\}$ be a set of n distinct natural numbers and $n \geq 8$. Which of the following will always be a natural number?
(a) $a_1 + a_2 + a_3 - a_7$
(b) $(a_1 - a_n)^5$
(c) $a_n - a_1$
(d) $(a_1 - a_n)^7$
(e) $(a_{n-1} - a_n)^2$

20. M and N are two distinct natural numbers. HCF and LCM of M and N are K and L respectively. A is also a natural number. Which of the following relations is not possible?
(a) $K \times L = A$ (b) $K \times A = L$ (c) $L \times A = K$
(d) $M \times A = N$ (e) None of these

Directions for questions 21 and 22: Answer the questions based on the following information.

A defence code is defined by assigning the numbers 1 to 9 to the letters in the grid above such that by adding horizontally, or diagonally the sum of the numbers is the same, i.e.15, and also Y : S is 1 : 4 and S : W is 2 : 1 and W : Q is 2 : 3.

S	Z	Q
X	V	T
W	R	Y

21. Which letter has the highest numerical value?
(a) X   (b) T   (c) V
(d) W   (e) None of these

22. If the code is 1159, then the message will be
(a) ZZVR   (b) RRZV   (c) XXVT
(d) a or c   (e) b or c

Directions for questions 23 and 24: Answer the questions based on the following information.

$V_1, V_2, V_3, V_4, \ldots, V_{999}, V_{1000}$ are all natural numbers and $V_n + V_{n+1} = K$, $1 \leq n \leq 999$. n is also a natural number and K is a constant.

23. If $V_{987} = 987$, what is the value of V_{236}?
(a) 236   (b) 987   (c) $K - 987$
(d) $K - 236$ (e) Cannot be determined

24. If $V_{100} = 100$, what is the value of $V_{10} + V_{11} + V_{12} + V_{13} + V_{14} - V_{15} - V_{16} - V_{17} - V_{18} - V_{19}$?
(a) $V_{14} + 100 - K$
(b) $V_{14} - 100 + K$
(c) $200 - K$
(d) Both (a) and (c)
(e) Both (b) and (c)

Direction for questions 25 and 26: Answer the questions based on the following information.

'abcde' is a five-digit number (e is unit's place digit, etc., ...), which has the following characteristics.
I. $a \neq 0$; d is odd
II. $a - b + c = d - e$
III. $d! = a \times b \times c$

25. If $c = a + b$, then c can take values
(a) 3 and 6   (b) 3   (c) 6 and 8
(d) 3, 6 and 8   (e) 3 and 8

26. Which of the following is/are true?
I. If $e = 0$, then d has to be equal to 1.
II. If $d = 5$, then $a + b + c > d + e$
(a) I only
(b) II only
(c) Both I and II
(d) Neither I nor II
(e) Indeter minate

27. A chain smoker had spent all the money he had. He had no money to buy his cigarettes. Hence, he resorted to join the stubs and to smoke them. He needed 4 stubs to make a single cigarette. If he got a pack of 10 cigarettes as a gift, then how many cigarettes could he smoke in all?
(a) 11   (b) 12   (c) 9
(d) 10   (e) 13

28. Let X_n denotes the nth element of the sequence {1, 2, 2, 3, 3, 3, 4, 4, 4, 4, 5, …}, where n is a positive integer. How many of the following statements are true?
   I. X_n < n for all n if n > 2.
   II. $(X_n + 1)(X_n) \geq 2n$
   III. If $X_{n+1} - X_n = 1$, then n can be written as the sum of first X_n natural numbers.

   (a) 1
   (b) 2
   (c) 3
   (d) 0
   (e) Cannot be determined

29. Consider the number n(n + 1)(2n + 1), where n is a positive integer. Then, which of the following is necessarily false?
   (a) n(n + 1)(2n + 1) is always even
   (b) n(n + 1)(2n + 1) is always divisible by 3
   (c) n(n + 1)(2n + 1) is always divisible by the sum of squares of first 'n' integers
   (d) n(n + 1)(2n + 1) is never divisible by 237
   (e) n(n + 1)(2n + 1) may be a multiple of 5.

30. The number of pairs of positive integers (a, b), where a and b are prime numbers and $a^2 - 2b^2 = 1$ is
   (a) zero
   (b) one
   (c) two
   (d) eight
   (e) four

31. The number of positive integers not greater than 100, which are not divisible by 2, 3, or 5, is
   (a) 24
   (b) 18
   (c) 31
   (d) 28
   (e) 26

32. Rohan sells corn at Nehru Place traffic crossing. The light turns red for 2 minutes after every 3 minutes. Rohan gets the opportunity to sell only when the signal is red. He finds that it takes him 10 s to sell one pack of corn. What is the usual number of packs he sells in one day, considering that he starts at 8 a.m. and goes on till 7 p.m., stopping only for a short lunch from 2 p.m. to 2.30 p.m.?
   (a) 1,512
   (b) 1,260
   (c) 1,080
   (d) 1,124
   (e) None of these

My Doubts

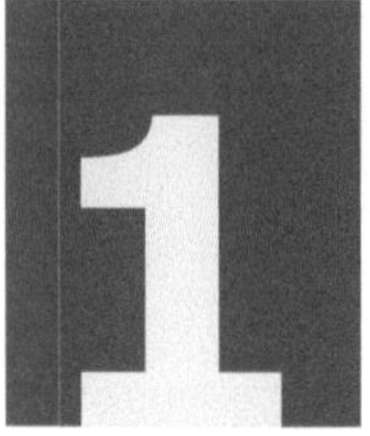

Set Theory

Introduction

A few disconnected topics make their appearances in the management entrance examinations. Usually, a few questions only are asked from these topics. Among these, set theory is an important topic to study. It is also not very complicated and a lot of day-to-day applications of set theory are there.

The treatment of trigonometry given here is elementary as, usually, problems related to only height and distance are known to be asked in these examinations.

Learning Objectives

At the end of this chapter you would have learnt:
*   Basic definitions in set theory
*   Venn diagram representation of sets

Miscellaneous Topics

We will cover the following topics in this chapter.
1.   Set theory
2.   Trigonometry
3.   Stocks and shares

Set Theory

Definition: A set is a well-defined collection of objects.

If A is a set and 'a' is an element of this set, we say that 'a' belongs to A or $a \in A$. A set 'A' which has a finite number of elements is called a finite set. The number of elements in a finite set is denoted by n(A).

The universal set is the set containing all the elements under consideration.

The empty set or null set (ϕ) is the set which has no element.

 *If a is an element of set A, then we write $a \in A$ (read a belongs to A or a is a member of set A). If a does not belong to A, then we write $a \notin A$. It is assumed that either $a \in A$ or $a \notin A$ and the two possibilities are mutually exclusive.*

Some important definitions:

Subset: If every element of A is an element of B, then A is called a subset of B and we write $A \subseteq B$. Every set is a subset of itself and the empty set is a subset of every set. A subset A of set B is called a proper subset of B if $A \neq B$ and we write $A \subset B$. If a set has n elements, then number of its subsets = 2^n.

Superset: If A is a subset of B, then B is known as the superset of A and we write $B \supseteq A$.

Power set: Let A be a set. Then thecollection or family of all subsets of A is called the power set of A and is denoted by P(A).
Example: Let A = $\{1, 2, 3\}$
Then the subsets of A are ϕ, $\{1\}$, $\{2\}$, $\{3\}$, $\{1, 2\}$ $\{1, 3\}$, $\{2, 3\}$ and $\{1, 2, 3\}$.
Hence P(A) = $\{ \phi, \{1\}, \{2\}, \{1, 2\} \{1, 3\}, \{2, 3\} \{1, 2, 3\}\}$

Universal set: A set that contains all the sets in a given context is called the universal set, i.e. It is the super set of all the sets under consideration e.g.
if A = $\{1, 2, 3\}$ and B = $\{2, 4, 5, 6\}$, then a set of all natural numbers (N) can be taken as a universal set.

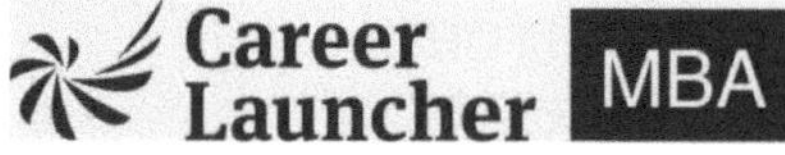

Introduction to Venn diagrams

The sets can be illustrated by means of Venn diagrams. A universal set U is represented by a rectangle and a subset by a circle within it.

Complement of a set

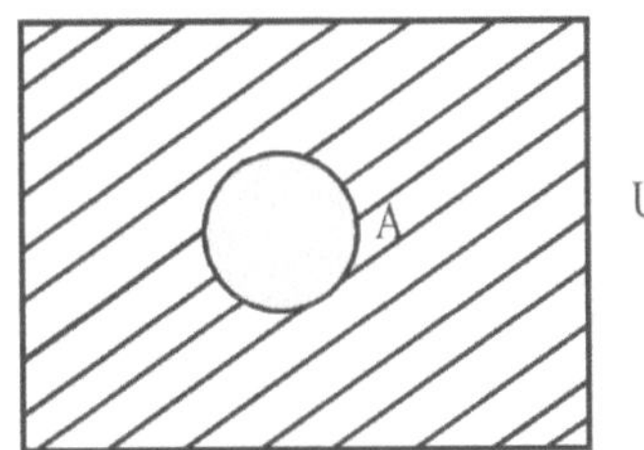

Let U and A be 2 sets such that $A \subseteq U$, then $(U - A)$ is simply called the complement of A.

It is denoted by $\overline{A}$ or A'.
e.g. U is the set of natural numbers, the complement of odd numbers will be a set of even numbers.

 *The following letter sets are standard notations:*
N: Set of natural numbers
Z: Set of integers
Q: Set of all rational numbers.
R: Set of all real numbers.
C: Set of all complex numbers.

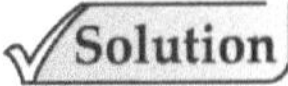 **Example 1**

U = {1, 2, 3, 4}, A = {3}.
What is the complement of A?

 **Solution**

A' = {1, 2, 4}

Remember the following
(i) $U' = \phi, \phi' = U$ (ii) $(A')' = A$

Union of Sets

If A and B are 2 sets, then the union of A and B, denoted by $A \cup B$, is the set of all elements which are **either** in A **or** in B or in both A and B.

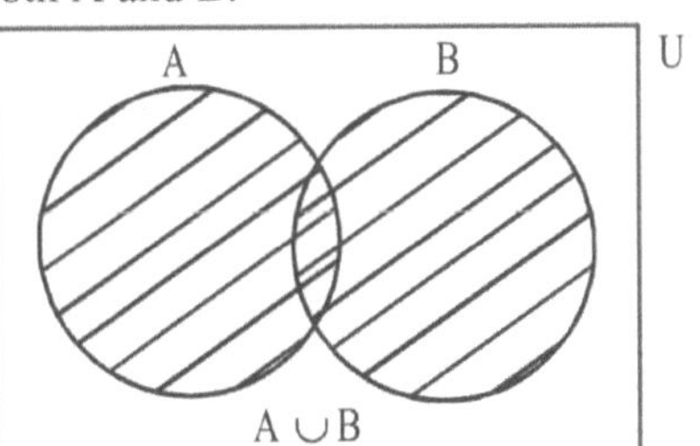

Union of even and odd non-negative integers is a set of natural numbers.

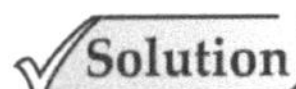 **Example 2**

If A = {1, 2, 5, 7, 9} and B = {3, 8, 9, 2, 0}. Find $A \cup B$.

Solution

$A \cup B$ = {0, 1, 2, 3, 5, 7, 8, 9}

Intersection of Sets

If A and B are sets, then the intersection of A and B, denoted by $A \cap B$, is the set of all elements which belong to **both** A **and** B.

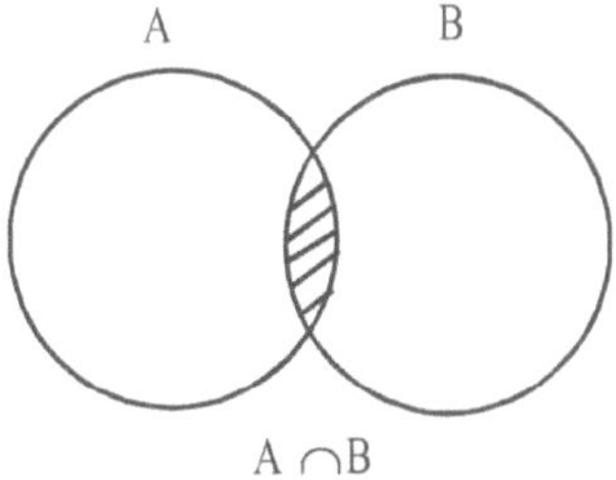

e.g. Intersection of set of prime numbers and set of even numbers is a set having only one element, which is 2, i.e. = {2}

 *Consider and verify the following identities:*
i. $A \cup A = A, \quad A \cap A = A$
ii. $A \cup \phi = A, \quad A \cap \phi = \phi$
iii. $A \cup U = U, \quad A \cap U = A$
iv. $A \cup B = B \cup A, \quad A \cap B = B \cap A$
v. $A \cup A' = U, \quad A \cap A' = \phi$

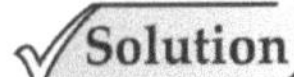 **Example 3**

A = {1, 2, 3, 4, 5} and B = {3, 7, 9, 4}. Find $A \cap B$.

Solution

$A \cap B$ = {3, 4}
If A and B have no elements in common, then they are called **disjoint sets**.

Difference of Sets

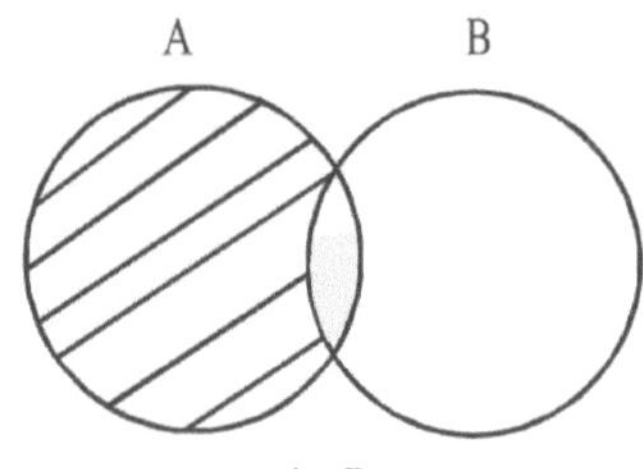

If A and B are sets, then the difference of A and B, written as A − B, is the set of all those elements of A which do not belong to B.

Note:

$A - B = A - A \cap B = A \cap B'$

Is $A - B = B - A$?
Find out for the sets A and B given in the example.

Example 4

$A = \{1, 2, 3, 4, 5\}$ and $B = \{3, 4, 6, 7\}$, find $A - B$.

Solution

$A - B = \{1, 2, 5\}$

Venn Diagrams

For three sets, the following diagram is valid.

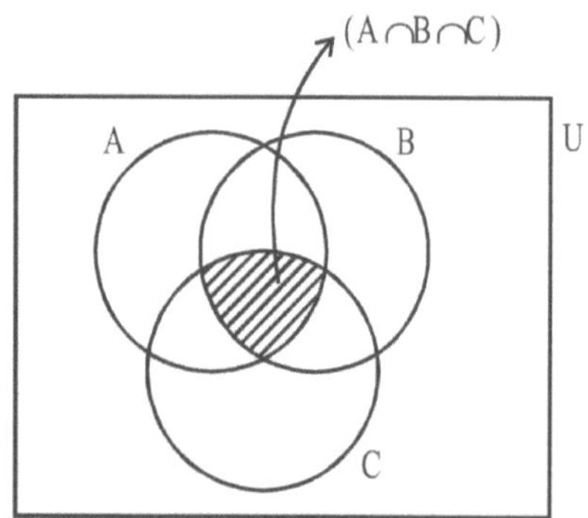

$n(A \cup B \cup C) = n(A) + n(B) + n(C) - n(A \cap C)$
$\qquad - n(A \cap B) - n(B \cap C) + n(A \cap B \cap C)$

$n(A \cup B) = n(A) + n(B) - n(A \cap B)$ *If $n(A \cup B)$ is not given and* $n(A \cap B)$ *is to be found, then we get a range of values for both in general. In specific cases, it might be a unique answer.*

Example 5

In a group of 800 persons, 600 can speak English and 400 can speak Telugu. If all the people speak at least one of the two languages, then find
a. how many can speak both the languages?
b. how many can speak exactly one language?

Solution

a. $n(E \cup T) = n(E) + n(T) - n(E \cap T)$
$800 = 600 + 400 - n(E \cap T) \Rightarrow n(E \cap T) = 200$
b. People speaking exactly one language is equal to $n(E \cup T) - n(E \cap T) = 800 - 200 = 600$

Example 6

A survey shows that 63% of the Americans like apples whereas 76% like guns. What percentage of Americans like both apples and guns?

Solution

The solution for the question cannot be determined. This is because we do not have the information whether all Americans like at least one of these.
(If we assume that 100% Americans like at least one of these)
Then n (A) = 63, n (G) = 76
and $n(A \cup G) = 100$
$\Rightarrow n(A \cap G) = n(A) + n(G) - n(A \cup G)$
$= 63 + 76 - 100 = 39$
Thus, 39% Americans like both guns and apples.

Example 7

In a certain city only 2 newspapers A and B are published. It is known that 25% of the city population reads A and 20% reads B, while 8% read both A and B. It is also known that 30% of those who read A but not B, look into advertisements and 40% of those who read B but not A, look into advertisements while 50% of those who read both A and B look into advertisements. What percentage of the population look into an advertisement?

Solution

Let A and B denote sets of people who read newspaper A and newspaper B respectively. Then
n(A) = 25, n(B) = 20, n (A ∩ B) = 8;
n(A − B) = n(A) − n (A ∩ B) = 25 − 8 = 17;
n (B − A) = n (B) − n(A ∩ B) = 20 − 8 = 12
Percentage of people reading an advertisement
= [(30% of 17) + (40% of 12) + (50% of 8)]% = 13.9%

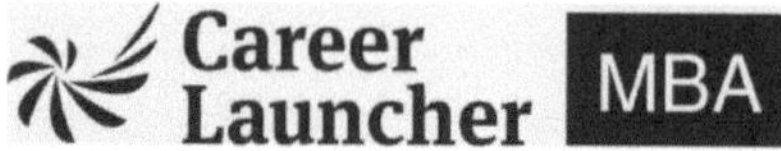

Fundamentals of Set Theory

Type I:

Example 8

In a school there are 200 students. 100 play cricket, 50 play hockey and 60 play basketball. 30 students play both cricket and hockey, 35 play both hockey and basketball and 45 play both basketball and cricket.

a. What is the maximum possible number of students who play at least one game?

b. What is the maximum possible number of students who play all the 3 games?

c. What is the minimum possible number of students playing at least one game?

d. What is the minimum possible number of students playing all the 3 games?

Solution

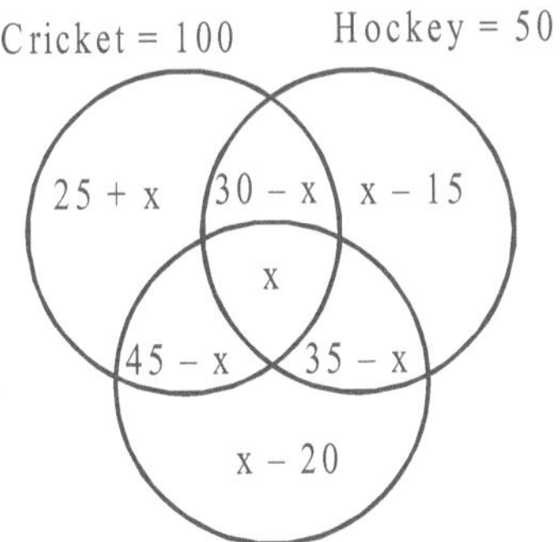

Let x be the number of students playing all the 3 games. Converting all values in terms of variable x, the number of students cannot be negative in any cell.

$\therefore$ x – 20 ≥ 0

$\therefore$ For minimum possible number of students playing all three games, i.e. x = 20

For maximum possible value of x, again none of the categories should have negative number of students.

$\therefore$ 30 – x ≥ 0

x ≤ 30

If x is more than 30, (30 – x) would be negative which is not possible.

$\therefore$ 20 ≤ x ≤ 30

Total number of students playing at least one game.
= 100 + (x – 15) + (35 – x) + (x – 20) = 100 + x

$\therefore$ Minimum possible number of students playing at least one game = 100 + 20 = 120
Maximum possible number of students playing at least one game = 100 + 30 = 130

Type II:

Example 9

In an office, where working in at least one department is mandatory, 78% of the employees are in operations, 69% are in finance and 87% are in HR. What are the maximum and minimum percentages of employees that could have been working in all three departments?

Solution

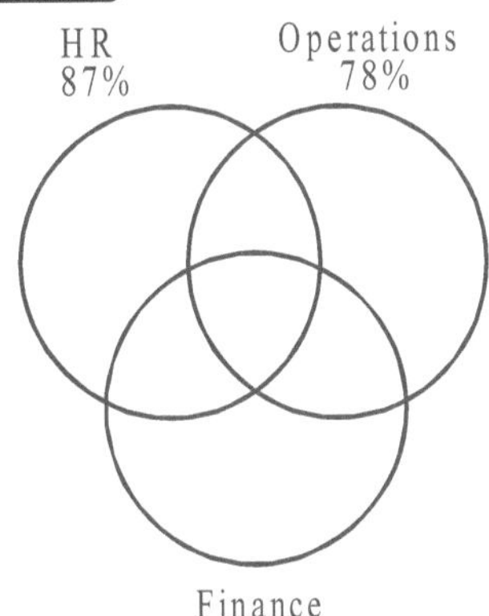

Let the total number of employees in the office be 100. Lets assume that x, y and z number of people are in exactly one, two and three departments of the office respectively.
Therefore, x + 2y + 3z = 78 + 69 + 87 = 234 and
x + y + z = 100
$\Rightarrow$ (x + 2y + 3z) – (x + y + z) = 134.
$\Rightarrow$ y + 2z = 134.

Maximum possible value of z is $\dfrac{134}{2}$ = 67

Therefore, maximum possible percentage of employees who could be working in all the three departments is 67%.

To minimize the value of z, we need to maximize the value of y, keeping in mind that x + y + z = 100.

Maximum possible value of y could be 66 and for this value of y, z = 34 and x = 0.

If we take a value of y greater than 66, lets say 68, then value of z comes out be 33, but here x + y + z is getting greater than 100, which is not possible.

Therefore, minimum possible percentage of employees who could be working in all the three departments is 34%.

Alternative method:

Minimum: 87% are in HR, it means at least 13% are in operations or finance or operations and finance both. In the same way, 78% are in operations.

So at least 22% are in HR or finance or HR and finance both.

Similarly, 31% are in HR, or operations or HR and operations.

Adding all three, 13% + 22% + 31% = 66%

It means that if there is no intersection among these three sets, 66% would be maximum number of employees in A, B, C alone or $(A \cap B)$, $(B \cap C)$, $(C \cap A)$.

This gives that at least 34% would be in all 3 departments.

The formula is $\left(\overline{\overline{A} + \overline{B} + \overline{C}} \right)$

Alternatively (for Example 8) the minimum value can be found by:
(78 + 69 + 87) —200 = 34%

Type III:

Example 10

There are 3 electives offered to the students in class of 92 (the students have a choice of not choosing any electives).

60 students opted for marketing, 80 for finance and 50 for systems, 40 students opted for both marketing and systems, 50 for both marketing and finance and 45 for both finance and systems. What is the maximum and the minimum possible number of students who opted for all 3 electives?

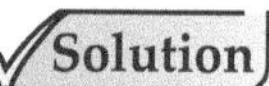

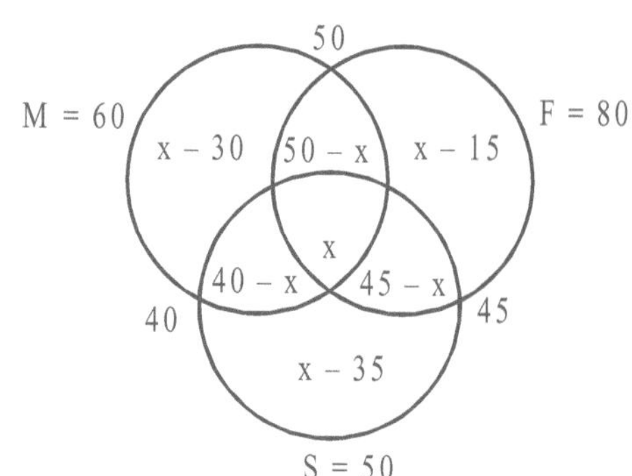

Total number of students = 60 + x – 5 = 55 + x

The minimum possible value of x, so that none of the categories becomes negative = 35

Now applying the same concept, maximum possible value of x = 40. For this value of x, total number of students = 55 + 40 = 95

Which exceeds the total number of students, i.e. 92 by 3, which is not possible.

So to make it equal to 92 the maximum possible value of x = 37

$\therefore 35 \leq x \leq 37$

Hence minimum possible number of students who opted for all 3 electives is 35. And maximum possible number of students who opted for all 3 electives is 37.

My Doubts

____

____

____

____

____

Career Launcher MBA

Fundamentals of Set Theory

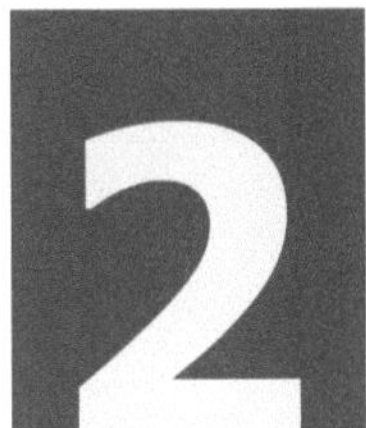

Practice Exercise

1. In a group there are 30 guys. 10 of them wear earrings, 15 of them wear ponytails. If the percentage of guys who wear neither is 30%, how many guys wear both earrings and ponytails?

2. Twenty friends, including the host decide to party on a festive Saturday night in a bar. The host knows that 15 of them can have whisky and 10 of them can have rum. He also knows that each of them have 4 pegs of any drink. None of them has both whisky and rum simultaneously. Every peg of whisky costs ₹60 and every peg of rum costs ₹30. What is the maximum and the minimum budget that the host would have planned for? [Assume that atmost 5 people can go without drink in that party]

3. In a class of 50 students, a test for 2 subjects was conducted. 30 passed in the first subject and 40 passed in the second subject.
(a) What is the maximum number of people who passed in both the subjects?
(b) What is minimum number of people who passed in both the subjects?

4. A survey was conducted on a car brand KHATARA. It was found that 60% of vehicles had a problem with their engines, 60% of vehicles had a problem with the doors, 50% of vehicles had a problem with the tyres. 20% of the vehicles had no problem. What is the minimum percentage of vehicles which had all the 3 problems?

5. In question 4, what is the maximum percentage of vehicles which could have had all the problems?

My Doubts

____

____

____

____

____

____

____

____

1. In a group of 500 students, selected for admission in a business school, 64% opted for finance and 56% for operations as specialisations. If dual specialisation is allowed, how many have opted for both?
    Each student opts for at least one of the two specialisations.
    (a) 200   (b) 100   (c) 150
    (d) 125   (e) 140

Directions for questions 2 to 4: Read the passage given below and answer the questions.

In a locality, 30% of the residents read *The Times of India* and 75% read *The Hindustan Times*. 3 people read neither of the papers and 6 read both. Only *The Times of India* and *The Hindustan Times* newspapers are available.

2. How many people are there in the locality?
    (a) 60   (b) 120   (c) 126
    (d) 130   (e) 90

3. What is the percentage of people who read only *The Times of India*?
    (a) 15%   (b) 20%   (c) 25%
    (d) 30%   (e) 35%

4. What percentage of residents read only one newspaper?
    (a) 11%   (b) 43%   (c) 85%
    (d) 20%   (e) 60%

Directions for questions 5 and 6: Answer the questions based on the following information.

In a sports centre 70 students play cricket, 50% play hockey, 25% play both hockey and cricket and 5% play none.

5. How many students are there in the class?
    (a) 80   (b) 85   (c) 95
    (d) 100   (e) 110

6. How many students play only one game?
    (a) 65   (b) 70   (c) 75
    (d) 80   (e) 90

Directions for questions 7 and 8: Read the following information and answer the questions.

In an examination there are 150 candidates. 40 candidates passed in papers A and B; 40 candidates passed in papers B and C; 30 candidates passed in papers C and A ; and 10 candidates passed in all the 3 papers.

7. How many students passed in paper B only?
    (a) 40   (b) 20   (c) 15
    (d) 25   (e) Cannot be determined

8. If no students failed in all the 3 subjects, what is the total number of students who passed in exactly one paper?
    (a) 25   (b) 45   (c) 60
    (d) 50   (e) 55

9. In a class of 60 boys, there are 45 boys who play cards and 30 boys play carrom. Find how many boys play both the games. (assuming that every boy plays either cards or carrom or both)
    (a) 15   (b) 17   (c) 20
    (d) 21   (e) 16

10. In question number 9, find the number of boys who only play cards.
    (a) 27   (b) 30   (c) 32
    (d) 25   (e) 35

11. In question number 9, find the number of boys who only play carrom.
    (a) 10   (b) 12   (c) 15
    (d) 20   (e) 14

12. Each student in a class of 40, studies at least one of the subjects namely English, Mathematics and Economics. 16 study English, 22 study Economics and 26 study Mathematics, 5 study English and Economics, 14 study Mathematics and Economics and 2 study English, Economics and Mathematics. Find the number of students who study English and Mathematics.
    (a) 10   (b) 7   (c) 17
    (d) 27   (e) None of these

13. In question number 12, find the number of students who study English and Mathematics but not Economics.
    (a) 8   (b) 12   (c) 7
    (d) 5   (e) 6

Fundamentals of Set Theory

Permutation and Combination

Introduction

The chapter covers permutation and combination which are efficient methods of counting numbers.

- Permutations are different ways of arranging things, we will learn to arrange different objects in different ways in this chapter.

Do you know ?

8 different books can be arranged in   40320 ways!!

- Combination deals with choosing the objects .

Do you know in how many ways , we can select 3 books out of 8 different books ?
56 ways!!

Learning Objectives

- Fundamental principles of counting
- Permutation - Linear and Geometrical
- Grouping and Distribution

Principal of Counting

Factorial:

Factorial of a natural number is defined as the product of all the consecutive natural numbers from 1 to that particular number. For example factorial of 5 is $1 \times 2 \times 3 \times 4 \times 5$. 'Factorial' word is represented with a symbol '!'. or 'L'. For example, factorial of 5 is written as L5 or 5!.

Example: $\dfrac{10!}{8!} = ?$

$$\dfrac{10!}{8!} = \dfrac{10 \times 9 \times 8!}{8!} = 10 \times 9 = 90 .$$

Note:

Factorial of zero is 1 (0! = 1)

Fundamental Principal of Counting

I. Product Rule:

In how many different ways can a person reach Mumbai from Ahmedabad (via Surat) if there are 4 different routes from Ahmedabad to Surat and 3 different routes from Surat to Mumbai?

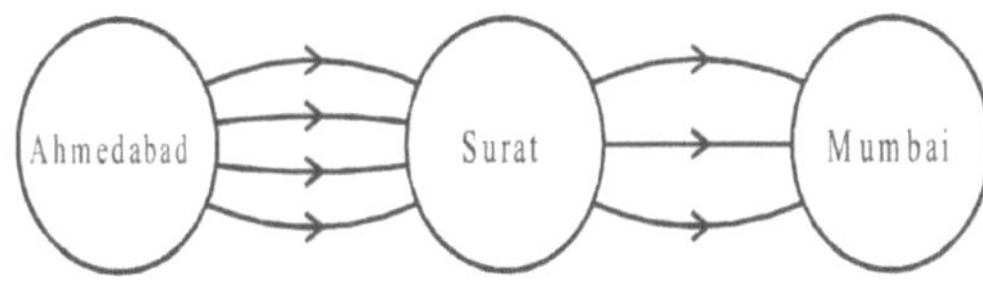

Total number of ways = 4 × 3 = 12 ways.

So according to fundamental principle of counting, if there are m ways of doing a first thing and for each of them there are n ways of doing a second thing, then the total number of ways of doing both the things together is m × n.

Most of the problems are based on the fundamental principle of counting.

Example: In how many different ways can 3 travellers stay in 4 hotels when each one should stay in different hotel?

Answer: For first traveller there are 4 choices; for second traveller 3 choices; for third traveller only 2 choices.

$\therefore$ Total ways = $4 \times 3 \times 2 = 24$ ways.

All problems of counting are based on fundamental principle of counting.

II. Addition rule

If there are 4 different ways from Surat to Ahmedabad and 3 different ways from Surat to Mumbai, then in how many different ways can a person go to Ahmedabad or Mumbai from Surat?

The answer is $4 + 3 = 7$ ways.

The addition rule and Product rules signify the cases of "or" & "and".

Identify and understand clearly when addition rule is applied and when product rule is applied. Addition rule is applied when you take different cases and product rule is applied for the same case.

Example:

From Surat a person can go either to Mumbai OR to Ahmedabad. When we have OR it is two different cases hence the number of ways is $4 + 3$. But to go from Ahmedabad to Mumbai you have to go from Ahmedabad to Surat AND from Surat to Mumbai. Hence they constitute single case. Hence number of ways = 4×3 and not $4 + 3$.

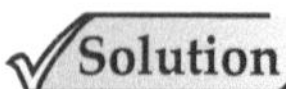 **Example 1**

There are 10 boys and 8 girls in a class . For the post of class monitor, the teacher wants to select either a boy or a girl. In how many ways can he do this function?

Solution

He can select one boy out of 10 boys in 10 ways.
He can select one girl out of 8 girls in 8 ways.
He can select either a boy or a girl in $10 + 8$
= 18 ways.

Note:

1. If all the functions are correlated, then basic principle of multiplication is used

2. If all the functions are independent, then basic principle of addition is used.

Example 2

How many three-digit numbers are there?

Solution

We know that there are 10 digits 0, 1, 2, 3, 4, 5, 6, 7, 8, 9
'0' cannot be at the hundreds place
So, 100th place can be filled in 9 ways.
Tens place can be filled in 10 ways.
Units place can be filled in 10 ways.
So the total number of three digit numbers
$= 9 \times 10 \times 10 = 900$

Example 3

How many three-digit numbers are there in which all the digits are distinct?

Solution

100th place can be filled in 9 ways.
10th place can be filled in 9 ways.
Units place can be filled in 8 ways because all the digits should be distinct.
So, the total number of three digit numbers in which all digits are distinct $= 9 \times 9 \times 8 = 648$

Example 4

There are 5 multiple choice questions in an examination. First three questions have 4 choices each and the remaining two questions have 5 choices each. How many sequences of answers are possible?

Solution

Each one of the first three questions can be solved in 4 ways, and each one of the last two questions can be solved in 5 ways.
So, the total number of different sequences of answers are $4 \times 4 \times 4 \times 5 \times 5 = 4^3 \times 5^2 = 1600$

Example 5

How many even numbers less than 1000 can be formed by using the digits 2, 4, 3 and 5, if repetition of the digits is allowed?

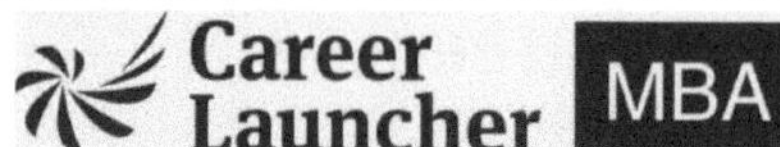

All the numbers of one digit, two digits and three digits are less than 1000. So take these cases one by one

1. Single-digit even numbers are 2 and 4
2. Two-digit even numbers:
   Unit's place can be filled in 2 ways, by 2 and 4 because unit's place digit must be an even number
   Ten's place can be filled in 4 ways.
   So the total number of two-digit even numbers $= 2 \times 4 = 8$
3. Three-digit even numbers
   Unit's place can be filled in 2 ways.
   Ten's place can be filled in 4 ways.
   Hundred's place can be filled in 4 ways
   So the total number of three-digit even numbers $= 2 \times 4 \times 4 = 32$
   Total number of three-digit even numbers (by using the digits 2, 4, 3 and 5) less then $1000 = 2 + 8 + 32 = 42$

Permutations

Suppose there are three persons A, B and C contesting for the post of president and vice president of an organization and we have to select two persons. We can do it in 3 ! ways. For example, (A, B), (B, C), (A, C) (B, A), (C, B) and (C, A). Here, the first person can be the president and the second person can be the vice president, means here we are talking about the order of arrangement.

The arrangements of a number of things taking some or all of them at a time are called permutations.

For example, if there are 'n' number of persons and we have to select 'r' persons at a time, then the total number of permutations is denoted by $^{n}P_{r}$ or by P(n, r).

First person can be selected in 'n' ways. Second person can selected in 'n – 1' ways. Third person can be selected in 'n – 2' ways.

Similarly, the rth person can be selected in 'n – (r – 1)' = '(n – r + 1)' ways.

∴ Total number of ways of arranging these 'r' selected persons

$$= n \times (n-1) \times (n-2) \times ....(n-r+1)$$

$$= \frac{n \times (n-1)(n-2) \times ....1}{(n-r)(n-r-1) \times ....1} = \frac{n!}{(n-r)!}$$

$$\therefore {}^{n}P_{r} = \frac{n!}{(n-r)\,!} \cdot$$

Example 6

There are four persons A, B, C and D and at a time we can arrange only two persons. Find the total number of arrangements.

Solution

Total number of arrangements (**permutations**) is AB, BA, AC, CA, AD, DA, BC, CB, CD, DC, BD and DB or we can say that out of 4 persons we have to arrange only 2 at a time, so the total number of permutations is $^{4}P_{2}$.

$$^{4}P_{2} = \frac{4!}{(4-2)\,!} = \frac{4!}{2!} = \frac{4 \times 3 \times 2}{2!} = 12$$

Example 7

In the above question, if all the persons are selected at a time, then how many arrangements are possible?

Solution

We have to arrange 4 persons, so this can be

$$^{4}P_{4} = \frac{4!}{(4-4)\,!} = \frac{4!}{0!} = \frac{4!}{1}$$
$$= 4 \times 3 \times 2 \times 1 = 24$$

Example 8

There are 4 flags of different colours. How many different signals can be given, by taking any number of flags at a time?

Solution

Signals can be given either taking all or some of the flags at a time.

Number of signals that can be given by taking 1 flag $= {}^{4}P_{1}$

Number of signals that can be given by taking 2 flags $= {}^{4}P_{2}$

Number of signals that can be given by taking 3 flags $= {}^{4}P_{3}$

Number of signals that can be given by taking 4 flags $= {}^{4}P_{4}$

So the total number of signals

$$= {}^{4}P_{1} + {}^{4}P_{2} + {}^{4}P_{3} + {}^{4}P_{4}$$

$$= \frac{4!}{(4-1)!} + \frac{4!}{(4-2)!} + \frac{4!}{(4-3)!} + \frac{4!}{(4-4)!}$$

$$= 4 + 12 + 24 + 24 = 64$$

? Example 9

Find the number of ways in which 5 boys and 5 girls be seated in a row so that:

I. All the boys sit together and all the girls sit together.
II. Boys and girls sit at alternate positions.
III. No two girls sit together.
IV. All the girls always sit together.
V. All the girls are never together.

✓ Solution

I. All the boys can be arranged in 5! ways and all the girls can be arranged in 5! ways.
   Now we have two groups (boys, girls) and these 2 groups can be arranged in 2! ways.
   [boys–girls and girls–boys]
   So total number of arrangements is
   $5! \times 5! \times 2! = 28,800$

II. Boys and girls sit alternately, this can be arranged like this
   B G B G B G B G B G or G B G B G B G B G B
   In the first case boys can be arranged in 5! and girls can be arranged in 5! ways.
   In the second case also, the number of arrangement is same as first case
   So the total number of arrangement
   $$= 5! \times 5! + 5! \times 5! \text{ or } {}^5P_5 \times {}^5P_5 + {}^5P_5 \times {}^5P_5$$
   $$= 120 \times 120 + 120 \times 120$$
   $$= 14,400 + 14,400 = 28,800 \text{ ways}$$

III. No two girls sit together - In this case
   __B__B__B__B__B__ there are 6 spaces where a girl can find her seat.

   5 girls can be arranged in ${}^6P_5$

   $$\frac{6!}{(6-5)!} = 6 \times 5 \times 4 \times 3 \times 2 = 720 \text{ ways}$$

   5 boys can be arranged in ${}^5P_5$
   $$= 5 \times 4 \times 3 \times 2 \times 1 = 120 \text{ ways}$$
   Total number of arrangements
   $$= 720 \times 120 = 86,400$$

IV. When all the girls are always together, then treat them as one group. So now we have 5 boys and 1 group of 6 girls and this can be permutated in 6! ways at the same time 5 girls in the group can be permutated in 5! ways, so total number of required ways is 6! × 5! = 720 × 120 = 86400

V. All the girls are never together
   Total number of arrangements of 5 boys and 5 girls is 10!
   Number of arrangements in which all the girls are always together

   $= B_1, B_2, B_3, B_4, B_5$ [All 5 girls]
   $= 6! \times 5! = 8,64,00$
   So number of arrangements in which all the girls are never together = total arrangement – number of arrangements when girls are always together.
   $= 10! - (6! \times 5!) = 3,54,2400$

? Example 10

Find the number of permutation of the letters of the word FOLDER taking all the letters at a time?

✓ Solution

Number of letters in the word FOLDER is 6

So the number of arrangements = ${}^6P_6 = 6!$

Alternative method:
First place can be filled by any one of the six letters. The second place can be filled by any one of the five remaining letters, the third place can be filled by any one of the four remaining letters and so on. So the total number of arrangements is
$6 \times 5 \times 4 \times 3 \times 2 \times 1 = 720$.

? Example 11

How many four-digit numbers greater than 5000 can be formed by using the digits 4, 5, 6 and 7? (Repetition of the digits is not allowed.)

✓ Solution

Total number of arrangements possible is ${}^4P_4 = 4!$
Total number of arrangements by using the digits 5, 6 and 7 is = 3!
So the total number of required arrangements is
$4! - 3! = 24 - 6 = 18$

Alternative method:

Thousand's place can be filled in 3 ways.

Hundred's place can be filled in 3 ways.

Ten's place can be filled in 2 ways.

Unit's place can be filled in 1 ways.

So total number of arrangements = $3 \times 3 \times 2 \times 1 = 18$

Example 12

In Q. 11, find the number of four-digit numbers that can be formed if the repetition of digits is allowed.

Solution

If the repetition is allowed, then the total number of arrangements is $4 \times 4 \times 4 \times 4 = 256$ ways

Because on the first place any one of the four number can come, similarly on the 2nd, 3rd and 4th place also.

Total number of arrangements beginning with 4 is $4 \times 4 \times 4 = 64$

So, total number of required arrangements = $256 - 64 = 192$

Alternative method:

Thousand's place can be filled in 3 ways

Hundred's place can be filled in 4 ways.

Ten's place can be filled in 4 ways.

Unit's place can be filled in 4 ways.

So the total number of arrangements = $3 \times 4 \times 4 \times 4 = 192$

Example 13

There are 5 friends: A, B, C, D and E. They wanted to take a group photograph of all of them sitting in a single row.

  a. How many distinctly different photographs can be clicked?

  b. In how many of these photographs would A be sitting in the middle?

  c. In how many of these photographs would A and B be sitting next to each other?

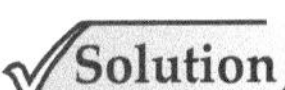

Solution

  a. There are 5 friends: A, B, C, D and E. The total number of photographs that can be taken each of which is distinctly different from the other is same as the total number of ways A, B, C, D and E can be permuted taken all at a time.

  Hence, the total number of photographs

  $$= {}^5P_5 = 5! = 120$$

  b. If we fix the position of A in the middle, then the other 4 can be seated in 4! ways. Hence, the number of ways in which A is in the middle $= 4!$.

  c. Take A and B as one unit.

  Then there are 4 units that have to be arranged (A B) CDE. They can be arranged in 4! ways. A and B among themselves can be arranged in 2! ways. Hence, by the fundamental principle of counting we have $4! \times 2!$ ways of arrangement.

$$ {}^nC_r = \frac{n!}{r!\,(n-r)!} $$

But a simpler way to look at

$$ {}^{10}C_3 = \frac{10 \times 9 \times 8}{1 \times 2 \times 3} $$

numerator has 3 numbers starting from 10 and denominator has 3 numbers starting from 1.

Similarly, $ {}^nP_3 = \dfrac{n!}{(n-r)!} $

$$ {}^{10}P_3 = 10 \times 9 \times 8 $$

This helps in faster calculation.

Example 14

A letter lock contains 4 rings, each ring containing 5 letters. In how many different ways can the 4 rings be combined? If the lock opens in only one arrangement of 4 letters, how many unsuccessful events are possible?

Solution

Each ring contains 5 letters. Therefore, for each of the ring we have 5 different ways of bringing a letter to the opening position.

$\therefore$ The number of ways in which the 4 rings can be combined = $5 \times 5 \times 5 \times 5 = 625$

But of these attempts to open the lock, only one will be successful.

Hence, the possible number of unsuccessful events = $625 - 1 = 624$

If certain objects have to appear together, we can treat them as a single set in certain problems

A group of 6 students comprised of 3 boys and 3 girls. In how many ways could they be arranged in a straight line such that
a. the girls and the boys occupy alternate positions?
b. no two boys were sitting together?

Solution

a. The positions could be BG BG BG or GB GB GB
Hence, the number of arrangements is
$3! \times 3! + 3! \times 3! = 2 \times 3! \times 3!$

b. First of all we will arrange 3 girls in 3! ways.
$|\,G_1\,|\,G_2\,|\,G_3\,|$
Now we have 4 positions for 3 boys that can be filled in $^4P_3$ ways.
Hence, the total number of arrangements
$= {}^4P_3 \times 3!$

Example 16

The letters of the word FIGMENT are to be arranged in the following manner.
a. There is no restriction.
b. Start with F.
c. All vowels together
d. Vowels at first and last positions

Solution

a. There are 7 letters which can be arranged at 7 positions in 7! ways = 5040 ways.

b. Starting with F, remaining 6 letters can be arranged in 6! ways = 720 ways.

c. Tying all vowels with a string, we have F, G, M, N, T and (I, E), i.e. 6 sets. These can be arranged in 6! ways and the 2 vowels can exchange their positions in 2! ways.
Total number of ways = 6! × 2! = 1440 ways.

d. For vowels at first and last positions, first place can be taken by I and last by E, or vice versa. Remaining 5 positions can be filled by 5 letters in 5! ways.
So total words formed = 5! × 2! = 240 words.

Combinations

Suppose three persons A, B and C are contesting for the post of president and vice president of an organization and we have to select two persons. We can select either (a, b) or (b, c) or (a, c) = 3 ways because here we are talking about the selection, not about the order. Whether 'a' is a president or 'b' is a vice president or vice-versa, doesn't matter.

Suppose there are 10 persons in class and we have to select any 3 persons at a point regardless of the order, it is a case of combination.

If there are n number of things and we have to select some or all of them it is called combinations.
If out of n things we have to select r things ($1 \le r \le n$), then the number of combinations is denoted by

$$^nC_r = \frac{n!}{(n-r)!\, r!}$$

We already know that the number of arrangements of 'r' things out of the 'n' things is given by $^nP_r = \dfrac{n!}{(n-r)!}$

Combination does not deal with the arrangements of the selected things.
∴ 'r' selected things can be arranged in r! ways.

$$\therefore (r!) \times \left({}^nC_r \right) = {}^n P_r$$

$$\Rightarrow {}^nC_r = \frac{{}^nP_r}{r!} = \frac{n!}{r!(n-r)!}$$

Difference between permutations and combinations

Suppose that there are five persons A, B, C, D and E and we have to choose two persons at a time then in

Permutation	**Combinations**
Number of required ways	$= \dfrac{5!}{2!\,(5-2)!}$
$= \dfrac{5!}{(5-2)!}$	
$= \dfrac{5!}{3!} = 5 \times 4 = 20$	$= \dfrac{5!}{2! \times 3!} = \dfrac{5 \times 4}{2} = 10$

So it is clear that in permutations (rearrangement) order matters but in combinations (selections) order does not matter.

Example 17

In a class there are 5 boys and 6 girls. How many different committees of 3 boys and 2 girls can be formed?

Out of 5 boys we have to select 3 boys, this can be done in $^5C_3$ ways.

Out of 6 girls we have to select 2 girls, this can be done in $^6C_2$ ways.

So, selection of 3 boys and 2 girls can be done in

$$\left(^5C_3\right) \times \left(^6C_2\right) \text{ ways}$$

[Basic rule of multiplication]

$$= \left(\frac{5!}{3!(5-3)!}\right) \times \left(\frac{6!}{2!\ (6-2)!}\right)$$

$$= \left(\frac{5 \times 4}{2}\right) \times \left(\frac{6 \times 5}{2}\right) = 10 \times 15 = 150 \text{ ways}$$

Example 18

If there are 10 persons in a party, and each person shake hands with all the persons in the party, then how many hand shakes took place in the party?

Solution

It is very obvious that when two persons shake hands, it is counted as one handshake. So we can say that there are 10 hands and every combination of 2 hands will gives us one handshake.

So, the number of handshakes

$$= {}^{10}C_2 = \frac{10!}{2!\ (10-2)\ !}$$

$$= \frac{10 \times 9 \times 8!}{2!\ \times\ 8!} = 45$$

Example 19

For the post of Maths faculty in Career Launcher there are 6 vacant seats. Exactly 2 seats are reserved for MBA's. There are 10 applicants out of which 4 are MBA's. In how many ways the selection can be made?

Solution

There are 4 MBA's and 6 other candidates.

So we have to select 2 candidates out of the 4 MBA's and the rest 4 candidates out of 6 other candidates.

So the total number of ways of selection

$$= \left(^4C_2\right) \times \left(^6C_4\right)$$

$$= \left(\frac{4!}{2! \times (4-2)\ !}\right) \times \left(\frac{6!}{4!(6-4)\ !}\right)$$

$$= \left(\frac{4 \times 3 \times 2!}{2 \times 1 \times 2!}\right) \times \left(\frac{6 \times 5 \times 4!}{4! \times 2 \times 1}\right)$$

$$= 6 \times 15 = 90 \text{ ways}$$

Example 20

There are 10 points out of which no three are collinear. How many straight lines can be formed using these 10 points?

Solution

By joining any two points we will get one line.

So the total number of lines formed

$$= {}^{10}C_2 = \frac{10 \times 9 \times 8!}{2 \times (10-2)\ !} = \frac{10 \times 9 \times 8!}{2 \times 8!} = 45$$

Example 21

Find the number of diagonals that can be drawn by joining the vertices of a decagon.

Solution

In decagon there are 10 vertices and by joining any two vertices we will get one line.

So in a decagon total number of lines formed

$$= {}^{10}C_2 = \frac{10!}{2!\ (10-2)!} = \frac{10 \times 9 \times 8!}{2! \times 8!} = 45$$

But out of these 45 lines, 10 lines will be the sides of the decagon. So total number of diagonals $= 45 - 10 = 35$

Example 22

In the above question how many triangles can be formed?

Solution

We know that in a triangle there are three vertices and by joining any three points we will get a triangle.

So number of triangles formed

$$= {}^{10}C_3 = \frac{10 \times 9 \times 8 \times 7!}{3! \times (10-3)!} = \frac{10 \times 9 \times 8 \times 7!}{3! \times 7!} = 120$$

There are 5 boys and 6 girls. A committee of 4 is to be selected so that it must consist at least one boy and at least one girl?

Solution

The different possibilities are
I.   1 boy and 3 girls
II. 2 boys and 2 girls
III. 3 boys and 1 girl
In the first possibility total number of combinations

is $^5C_1 \times {}^6C_3$

In the second possibility total number of combinations

is $^5C_2 \times {}^6C_2$

In the third possibility total number of combinations

is $^5C_3 \times {}^6C_1$

So the total number of combinations are

$$^5C_1 \times {}^6C_3 + {}^5C_2 \times {}^6C_2 + {}^5C_3 \times {}^6C_1 = 310$$

Permutation of things when some are identical

Above was the case when all letters in the word were different. What if some letters are identical?

$\Rightarrow$ If out of n things, p are exactly alike of one kind, q exactly alike of second kind and r exactly alike of third kind and the rest are different, then the number of permutations of

n things taken all at a time = $\dfrac{n!}{p!q!r!}$

Example 24

How many different words can be formed using the letter of "HALLUCINATION"
i.   Using all the letters.
ii. If all vowels are together?
      There are 6 vowels: two **A**s, two **I**s, one **U**, one **O**.
iii. All vowels occupy odd places only.

Solution

i.   Total letters in the word are 13 and the identical letters are 2L, 2A, 2I, 2N.
      So total number of arrangements possible

      $= \dfrac{13!}{2!2!2!2!}$

ii. Tie all vowels together and considering as a single letter, now we have 8 letters, out of these 8 letters 2L and 2N are identical. These 8 letters can be

arranged in $\dfrac{8!}{2!2!}$ ways .

In group of 6 vowels, 6 letters can be arranged

themselves in $\dfrac{6!}{2!2!}$ ways.

So total number of words formed

$= \dfrac{8!}{2!2!} \times \dfrac{6!}{2!2!}$

iii. Out of 7 odd places (1, 3, 5, 7, 9, 11, 13), 6 odd places for 6 vowels can be selected in $^7C_6$ ways. On these 6 places, 6 letters can be arranged

in $\dfrac{6!}{2!2!}$ ways.

Remaining 7 letters can be arranged in

7 remaining places in $\dfrac{7!}{2!2!}$ ways.

Total words formed $= {}^7C_6 \times \dfrac{6!}{2!2!} \times \dfrac{7!}{2!2!}$

Note that you would apply the formula for arrangement of objects some of which are identical, only if all the objects are permuted. If "r" objects are selected, we will apply the rule to those "r" objects that are selected.

Example 25

In how many ways can the letters of the word SUCCESSFUL be arranged? In how many of them will (i) all Ss come together, (ii) all Ss not come together, (iii) the Ss come together and Us also come together?

Solution

The word contains 10 letters of which 3 are Ss, 2 are Cs, and 2 are Us and the rest all are different.

$\therefore$ The letters of the word SUCCESSFUL can be

arranged in $\dfrac{10!}{3!2!2!} = 151\,200$ ways.

i.   Since the Ss are to come together, treat 3 Ss as one letter. Now with this restriction there will be 8 letters of which 2 are Cs and 2 are Us and the rest all are different.

$\therefore$ The arrangement in which Ss will come

together $= \dfrac{8!}{2!\,2!} = 10080$

ii. The arrangements in which all Ss will not come together = Total number of arrangements – The number of arrangements in which all the Ss will come together
$= 151200 - 10080 = 141120$

iii. Since the Ss and Us are to come together, treat 3 Ss as one letter and 2 Us as one letter. Now there will be 7 letters of which 2 are Cs and the rest all are different.
$\therefore$ The arrangements in which Ss and Us will come

together $= \dfrac{7!}{2!} = 2520$

 *Note that in the case of repetition of digits all those cases where no digits are repeated are also included.*

Example 26

There are 10 digits from 0 to 9 in the decimal system. Find the following using this data.

a. How many 5-digit numbers can be formed, such that no 2 digits are the same?
b. How many 4-digit numbers can be formed using these 10 digits?
c. How many numbers more than 1,000 and less than 10,000 can be formed such that they are divisible by 5 and no 2 digits are the same?
d. What is the number of arrangements in which 3 appears exactly twice in part (b)?

Solution

a. The total number of digits that can occupy the 1st place = 9 (zero cannot occupy the first place). Consequently, the number of digits that can fill the 2nd, 3rd, 4th and 5th places are 9, 8, 7 and 6 respectively.
So total number of 5-digit numbers with distinctly different digits is
$9 \times 9 \times 8 \times 7 \times 6 = 27216$

b. The number of digits that can occupy the first place = 9
For the 2nd, 3rd and 4th places any of the 10 digits can occupy the distinct places.
Hence, the total number of 4-digit numbers is
$9 \times 10 \times 10 \times 10 = 9000$

Note: Repetition of digits occur in these arrangements.

c. The number has to be a 4-digit number. Since the number is divisible by 5. It has to end in either a 5 or a 0.
Take each of these cases separately.

Case 1: If it ends in a 5, the 1st, 2nd, 3rd places could be filled in 8, 8 and 7 ways respectively. Hence, the number of 4-digit numbers with distinctly different digits and ending in a 5 is $8 \times 8 \times 7 = 448$

Case 2: If the number ends in a 0, the 1st, 2nd, 3rd places could be filled in 9, 8 and 7 ways respectively. Hence, the total number of such numbers possible is $9 \times 8 \times 7 = 504$
So total number of 4-digit numbers divisible by 5 and having distinctly different digits is $448 + 504 = 952$

d. Out of the 4-digit numbers formed with repetition we need to find how many of them have two 3s. The cases are:
(i) When one of the 3s is in the first place.
(ii) When none of the 3s is in the first place.

Case (i)
If we fix a 3 in the first position, then the total number of ways of forming the remaining 3 digits is $9 \times 9 \times {}^3C_1 = 243$
[The second 3 can occupy 3 possible position.]

Case (ii)
If we let the first digit be anything other than 3, then the number of arrangements $= 8 \times 9 \times {}^3C_2 = 216$
Total such numbers $= 243 + 216 = 459$

 *In (2 + 3 + 4 + 5 + 6) (11111) (4!)*
(2 + 3 + 4 + 5 + 6) $\Rightarrow$ Sum of the digits
(11111) $\Rightarrow$ As many 1's as there are digits in the number.
(4!) $\Rightarrow$ Indicates number of times any digit appears in any place.

Example 27

Using the digits 2, 3, 4, 5 and 6, find the following.

a. Sum of all 5-digit numbers that can be formed such that no 2 digits are the same.
b. Sum of all 4-digit numbers that can be formed such that no 2 digits are the same.
c. Sum of all 4-digit numbers that can be formed such that digits can be repeated.

a. Each of the numbers would be in any place 4! times.

Hence, their contribution when in the ten thousand's place is $(2 + 3 + 4 + 5 + 6)(10000) \times 4!$

Similarly, when in thousand's place they contribute $(2 + 3 + 4 + 5 + 6)(1000) \times 4!$.

For hundred's, ten's and unit's places the contributions are

$(2 + 3 + 4 + 5 + 6)(100) \times 4!$,

$(2 + 3 + 4 + 5 + 6)(10) \times 4!$,

$(2 + 3 + 4 + 5 + 6)(1) \times 4!$ respectively.

Hence, the total contribution to the sum is

$(2 + 3 + 4 + 5 + 6)(11111)(4!)$.

b. The method is similar as in the previous question.

Each of these digits would be in any place in $^4P_3$ times.

Hence, the sum of all 4-digit numbers, with no repetitions, is

$$(2 + 3 + 4 + 5 + 6)(1111)(^4P_3)$$

c. Each of these digits would appear in the thousand's place 5^3 times.

Hence, their total contribution when in that position is $(2 + 3 + 4 + 5 + 6)(1000)(5^3)$

Extending the same principle to the rest of the problem, we get the sum of all such numbers with repetitions is

$(2 + 3 + 4 + 5 + 6)(1111)5^3$.

Example 28

Using the digits 0, 1, 2 and 4, find the sum of all four-digit numbers that can be formed. (Repetition of digits is not allowed.)

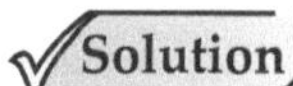

Using the principle as in # 8 (b), we would have sum of all 4-digit numbers $= (0 + 1 + 2 + 4)(1111)(3!)$

But some of these numbers will have 0 in the thousand's place and such cases are to be taken away. Such numbers would be same as the 3-digit numbers formed using digits 1, 2 and 4.

Hence, the sum of all such 3-digit numbers are $(1 + 2 + 4)(111)(2!)$.

Total sum

$= (0 + 1 + 2 + 4)(1111)(3!) - (1 + 2 + 4)(111)(2!)$

Example 29

Find the total number of triangles that can be formed by joining the vertices of the polygon of n sides. If the polygon has the same number of diagonals as its sides, find the number of triangles?

✓ Solution

The triangle is formed by joining any 3 vertices of the polygon of n vertices.

∴ The number of triangles formed by n vertices $= {}^nC_3$

The number of diagonals $= {}^nC_2 - n$

If a polygon with n sides has the same number of diagonals as sides, we have $n = {}^nC_2 - n$ Solving for n, we get n = 0 or 5.

Since $n \neq 0$, n = 5. Hence, the number of triangles $= {}^5C_3 = 10$

Example 30

There are 10 points in a plane. Except for 4 points which are collinear no three points are in a straight line. Find

(i) the number of straight lines obtained by joining these points,

(ii) number of triangles that can be formed with the vertices as these points.

✓ Solution

i. Two points form a straight line.

∴ Number of lines formed by joining 10 points

$$= {}^{10}C_2 = \frac{10.9}{2!} = 45$$

Number of straight lines formed by joining 4 points $= {}^4C_2 = 6$

But 4 collinear points give only one line. So these lines should be excluded.

∴ Required number of straight lines $= 45 - 6 + 1 = 40$

ii. Number of triangles formed by joining the points

taking 3 at a time $= {}^{10}C_3 = \frac{10.9.8}{3!} = 120$

Number of triangles formed by 4 points $= {}^4C_3 = 4$

But 4 collinear points cannot form any triangle.

∴ Required number of triangles $= 120 - 4 = 116$

The number of different relative arrangement for n different things arranged on a circle is (n —1)!

In how many ways can the letters of the word 'PROPORTION' be arranged without changing the relative positions of the vowels and consonants.

Solution

In the word PROPORTION, there are 6 consonants of which 2 are Ps, 2 are Rs and the rest are different and there are 4 vowels of which 3 are Os and one I. The positions originally occupied by vowels must be occupied by vowels and those occupied by consonants, by consonants only. The vowels must be permuted among themselves and similarly the consonants.

$\therefore$ The consonants can be permuted among themselves in $\dfrac{6!}{2!\,2!}$ ways and the vowels can be permuted among themselves in $\dfrac{4!}{3!}$.

Since the two operations are independent, the required number of ways is $\dfrac{6!}{2!\,2!} \times \dfrac{4!}{3!}$.

Geometrical Arrangements

Sitting in a circle is not same as sitting in a straight line. A circle has no starting point and no ending point. We will also talk about relative arrangements in a circle, which means the positions of others relative to a point being the same or different. The moment we label the positions on a circle the relative arrangements though same can yield "n" circular arrangements.

Circular Permutation: Number of circular permutation of n different things taken all at a time = (n – 1)! ways. Fix any one as reference point, other (n – 1) things can be arranged in (n – 1)! ways. Three persons around a circular table can be arranged in 2 ways, i.e. (3 – 1)! ways

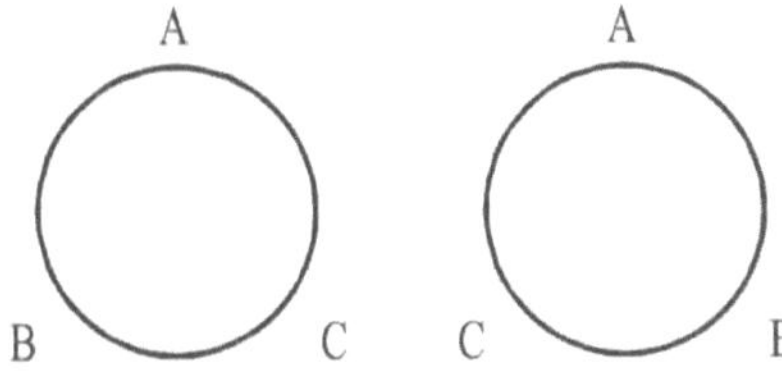

Necklace: In case of the necklace or garland, anticlockwise and clockwise arrangements are same. So total number of arrangements of n beads for forming a necklace is $\dfrac{1}{2}(n-1)!$

Example 32

In how many ways can 7 boys be seated at a round table so that 2 particular boys are

i. next to each other,

ii. separated.

Solution

Number of boys = 7

i. Let the 2 particular boys be taken together as one unit.

Then the number of units will be 6. They can sit around the table in 5! ways. For each of this arrangement, the 2 can be interchanged in 2! ways.

$\therefore$ The total number of arrangements = 5! 2!

ii. The arrangements that the 2 persons are separated = 6! – 5! 2!

Example 33

There are 25 gangsters including 2 brothers, 'Munna Mobile' and 'Pappu Pager'. In how many ways can they be arranged around the circular table if

a. there is exactly one person between these 2 brothers,

b. the 2 brothers are always separated?

Solution

a. One person between 2 brothers can be selected in 23 ways.

Remaining 22 persons can be arranged in 22! ways.

2 brothers can interchange their positions.

So total number of ways $= 2 \times 23 \times 22!$

$= 2 \times 23!$ ways

b. Total ways of arranging 25 people = 24!

Subtract those ways in which 2 brothers are together = 2 × 23!

$\therefore$ Number of ways when 2 brothers are always separated = 24! – 2 × 23!

Arrangement around a regular polygon:

If N people are to be arranged around a K sided regular polygon, such that each side of that polygon contains same number of people, then the number of arrangements will be $\dfrac{N!}{K}$

For example, 24 people are to be arranged around a square table having six people on each side of the table, number of arrangements will be $\dfrac{24!}{4}$.

Please remember if the polygon is not regular, i.e., if the sides of that polygon are uneven in length, then the number of arrangements will be just N!, whatever be the number of sides of that polygon.

Special case of a rectangular table:

If N people are to be arranged around a rectangular table, such that there are 6 people on each side of the table, then

total number of arrangements will be $\dfrac{N!}{2}$. Here '2' signifies

the degree of symmetry of a rectangle.

Example 34

A group of 11 people went to a party. There were 5 girls and 6 boys. They were seated on a rectangular table with 6 chairs on either side of the longer edge.

a. What is the total number of ways the group could be seated? [Sides are indistinguishable.]

b. What is the number of ways they can be seated so that all the 5 girls were sitting on the same side?

Solution

a. The total number of ways we can form 2 groups of

6 and 5 is $^{11}C_6$ or $^{11}C_5$. The total number of

ways these 2 groups can be seated on either side

is $^{11}C_6 \times 6! \times {}^6P_5$.

b. There will be 2 cases here.

Case (i)

When there are 5 girls, and a guy is sitting on one side and the remaining 5 guys are on the other side:

This is possible in $^6C_1 \times 6! \times 6!$ ways.

Case (ii)

When there are 5 girls on one side and all the guys are on the other side:

This is possible in $^6P_5 \times {}^6P_6 = 6! \times 6!$ ways.

∴ Total number of required arrangement

$= 6 \times 6! \times 6! + 6! \times 6!$

$= 7 \times 6! \times 6!$

Grouping and Distribution

This is another very important concept of permutation and combination. To distribute something, first grouping is done. Then permute these groups if required.

To illustrate the difference take the example of a case where you have 2 items I_1, I_2, of you have to split into 2 groups there is only 1 way of doing it. I_1 goes into one group and I_2 into another group. If you have to distribute among 2 people A, B then these 2 groups can be permuted in 2! ways. Similarly if there are 3 items I_1, I_2, I_3 the number of ways of splitting into 2 groups is $^3C_2$ i.e. $(I_1, I_2), (I_3)(I_1, I_3), (I_2)$ (or) $(I_2, I_3), (I_1)$

They can be distributed among 2 people in 2! ways. So it is important to distinguish between grouping and distribution.

Important points for grouping:

(i) The number of ways in which (m + n) things can be divided into two groups containing m and n things

respectively $= \dfrac{(m+n)!}{m!\,n!}$

(ii) If the numbers of things are equal, say m = n,

total ways of grouping $= \dfrac{(2\,m!)}{2!(m!)^2}$

It means divide by p! if there are p groups having same number of things or in other words, p groups are identical.

Example 35

I. In how many ways can 15 soldiers be divided into 3 groups equally?

Answer: $\dfrac{15!}{3!\,(5!)^3}$. Here we are dividing by 3!

because 3 groups are having same number of persons.

II. But if the question is, in how many ways can 15 soldiers be drafted into 3 regiments (JAT, SIKH, GORKHA)?

Answer: $\dfrac{15!}{3!\,(5!)^3} \times 3! = \dfrac{15!}{(5!)^3}$ i.e. the concept is

same. Dividing or grouping first, then permutating if groups are named, i.e. if groups are different. All questions of distributions can be solved easily if you are very clear about grouping.

Example 36

In how many different ways can 5 different balls be distributed to 3 different boxes, when each box can hold any number of balls?

Fundamentals of
Permutations & Combinations

Every ball has 3 ways of distribution. It can go to any of 3 boxes. So applying fundamental principle of counting, we get $3 \times 3 \times 3 \times 3 \times 3 = 3^5$ ways.

Note: We cannot say every box has 5 ways of chosing a ball. So 5^3 is wrong.

Example 37

In how many different ways can 5 identical balls be distributed to 3 different boxes, when each box can have any number of balls?

In this question, now the balls are identical. So number of balls in each box will matter. This question is exactly same as find non-negative integral solution of the equation $x_1 + x_2 + x_3 = 5$

These 3 variables are representing the number of balls in 3 different boxes. Insert 2 partitions in between these 5 balls.

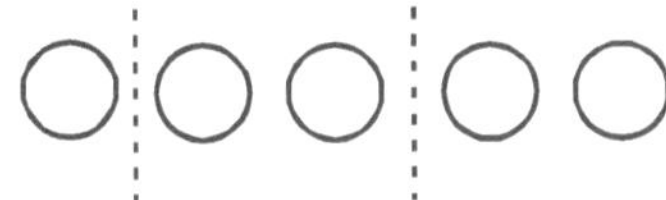

These 2 partitions will divide these 5 balls in 3 groups. Total number of ways of arranging these $(5 + 2)$ things

is $= \dfrac{(5+2)!}{2!\,5!}$ (Because 2 partitions are alike, 5 balls

are identical.) $= {}^7C_2$

So, distributing 'n' identical things in 'r' different

boxes $= {}^{n+r-1}C_{r-1}$

The number of ways of picking up any number of items from n different items is 2^n. Here the case of not picking up any item is also considered

Example 38

If $x + y + z = 12$, then what is the total number of positive integral solutions?

The difference in this question from above question is that it is asking for positive integral solution. It means now none of the variables can take 0 value. So

giving one ball to each of 3 boxes initially will ensure positive integral solution of $x + y + z = 12$. Total non-negative integral solutions of $x + y + z = 9$ is

$${}^{9+3-1}C_{3-1} = {}^{11}C_2$$

Note that from 10 identical items the number of distinct ways of choosing r items is not ${}^{10}C_r$ but just 1. The key word here is <u>distinct</u>.

Example 39

What is the total number of ways of selecting at least one object from 2 sets of

i. 10 distinctly different objects?
ii. 10 identical objects?
iii. 10 distinctly different objects picking at least one from each set?
iv. 10 identical objects picking at least one from each set?

i. Number of ways of selecting an item from 10 distinctly different items of one set

$$= {}^{10}C_0 + {}^{10}C_1 + {}^{10}C_2 + \cdots + {}^{10}C_{10} = (1+1)^{10}$$
$$= 2^{10}$$

Since there are 2 sets, the total number of

selections $= (2^{10}) \times (2^{10}) = 2^{20}$

Since at least one has to be selected, deduct the case where none has been selected from either sets, i.e. $2^{20} - 1$ cases.

ii. If all the objects are identical, then the number of ways is 11. (Select 0 or 1 or 2 or 3 ... or 10. Each one of these selections can be made in only 1 way.)

Since there are 2 sets there would be $11 \times 11 = 121$ cases. One of these cases would involve 0 selections from either of the sets. Hence, the total number of ways $= 121 - 1 = 120$

iii. If we have to pick at least 1 from each set, there

are $\left({}^{10}C_1 + {}^{10}C_2 + \cdots + {}^{10}C_{10}\right)\left({}^{10}C_1 + {}^{10}C_2 + \right.$

$\left. \cdots + {}^{10}C_{10}\right) = (2^{10} - 1)^2$ cases.

iv. If at least one item has to be selected from either of the sets, the total number of ways $= 10 \times 10 = 100$

[The case of 0 selection from each of the sets is not considered.]

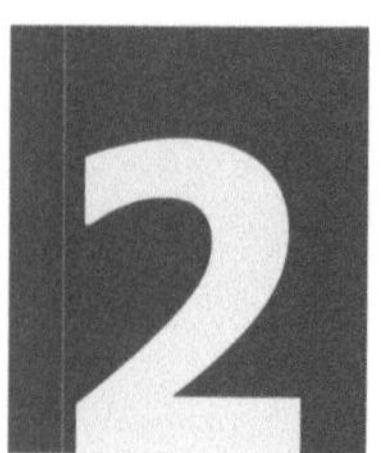

Probability

Introduction

- Probability is concerned with random outcomes, such as flipping coins or rolling dice.
- Probabilty is used to determine the possible outcome of a coin toss or a genetic sequence

Learning Objectives

- Probability
- Conditional Probability

Probability

Probability is the measure of the likelihood of occurrence of an event. Now we may define the probability of an event as follows:

Probability of an event

$$= \frac{\text{Number of favourable outcomes}}{\text{Number of all possible outcomes}}$$

 *An event is any outcome or a set of outcomes from an experiment.*

1. If an event E is sure to occur, we say that the probability of the event E is equal to 1 and we write P (E) = 1. Such events are known as certain events.

2. If an event E is sure not to occur, we say that the probability of the event E is equal to 0 and we write P (E) = 0. Such events are known as impossible events.

   Therefore, for any event E, $0 \le P(E) \le 1$.

   For example, if we toss a coin, is it more likely for a 'head' or a 'tail' to come up? If the coin is unbiased, we find that there is an equal chance for a 'head' or a 'tail' to come up. Thus, the chance for a 'head' (or a 'tail') to come up is $\frac{1}{2}$. An alternative word used for 'chance' is 'probability' and it is generally represented by 'P'.

Mathematical definition of probability:

A. If the outcome of an operation can occur in n equally likely, mutually exclusive and exhaustive ways, and if m of these ways are favourable to an event E, then probability of E, denoted by P (E), is given by $P(E) = \dfrac{m}{n}$

B. As $0 \le m \le n$, therefore for any event E, we have $0 \le P(E) \le 1$.

C. The probability of E not occuring, denoted by P (not E), is given by P (not E) or $P(\overline{E}) = 1 - P(E)$

D. Odds in favour

$$= \frac{\text{Number of favourable cases}}{\text{Number of unfavourable cases}}$$

E. Odds against

$$= \frac{\text{Number of unfavourable cases}}{\text{Number of favourable cases}}$$

Mutually exclusive events and addition law

(A) Mutually exclusive events:

If two events are said to be mutually exclusive then if one happens, the other cannot happen and vice versa. In other words, the events have no simultaneous occurence. For example,

1. In rolling a die:
   E : – The event that the number is odd
   F : – The event that the number is even
   G : – The event that the number is a multiple of three.

2. In drawing a card from a deck of 52 cards:
   E : – The event that it is a spade.
   F : – The event that it is a club.
   G : – The event that it is a king.

In general P(A or B) = P(A) + P(B) –P(A∩B)

If A, B are mutually exclusive then $P(A \cap B) = 0$

If A, B are independent then $P(A \cap B) = P(A) \cdot P(B)$

In the above 2 cases events E and F are mutually exclusive but the events E and G are not mutually exclusive or disjoint since they may have common outcomes.

(B) Additional law of probability:

If E and F are two mutually exclusive events, then the probability that either event E or event F will occur in a single trial is given by:

P(E or F) = P(E) + P(F)

If the events are not mutually exclusive, then

P(E or F) = P(E) + P(F) – P(E and F together).

Note:

Compare this with of set theory.

Similarly, **P (neither E nor F) = 1 – P(E or F).**

Independent Events And Multiplication Law

(A) Two events are independent if the occurence of one has no effect on the occurence of the other.

For example,
1. On rolling a die and tossing a coin together:
   E : – The event that number 6 turns up.
   F : – The event that head turns up.
2. In shooting a target:
   E : – Event that the first trial is missed.
   F : – Event that the second trial is missed.
   In both these cases events E and F are independent.
3. In drawing a card from a well–shuffled pack:
   E : – Event that first card is drawn.
   F : – Event that second card is drawn without replacing the first .
   G : – Event that second card is drawn after replacing the first.

In this case, E and F are not independent but E and G are independent.

(B) Multiplication law of probability:

If the events E and F are independent, then
P(E and F) = P (E) × P (F)

Example 1

In a single throw of a fair dice what is the probability that the number the appearing on the top face of the dice is more than 2?

Solution

In a dice there are 6 faces numbered 1, 2, 3, 4, 5 and 6. So, the total number of possible events are 1, 2, 3, 4, 5 and 6 = 6 and the total number of favourable events are 3, 4, 5 and 6 = 4

So, the required probability is $\dfrac{4}{6} = \dfrac{2}{3}$

Example 2

If two fair dice are thrown simultaneously, then what is the probability that the sum of the numbers appearing on the top faces of the dice is less than 4?

Solution

Total number of possible events = (1, 1), (1, 2), (1, 3), (1, 4), (1, 5), (1, 6), (2, 1), (2, 2) ….and so on. There will be 6 × 6 = 36 possible events.
Number of favourable events
= (1, 1), (1, 2) and (2, 1) = 3 events

So, the required probability = $\dfrac{3}{36} = \dfrac{1}{12}$

Example 3

If out of the first 20 natural numbers Mr. X selects a number at random, then what is the probability that this number will be a multiple of 4?

Solution

Total number of possible events = 1, 2, 3, …, 20 = 20 such numbers
Total number of favourable events
= 4, 8, 12, 16 and 20 = 5 such numbers

So, the required probability = $\dfrac{5}{20} = \dfrac{1}{4}$

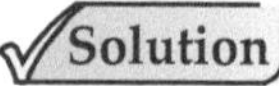

In the example 3, what is the probability that this number will be a multiple of 4 or 7?

Solution

Total number of possible events
= 1, 2 … 20 = 20 such numbers
Numbers divisible by 4 = 4, 8, 12, 16, 20
= 5 such numbers
Number divisible by 7 = 7 and 14 = 2 such numbers
Since from 1 to 20 there is no number which is divisible by both 4 and 7. It is a case of mutually exclusive events.
So number of possible outcomes = 5 + 2 = 7

So, the required probability is = $\dfrac{7}{20}$

Example 5

In the example 3, what is the probability that the selected number is divisible by 2 and 4?

Solution

The total number of possible events
= 20 such numbers
Number divisible by 2 and 4 means the number should be divisible by 4 (LCM of 2 and 4 is 4) = 4, 8, 12, 16, 20 = 5 such numbers

So, the required probability is $\dfrac{5}{20} = \dfrac{1}{4}$

Example 6

In the example 3, what is the probability that this number is divisible by 2 or 4?

Solution

The total number of possible outcomes = 20 in number
Number divisible by 2 = 2, 4, 6, 8, 10, 12, 14, 16, 18, 20 = 10 such numbers
Number divisible by 4 = 4, 8, 12, 16 and 20
= 5 such numbers
There are certain numbers which are divisible by both 2 and 4, so it is case of non mutually exclusive events.
Number divisible by both 2 and 4 are 4, 8, 12, 16 and 20 = 5 such number
So, the required probability= P(A) + P(B) – P(C)

$= \dfrac{10}{20} + \dfrac{5}{20} - \dfrac{5}{20} = \dfrac{10}{20} = \dfrac{1}{2}$

Conditional Probability

Let A and B are two dependent events, then probability of occurence of event A when B has already occurred is given

by $P(A\,|\,B) = \dfrac{P(A \cap B)}{P(B)}$

Example 7

From a pack of 52 cards, 4 cards were picked one at a time.
a. If the card picked is not replaced, find the probability that all the cards were aces.
b. If the card picked was replaced, what is the probability that all the 4 pickings were aces?
c. If the cards were picked all at a time, find the probability that all the 4 cards were aces.

Solution

a. Probability that the first card is an ace is $\dfrac{^{4}C_1}{^{52}C_1}$.

Probabilities that the 2nd, 3rd and 4th cards are all

aces are $\dfrac{^{3}C_1}{^{51}C_1}$, $\dfrac{^{2}C_1}{^{50}C_1}$ and $\dfrac{^{1}C_1}{^{49}C_1}$ respectively.

Hence, the total probability is

$\dfrac{^{4}C_1}{^{52}C_1} \times \dfrac{^{3}C_1}{^{51}C_1} \times \dfrac{^{2}C_1}{^{50}C_1} \times \dfrac{^{1}C_1}{^{49}C_1}$

$= \dfrac{4 \times 3 \times 2 \times 1}{52 \times 51 \times 50 \times 49} = \dfrac{1}{^{52}C_4}$.

b. With replacement, the probability is

$\left(\dfrac{^{4}C_1}{^{52}C_1}\right)^4 = \dfrac{1}{13^4}$

c. If all the 4 cards were picked simultaneously, then

the required probability is $\dfrac{^{4}C_4}{^{52}C_4} = \dfrac{1}{^{52}C_4}$.

Compare the cases (a) and (c). You would note that they are one and the same.

Career Launcher MBA

Fundamentals of Permutations & Combinations

One card is drawn from a pack of 52 cards, each of the 52 cards being equally likely to be drawn. Find the probability that the card drawn is

i.   a king,
ii. either red or king,
iii. red and a king.

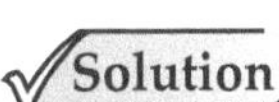 Solution

Out of 52 cards, one card can be drawn in $^{52}C_1$ ways. Therefore, exhaustive number of cases = $^{52}C_1 = 52$

i. There are 4 kings in a pack of cards, out of which one can be drawn in $^4C_1$. Therefore, favourable number of cases = $^4C_1 = 4$.

So, the required probability = $\dfrac{4}{52} = \dfrac{1}{13}$

ii. There are 28 cards in a pack of cards which are either a red or a king. Therefore, one can be drawn in $^{28}C_1$ ways. Therefore, favourable number of cases = $^{28}C_1 = 28$

So the required probability = $\dfrac{28}{52} = \dfrac{7}{13}$

iii. There are 2 cards which are red and king, i.e. red kings. Therefore, favourable number of cases = $^2C_1 = 2$.

So, the required probability = $\dfrac{2}{52} = \dfrac{1}{26}$

Example 9

Three unbiased coins are tossed. What is the probability of getting the following?

i.   All heads
ii. 2 heads
iii. Exactly 1 head

Solution

If 3 coins are tossed together, we can obtain any one of the following as an outcome.
HHH, HHT, HTH, THH, TTH, THT, HTT, TTT
So exhaustive number of cases = 8

i. All heads can be obtained in only one way, i.e. HHH.
So, the favourable number of cases = 1

Thus, the required probability = $\dfrac{1}{8}$

ii. Two heads can be obtained in any one of the following ways: HHT, THH, HTH. So favourable number of cases = 3.

Thus, required probability = $\dfrac{3}{8}$

iii. Required probability = $\dfrac{3}{8}$. The probability of exactly 1 head is same as probability of exactly 1 tail (or 2 heads) since the coin is unbiased.

Example 10

An urn contains 9 red, 7 white and 4 black balls. If 2 balls are drawn at random, find the probability that
i.   both the balls are red,
ii. one ball is white.

Solution

There are 20 balls in the bag out of which 2 balls can be drawn in $^{20}C_2$ ways. So the exhaustive number of cases = $^{20}C_2 = 190$

i. There are 9 red balls out of which 2 balls can be drawn in $^9C_2$ ways. Therefore, favourable number of cases = $^9C_2 = 36$.

So, the required probability = $\dfrac{36}{190} = \dfrac{18}{95}$

ii. There are 7 white balls out of which one white can be drawn in $^7C_1$ ways. One ball from the remaining 13 balls can be drawn in $^{13}C_1$ ways. Therefore, one white and one other colour ball can be drawn in $^7C_1 \times {}^{13}C_1$ ways.
So the favourable number of cases = $^7C_1 \times {}^{13}C_1 = 91$

So, the required probability = $\dfrac{91}{190}$

 *Let p be the probability of getting a head, q be the probability of not getting a head (i.e. a tail). If n coins are tossed simultaneously or one coin is tossed n times, $^nC_r \cdot p^r \cdot q^{n-r}$ gives the probability of having r heads and (n —r) tails.*

Example 11

Four coins were tossed. What is the probability that
a. all the 4 coins showed a head?
b. exactly 3 coins showed a head and the fourth showed a tail?

The problem is based on binomial distribution of probabilities.

If $p + q = 1$, then the term $^nC_r \cdot p^r \cdot q^{n-r}$ in the expansion $(p + q)^n$ gives the probability that when n such experiments are conducted r events are favourable and n–r events are unfavourable.

a. The probability that 4 heads occur when a coin is tossed 4 times is $^4C_4 \cdot \left(\dfrac{1}{2}\right)^4 = \left(\dfrac{1}{2}\right)^4$

b. The probability that there are 3 heads and 1 tail corresponds to $^4C_3 \left(\dfrac{1}{2}\right)^3 \left(\dfrac{1}{2}\right) = \dfrac{1}{4}$

Example 12

Two dice were thrown. What is the probability that
a. both of them showed a 6?
b. the sum of the numbers on the dice was 10?

✓ Solution

a. The probability that 1 die shows a 6 is $\dfrac{1}{6}$. The probability that both the dice show a 6 is $\dfrac{1}{6} \times \dfrac{1}{6} = \dfrac{1}{36}$.

b. The total number of cases in the sample space = 6 × 6 = 36

The cases satisfying a sum of 10 is {(4, 6) (5, 5)(6, 4)}, i.e. 3 events. Hence, the probability of having a sum of 3 is $\dfrac{3}{36} = \dfrac{1}{12}$

Example 13

Ramesh and Geeta were in the same class. The probability of Ramesh attending the class is 0.6. The probability of Geeta attending the class is 0.4. (Assume they behave independent of each other)
a. What is the probability that both of them attended the class?
b. What is the probability that at least one of them attended the class?

✓ Solution

a. Since the 2 events happen independent of each other, the probability of both Ramesh and Geeta attending the class simultaneously is 0. 6 × 0. 4 = 0.24

b. The probability of at least one of them attending the class is

P (Ramesh attends) + P (Geeta attends) – P (Both attend)

$\Rightarrow 0.6 + 0.4 – 0.24 = 0.76$

Example 14

Two machines A and B produce 100 and 200 items every day. Machine A produce 10 defective items and machine B produces 40 defective items. On one particular day the supervisor of the shop floor picked up an item and found that it was defective. Find the probability that it came from machine A.

✓ Solution

Method 1:
The total number of defective items produced on any single day = 50
The number of defective items from machine A = 10
Hence, probability of that item having come from machine A $= \dfrac{10}{50} = \dfrac{1}{5}$

Method 2:
Probability of finding a defective item = Probability that it is from machine A and is defective + Probability that it is from machine B and is defective

$\Rightarrow \dfrac{100}{300} \times \dfrac{10}{100} + \dfrac{200}{300} \times \dfrac{40}{200} = \dfrac{50}{300} = \dfrac{1}{6}$

Hence, probability that the defective item is from machine A $= \dfrac{\dfrac{100}{300} \times \dfrac{10}{100}}{\dfrac{1}{6}} = \dfrac{1}{5}$

Method 2, Example 14
This illustrates Bay's theorem.
P (finding defective) = P (Def from A) + P (Def from B) = y + z (say)

If given that you have found a defective the probability that it is produced by machine A $= \dfrac{y}{y+z}$.

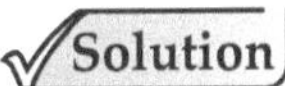 Example 15

Three black marketers A, B and C were selling the tickets of Jerry Maguire. The odds in favour of their selling all the tickets was 1 : 4, 2 : 3 and 4 : 1 respectively. What is the probability that at least one of them could sell all his tickets?

Solution

Probabilities of the three selling all their tickets are

$\dfrac{1}{5}, \dfrac{2}{5}$ and $\dfrac{4}{5}$.

Hence, probability that at least one of them sells all the ticket is equal to 1 – (None of them sells all his tickets)

$= 1 - \dfrac{4}{5} \times \dfrac{3}{5} \times \dfrac{1}{5} = 1 - \dfrac{12}{125} = \dfrac{113}{125}$

Example 16

A drawer contains 50 bolts and 150 nuts. Half of the bolts and half of the nuts are rusted.
If one item is chosen at random, what is the probability that it is rusted or a bolt?

Solution

Let A be the event that the item chosen is rusted and B be the event that the item chosen is a bolt.
Clearly, there are 200 items in all, out of which 100 are rusted.

$\therefore P(A) = \dfrac{100}{200}, \; P(B) = \dfrac{50}{200}$ and $P(A \cap B) = \dfrac{25}{200}$

Required probability

$= P(A \cup B) = P(A) + P(B) - P(A \cap B)$

$= \left(\dfrac{100}{200}\right) + \left(\dfrac{50}{200}\right) - \left(\dfrac{25}{200}\right) = \dfrac{5}{8}$

Example 17

An urn contains 5 white and 8 black balls. Two successive drawings of 3 balls at a time are made such that the balls are not replaced before the second draw. Find the probability that the first draw gives 3 white balls and second draw gives 3 black balls.

Solution

Consider the following events.
A = Drawing 3 white balls in first draw,

B = Drawing 3 black balls in the second draw
Required probability

$= P(A \cap B) = P(A) \; P(B \mid A) \qquad \ldots (i)$

Now $P(A) = \dfrac{{}^{5}C_{3}}{{}^{13}C_{3}} = \dfrac{10}{286} = \dfrac{5}{143}$

After drawing 3 white balls in first draw,
10 balls are left in the bag, out of which 8 are black balls.

$\therefore P(B \mid A) = \dfrac{{}^{8}C_{3}}{{}^{10}C_{3}} = \dfrac{56}{120} = \dfrac{7}{15}$

Hence, the required probability

$= P(A \cap B) = P(A) \; P(B \mid A) = \left(\dfrac{5}{143}\right) \times \left(\dfrac{7}{15}\right) = \dfrac{7}{429}$

Example 18

A dart is thrown at a dart board whose dimensions are 5 m × 5 m. If the probability of missing the dart board 0.25, find the probability of hitting the board at a point that is at a maximum distance of 2 m from the centre of the board.

Solution

Probability of hitting the dart board = 1 – 0.25 = 0.75
If the dart hits, then probability of hitting within the

circle of radius 2 m $= \dfrac{\pi r^{2}}{a^{2}} = \dfrac{\pi(2)^{2}}{5^{2}} = \dfrac{4\pi}{25}$

Hence, the resultant probability $= 0.75 \times \dfrac{4\pi}{25} = \dfrac{3\pi}{25}$

 *Example 18 is a case of infinistic probability, we cannot count the number of favourable outcomes because they are infinite. Hence, we take the ratio of favourable area to total area.*

 Example 19

If n persons are seated on a round table, what is the probability that 2 of them are always together?

Solution

Total number of ways in which n persons can sit on a round table is (n – 1)! Therefore, exhaustive number of cases = (n – 1)!. Considering 2 individuals as one persons there are (n – 1) persons who can sit on a round table in (n – 2)! ways. But the 2 individuals can be seated together in 2! ways. Therefore, favourable number of cases = $(n-2)! \times 2!$

So required probability = $\dfrac{(n-2)! \times 2!}{(n-1)!} = \dfrac{2}{n-1}$

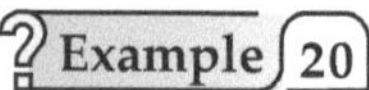

Example 20

Three different prizes have to be distributed among 4 different students. Each student could get 0 to 3 prizes. If all the prizes were distributed, find

a. the number of ways the prizes are distributed,

b. the probability that exactly 2 students did not receive a prize.

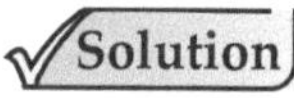

Solution

a. Each of the prizes could have been given to any of the 4 students.

Hence, the total number of ways of distributing the prizes = 4^3

Note: This will include all the cases when the prizes are distributed among 3 or 2 or only 1 student.

b. The total number of ways of distributing the prizes among exactly 2 students is $\left(^4C_2\right)\left(2^3 - 2\right)$ ways.

$^4C_2$ gives the selection of 2 boys.

$2^3 - 2$ gives the total number of ways of distributing 3 prizes among those 2 students. The subtraction of the 2 cases is to take care of those cases when all the prizes are distributed to only one among the two.

$\therefore$ The required probability $= \dfrac{36}{64} = \dfrac{9}{16}$

My Doubts

Career Launcher MBA

Introduction

There are 4 practice exercises out of which 1 is of level-1, 2 are of level 2 and 1 is of level 3 apart from the non MCQ to strengthen you fundamentals. While solving the exercises make sure that each and every concept is understood properly.

Problems for Practice (Non MCQ)

Level – 1

1. (a) Find r if
   (i) $^{10}P_r = 720$ (ii) $^9P_r = 3024$
   (b) Find n and r if
   (i) $^nP_r = 1680$ (ii) $^nP_r = 5040$

2. (a) Find n if $^nP_5 : {^nP_3} = 2 : 1$
   (b) Find r if $^9P_5 + 5 \cdot {^9P_4} = {^{10}P_r}$

3. In how many ways can 3 scholarships of unequal value be awarded to 17 candidates, such that no candidate gets more than one scholarship?

4. A man has 4 sons. There are 6 schools near his house. In how many ways can he send his sons to school, if no 2 of his sons are to study in the same school?

5. How many different 7-digit numbers can be formed from 0, 1, 2, 3, 4, 5, 6, 7, 8, 9?

6. There are 15 railway stations between Bangalore and Hyderabad. How many different kinds of second class tickets must be printed so as to enable a passenger to travel from every place in the route to other?

7. In how many ways can 7 letters be posted in 4 letter boxes?

8. How many natural numbers can be formed by using any number of digits from 0, 1, 2, 3, 4? (Repetition is not allowed.)

9. Five persons are to address a meeting. If a specified speaker is to speak before another specified speaker, find the number of ways in which this can be scheduled.

10. In how many permutations of 10 things taken 4 at a time will one particular thing (i) always occur and (ii) never occur?

11. The letters of the word LABOUR are permuted in all possible ways and the words thus formed are arranged as in a dictionary. What is the rank of the word LABOUR?

12. In how many ways can 17 billiard balls be arranged in a row if 7 of them are black, 6 red and 4 white?

13. A round table conference is to be held between 20 delegates of 20 countries. In how many ways can they be seated if 2 particular delegates always sit together?

14. In how many ways can a committee of 6 men and 3 women be formed from a group of 10 men and 7 women?

15. Out of 8 gentlemen and 5 ladies a committee of 5 is to be formed. Find the number of ways in which this can be done so as to include at least 3 ladies.

16. There are 20 points in a plane. Five of them are collinear.
   i. How many triangles can be made using these points as the vertices?
   ii. How many straight lines can be drawn passing through at least 2 of these points?

17. What is the total number of 4-digit numbers that can be formed using the digits 0 to 5 without repetition, such that the number is divisible by 9?

Directions for questions 18 to 29: Answer the questions based on the information given below.

There are 5 different boxes B1, B2, B3, B4, B5, and 5 different hats H1, H2, H3, H4, H5. The hats are to be distributed among the different boxes. Each box can accomodate all the hats.

18. If any box can have any number of hats, in how many ways can all the hats be distributed?

19. If all the hats are identical, in how many ways can the hats be arranged in the different boxes such that no box is without a hat?

20. If all the hats have different colours and each box can have only one hat, in how many ways can you arrange all the hats among the different boxes?

21. If the hats have to be arranged such that any box can have a maximum of one hat only, in how many ways can you arrange the hats among the 5 boxes? (At least one hat has to be distributed.)

22. If hats H1 and H2 are similar in all aspects, in how many ways can you arrange the hats in such a way that all the boxes have one hat?

23. If B1 can keep only hat H1 or H2, in how many ways can you arrange the hats such that all boxes have one hat?

24. What is the probability that B1 has either H1 or H2, but not both?

25. If B1 and B2 have the hats H1 and H2 among themselves, in how many ways can you arrange the hats among the 5 boxes?

26. In how many arrangements does B3 have hat H3?

27. If another hat H6 is also there, such that H6 has a different colour in comparison to all the other hats, in how many ways can you arrange the hats such that all the boxes have only one hat?

28. In question 27, if hat H6 has the same colour as H5, how many arrangements are there?

29. If it is known that hat H6 has the same colour as one of the other 5 hats, how many arrangements are possible in question 27?

30. In how many ways can 3 prizes be given to 4 contestants, if any contestant can receive any number of prizes?

31. m parallel lines in a plane are intersected by a family of n parallel lines. How many parallelograms are formed in the network thus formed?

32. In how many ways can 100 scouts be divided into squads of 50, 30 and 20 respectively?

33. There are 10 identical mangoes. In how many ways can you divide them among 3 brothers?

34. A person has to climb 10 steps. He climbs either a single step or 2 steps at a time. In how many ways can he do it?

35. The odds in favour of India winning a match against England is 4 : 3 and the odds against South Africa winning a match against Pakistan is 7: 5. Find the probability that at least one of them will win their respective matches.

36. A problem in mathematics is given to 3 students whose chance of solving it are $\frac{1}{2}, \frac{1}{3}$ and $\frac{1}{4}$ respectively. What is the probability that the problem is solved?

37. A bag contains 3 red and 5 black balls and a second bag contains 6 red and 4 black balls. A ball is drawn from each bag. Find the probability that both are (i) red, and (ii) black.

Level – 2

38. How many 5-digit numbers exist having exactly two 4s in them?

39. What is the sum of all 5-digit numbers formed using the digits 0, 2, 3, 4, 5?

40. There are 9 books of different subjects.
    i. What is the total number of selections of 3 books that can be made?
    ii. What is the total number of ways can 3 of these books be arranged on a shelf?
    iii. What is the total number of ways of dividing them into groups of 3 each?

41. What is the probability that when 2 dice and 4 coins are thrown simultaneously, there is a sum of 9 on the dice and at least 2 heads on the coins?

42. The probabilities of A, B, C solving a problem are $\frac{1}{3}, \frac{2}{7}$ and $\frac{3}{8}$ respectively. If all the three try to solve the problem simultaneously, find the probability that exactly one of them will solve it.

43. A gangster fires 4 bullets at the police inspector. The probability that the inspector will be killed by a bullet is 0.4. What is the probability that the inspector survives?

44. Two integers are selected at random from first 11 natural numbers. If the sum is even, find the probability that both the numbers are odd.

1. Find the value of $^8P_6$
   (a) 33425   (b) 20160   (c) 18972
   (d) 6625   (e) 6620

2. Find the value of $^8C_6$
   (a) 33   (b) 32   (c) 30
   (d) 28   (e) 35

3. Find the number of ways in which the letters of the word BIHAR can be rearranged.
   (a) 99   (b) 129   (c) 119
   (d) 125   (e) 130

4. Find the number of ways in which the letters of the word AMERICA can be rearranged.
   (a) 2519   (b) 2620   (c) 1250
   (d) 2500   (e) 2000

5. Find the number of ways in which the letters of the word CALCUTTA can be rearranged.
   (a) 3000   (b) 5009   (c) 5029
   (d) 5039   (e) 5150

6. In how many ways can you arrange the letters of the word AKSHAY such that vowels do not start the words?
   (a) $\dfrac{6!}{2!} - 1$ (b) $\dfrac{6!}{2!} - 2$ (c) $2 \times 5!$
   (d) 248   (e) 120

7. In how many ways can 2 cards be drawn from a full pack of 52 cards such that both the cards are red?
   (a) 275   (b) 325   (c) 350
   (d) 375   (e) 300

8. How many four-digit numbers each consisting of 4 different digits can be formed with the digits 0, 1, 2, 3?
   (a) 10   (b) 12   (c) 18
   (d) 20   (e) 16

9. In a tournament 7 teams are participating. Each team plays with every other participating team once and the winner is decided by the total points accumulated by the teams at the end of all these matches. Find the total number of matches in the tournament.
   (a) 7!   (b) 7! − 1   (c) 20
   (d) 21   (e) 25

10. Ram buys 7 novels from a book fair. Shyam buys 8 novels from the fair, none of which is common with those bought by Ram. They decide to exchange their books one for one. In how many ways can they exchange their books for the first time?
    (a) $7! \times 8!$ (b) $7 \times 8!$ (c) $7! \times 8$
    (d) 56   (e) None of these

11. In an Olympic 100 m race, 7 athletes are participating. Then the number of ways in which the first 3 prizes can be won is
    (a) 7!   (b) 7^3 (c) 3^7
    (d) 210   (e) 320

12. After group discussion and interview 6 candidates were selected for admission in a college. But unfortunately the number of seats left is 2. So it was left to the principal to select 2 candidates out of them. In how many ways can he select 2 candidates?
    (a) $^6P_2$ (b) $\dfrac{6!}{2!}$ (c) 15
    (d) 20   (e) 18

13. In an examination 10 questions are to be answered choosing at least 4 from each of part A and part B. If there are 6 questions in part A and 7 in part B, in how many ways can 10 questions be answered?
    (a) 212   (b) 280   (c) 272
    (d) 312   (e) 266

14. There are 2 parallel line segments AB and CD in a plane. AB contains 12 marked points whereas CD contains 8 marked points. How many triangle can be formed by using these marked points as vertices?
    (a) $12! \times 28 + 8! \times 66$
    (b) $12! \times 8!$
    (c) $^{20}C_3$
    (d) 864
    (e) 1024

15. In a box there are 5 distinct white and 6 distinct black balls. A person has to pick up 2 balls from the box such that there is one each of both the colours. In how many ways can he pick up the balls?
(a) 25 (b) 30 (c) 35
(d) 40 (e) 45

16. The product of any r consecutive positive integers must be divisible by
(a) r^2 (b) r! (c) $(r-1)!$
(d) $^{r-1}C_{r+1}$ (e) None of these

17. Two cards are drawn together from a pack of 52 cards at random. What is the probability that both the cards are spades?
(a) $\dfrac{^4C_2}{^{52}C_2}$ (b) $\dfrac{^{13}C_2}{^{52}C_2}$ (c) $\dfrac{^{26}C_2}{^{52}C_2}$
(d) $\dfrac{^8C_2}{^{52}C_2}$ (e) $\dfrac{^{13}C_2}{^{51}C_2}$

18. In question number 17, what is the probability that both the cards are kings?
(a) $\dfrac{^8C_2}{^{52}C_2}$ (b) $\dfrac{^{13}C_2}{^{52}C_2}$ (c) $\dfrac{^{26}C_2}{^{52}C_2}$
(d) $\dfrac{^4C_2}{^{52}C_2}$ (e) $\dfrac{^{10}C_2}{^{52}C_2}$

19. In question number 17, what is the probability that one card is a spade and one card is a heart?
(a) $\dfrac{^{13}C_1 \times ^{13}C_2}{^{52}C_2}$

(b) $\dfrac{^{13}C_1 \times ^{26}C_1}{^{52}C_2}$

(c) $\dfrac{13}{52} \times \dfrac{13}{52}$

(d) $\dfrac{^{13}C_1 \times ^{13}C_1}{^{52}C_2}$

(e) $\dfrac{^{13}C_2 \times ^{13}C_2}{^{52}C_2}$

20. In question number 17, what is the probability that exactly one card is a king ?
(a) $\dfrac{^{52}C_1}{^{52}C_2}$ (b) $\dfrac{4}{^{58}C_2}$ (c) $\dfrac{^4C_1 \times ^{48}C_1}{^{52}C_2}$
(d) $\dfrac{3}{^{52}C_2}$ (e) $\dfrac{1}{2}$

21. A telegraph has 5 arms and each arm is capable of 4 distinct positions including the position of rest. What is the total number of signals that can be made?
(a) 1,024 (b) 1,021 (c) 1,020
(d) 1,022 (e) 1,023

22. If A and B are 2 independent events and P(A) = 0.5 and P(B) = 0.4, find $P\left(\dfrac{A}{B}\right)$.
(a) 0.5 (b) 0.4 (c) 0.88
(d) 0.6 (e) 0.74

23. A set of cards bearing the numbers 100-199 is used in a game. If a card is drawn at random, what is the probability that it is divisible by 3?
(a) $\dfrac{2}{3}$ (b) 0.33 (c) $\dfrac{32}{99}$
(d) $\dfrac{1}{5}$ (e) None of these

24. A box contain 6 red balls, 7 green balls and 5 blue balls. Each ball is of a different size. The probability that the red ball being selected is the smallest red ball, is
(a) $\dfrac{1}{18}$ (b) $\dfrac{1}{3}$ (c) $\dfrac{1}{6}$
(d) $\dfrac{2}{3}$ (e) $\dfrac{1}{5}$

Fundamentals of
Permutations & Combinations

Practice Exercise 2 : Level 2

1. How many distinct 4 letter words can be formed by using the letters a, b, c and d? (Repetition of the letters is allowed).
   (a) 296   (b) 346   (c) 440
   (d) 256   (e) 361

2. How many four digit numbers can be formed by using the digits 2, 3, 4 and 5?
   (a) 58   (b) 512   (c) 64
   (d) 256   (e) None of these

3. How many numbers greater than 4000 can be made by using the digits 2, 3, 4 and 5? (Repetition of the digits is not allowed).
   (a) 12   (b) 14   (c) 20
   (d) 24   (e) 30

4. How many numbers greater than 4000 can be made by using the digits 2, 3, 4 and 5? (Repetition of digits is allowed).
   (a) 120   (b) 128   (c) 138
   (d) 130   (e) 125

5. If 4 dices and 3 coins are tossed simultaneously, then find the number of elements in the sample space.
   (a) $2^4 \times 6^3$ (b) $6^4 \times 2^3$ (c) 2156
   (d) $4^2 \times 3^6$ (e) $4^6 \times 3^2$

6. There are 3 roads from A to B, 4 roads from B to C, and 1 road from C to D. How many combinations of roads are there from A to D?
   (a) 11   (b) 15   (c) 14
   (d) 12   (e) 10

7. There are 5 questions in a question paper. In how many ways a candidate can attempt at least 1 question?
   (a) 30   (b) 34   (c) 32
   (d) 31   (e) 20

8. In how many ways can the letters of the word 'POSSESS' be arranged so that the four Ss are in alternate positions only?
   (a) 8   (b) 6   (c) 12
   (d) 10   (e) 16

9. In how many ways can a committee of 3 men and 2 women be formed out of a total of 4 men and 4 women?
   (a) 15   (b) 16   (c) 20
   (d) 28   (e) 24

10. A six-face die, an eight-face die and a ten-face die are thrown together. What is the probable number of outcomes?
    (a) 286   (b) 320   (c) 480
    (d) 492   (e) 360

11. In an entrance test, a candidate is required to attempt a total of 4 questions which are to be attempted from 2 sections each containing 5 questions. The maximum number of questions that he can attempt from any section is 3. In how many ways can he answer in the test?
    (a) 150   (b) 175   (c) 200
    (d) 250   (e) 240

12. In a cultural festival, 6 programmes are to be staged, 3 on a day for 2 days. In how many ways could the programmes be arranged?
    (a) 320   (b) 360   (c) 675
    (d) 720   (e) None of these

13. All the odd numbers from 1 to 9 are written in every possible order. How many numbers can be formed if repetition is not allowed?
    (a) 60   (b) 120   (c) 150
    (d) 180   (e) 90

14. How many numbers lying between 3000 and 4000 and made with the digits 3, 4, 5, 6, 7 and 8 are divisible by 5? Repetitions are not allowed.
    (a) 5!   (b) 4!   (c) 12
    (d) 6   (e) 20

15. Five persons A, B, C, D and E occupy seats in a row such that A and B sit next to each other. In how many possible ways can these 5 people sit?
    (a) 24   (b) 48   (c) 72
    (d) 96   (e) 40

16. Ten distinguishable balls are distributed into 4 distinct boxes such that a specified box contains exactly 2 balls. Find the number of such distributions.
(a) 3^8 (b) 3^{10} (c) 3^6
(d) 45×3^8 (e) None of these

17. Five speakers A, B, C, D and E are to be scheduled to speak such that A must speak immediately before B. In how many ways can their speeches be scheduled?
(a) 32 (b) 48 (c) 72
(d) 96 (e) 24

18. A production unit produces 10 articles of which 4 are defective. A quality inspector allows release of the products if he finds none out of the 3 articles he chooses at random to be defective. In how many ways can he pick up the 3 articles such that he clears the release?
(a) 10 (b) 6! (c) 20
(d) 18 (e) 24

19. $P_i = {}^iP_i$, where i is an integer. Then

$1 + 1P_1 + 2P_2 + 3P_3 + \cdots + nP_n =$

(a) n! (b) $(n+1)!$ (c) $(n+2)!$

(d) $\dfrac{(n+2)!}{n-1}$ (e) None of these

20. From a class of 12 students, 5 are to be chosen for an excursion. But 3 very close friends decide among themselves that either all 3 of them will go or none of them will go. In how many ways can the excursion party be chosen?
(a) 150 (b) 156 (c) 162
(d) 169 (e) 184

21. How many different words can be made from the word 'EDUCATION' so that all the vowels are always together? (Do not bother about many meaningless words.)
(a) 12,320 (b) 13,460 (c) 14,400
(d) 16,200 (e) 18,400

22. How many numbers are there between 100 and 1000 such that every digit is either 4 or 5?
(a) 1 (b) 6 (c) 5
(d) 4 (e) 8

23. A tea-expert claims that he can easily find out whether milk or tea leaves were added first to water just by tasting the cup of tea. In order to check this claim 10 cups of tea are prepared, 5 in one way and 5 in the other. Find the different possible ways of presenting these 10 cups to the expert.

(a) 100 (b) 10! (c) $\dfrac{10!}{(5!)^2}$

(d) 300 (e) 240

24. In how many ways can a leap year have 53 Sundays?
(a) $^{365}C_7$ (b) 7 (c) 4
(d) 2 (e) None of these

25. On their 10th wedding anniversary a Bengali couple bought 10 different sweets and then distributed it between 2 of their family friends such that both of them got 5 sweets each. Find the number of different ways in which this distribution can be done.
(a) 126 (b) 252 (c) 350
(d) 729 (e) None of these

26. In the country Utopia, the language contains only 4 letters. Find the maximum number of words that can exist in the Utopian dictionary if no letter can be repeated in a word.
(a) 26 (b) 4! (c) 40
(d) 64 (e) 80

27. A company could advertise about its new product in 4 magazines, 3 newspapers and 2 television channels. But in a later move it decided to give advertisements in only 2 of the magazines, one of the newspapers and one of the TV channels. In how many ways can they advertise their product?
(a) 30 (b) 36 (c) 44
(d) 40 (e) 48

28. The first 5 odd natural numbers are written in every possible order. How many numbers can be formed if no repetition is allowed and what is their sum?
(a) 5!, 6666600 (b) $^5C_1$, 10^5 (c) 51, 55555
(d) 50, 666660 (e) None of these

29. In how many ways one or more than one fruit can be selected from 6 varieties of fruits, given that there are 5 fruits of each variety? (All the fruits of one variety are identical.)

(a) 6^6 (b) $5^6 - 1$ (c) $6^6 - 1$
(d) 5^6 (e) None of these

Fundamentals of
Permutations & Combinations

1. In a staircase there are 4 steps. A person can jump one step, 2 steps, 3 steps or all 4 steps. In how many ways can he reach the top?
   (a) 2 (b) 4 (c) 6
   (d) 8 (e) 10

2. Kapil wishes to pay Rs. 255 with hundred notes. In how many ways can this task be performed if Kapil had hundred notes of value Re 1 and Rs. 5 only?
   (a) More than 100
   (b) More than 50 but less than 100
   (c) 50
   (d) 10
   (e) 0

3. A committee is to be formed comprising of 7 members such that there is a majority of men and at least 1 woman in the committee. The shortlisting for the committee is done out of 9 men and 6 women. In how many ways can this be done?
   (a) 3,724 (b) 3,630 (c) 3,526
   (d) 4,914 (e) 4312

4. A committee is to be formed comprising 7 members such that there is a simple majority of men and at least 1 woman. The shortlist consists of 9 men and 6 women. In how many ways can this committee be formed?
   (a) 3,724 (b) 3,630 (c) 4,914
   (d) 5,670 (e) 3,824

5. For the BCCI, a selection committee is to be chosen consisting of 5 ex-cricketers. Now there are 12 representatives from four zones. It has further been decided that if Srikanth is selected, Mohinder Amarnath will not be selected and vice versa. In how many ways can this be done?
   (a) 572 (b) 372 (c) 672
   (d) 472 (e) 362

6. How many five-digit positive integers have the product of their digits equal to 2000?
   (a) 15 (b) 20 (c) 22
   (d) 30 (e) 36

7. A bag contains 6 white balls and 4 red balls. Three balls are drawn one by one with replacement. What is the probability that all the 3 balls are red?
   (a) $\dfrac{8}{125}$ (b) $\dfrac{1}{20}$ (c) $\dfrac{1}{30}$
   (d) $\dfrac{1}{120}$ (e) $\dfrac{7}{20}$

8. In the above question, if 3 balls are drawn one by one with replacement, then what is the probability that 2 balls are white and 1 ball is red?
   (a) $\dfrac{54}{125}$ (b) $\dfrac{1}{4}$ (c) $\dfrac{1}{3}$
   (d) $\dfrac{1}{2}$ (e) $\dfrac{53}{125}$

9. In question 7, if the balls are drawn without replacement. What is the probability that 2 balls are red and 1 ball is white?
   (a) 0.1 (b) 0.2 (c) 0.3
   (d) 0.4 (e) 0.5

10. The probability that A will pass the examination is $\dfrac{1}{3}$ and the probability that B will pass the examination is $\dfrac{1}{2}$. What is the probability that both A and B will pass the examination?
    (a) $\dfrac{1}{6}$ (b) $\dfrac{1}{4}$ (c) $\dfrac{2}{3}$
    (d) $\dfrac{1}{3}$ (e) $\dfrac{1}{2}$

11. In Q. No. 10, what is the probability that only one person [either A or B] will pass the examination?
    (a) $\dfrac{1}{6}$ (b) $\dfrac{1}{2}$ (c) $\dfrac{1}{3}$
    (d) $\dfrac{2}{3}$ (e) $\dfrac{1}{4}$

12. In Q. No. 10, what is the probability that at least one person will pass the examination?

(a) 1   (b) $\dfrac{1}{2}$ (c) $\dfrac{1}{3}$

(d) $\dfrac{2}{3}$ (e) $\dfrac{1}{4}$

13. In Q. No. 10, what is the probability that no one will pass the examination?

(a) $\dfrac{2}{3}$ (b) $\dfrac{1}{2}$ (c) $\dfrac{1}{4}$

(d) $\dfrac{1}{3}$ (e) $\dfrac{1}{6}$

14. When 2 fair dice are thrown simultaneously, what is the probability that one die will show more value than the other?

(a) $\dfrac{1}{6}$ (b) $\dfrac{1}{16}$ (c) $\dfrac{5}{6}$

(d) $\dfrac{1}{2}$ (e) $\dfrac{15}{16}$

15. A basket contains 20 apples and 10 oranges out of which 2 oranges and 5 apples are defective. If a person takes out 2 at random, what is the probability that either both are apples, or both are good?

(a) $\dfrac{119}{435}$ (b) $\dfrac{338}{435}$ (c) $\dfrac{841}{870}$

(d) $\dfrac{217}{870}$ (e) None of these

16. What is the probability of getting a 2 in the roll of 2 fair dice, given that the sum is 7?

(a) $\dfrac{2}{3}$ (b) $\dfrac{25}{36}$ (c) $\dfrac{11}{36}$

(d) $\dfrac{1}{4}$ (e) $\dfrac{1}{3}$

17. In an urn there are 6 red, 4 black and 3 white balls. 3 balls are drawn out of it simultaneously. What is the probability that all the three are of the same colour?

(a) $\dfrac{7}{220}$ (b) $\dfrac{9}{44}$ (c) $\dfrac{25}{286}$

(d) $\dfrac{35}{286}$ (e) $\dfrac{21}{44}$

18. When 3 fair coins are tossed together, what is the probability of getting at least 2 tails?

(a) $\dfrac{1}{4}$ (b) $\dfrac{1}{2}$ (c) $\dfrac{1}{3}$

(d) $\dfrac{2}{3}$ (e) None of these

19. The probability that a bullet fired from a point will hit the target is $\dfrac{1}{3}$. Three such bullets are fired simultaneously towards the target from that very point. What is the probability that the target will be hit?

(a) $\dfrac{1}{27}$ (b) $\dfrac{1}{8}$ (c) $\dfrac{19}{27}$

(d) $\dfrac{8}{27}$ (e) $\dfrac{7}{8}$

20. In a management entrance examination there are 200 questions with four alternatives each. A student marks first alternative as the answer to all the questions. What is his probable net score if each right answer fetches +1 and each wrong answer fetches $-\dfrac{1}{4}$ marks?

(a) 0   (b) 10   (c) 12.5

(d) −12.5   (e) None of these

21. There are 2 positive integers a and b. What is the probability that a + b is odd?

(a) $\dfrac{1}{4}$ (b) $\dfrac{1}{3}$ (c) $\dfrac{1}{2}$

(d) $\dfrac{1}{5}$ (e) $\dfrac{2}{3}$

22. A 5-digit number is formed by the digits 1, 2, 3, 4 and 5 without repetition. What is the probability that the number formed is a multiple of 4?

(a) $\dfrac{1}{4}$ (b) $\dfrac{3}{5}$ (c) $\dfrac{2}{5}$

(d) $\dfrac{4}{5}$ (e) $\dfrac{1}{5}$

Fundamentals of
Permutations & Combinations

1. A garland is to be prepared with 10 different flowers such that 2 particular flowers will be next to each other. Find the number of different garlands that can be formed.
   (a) 8!   (b) 80,640
   (c) 26,880   (d) 40,000
   (e) None of these

2. In how many ways can 6 identical rings be worn in 4 fingers of one hand assuming any number of rings can be worn in one finger?
   (a) 6^4 (b) 4^6
   (c) $4! \times 6!$ (d) 84
   (e) 196

3. In a global conference there are 16 delegates who are to be seated along 2 sides of a long table with 8 chairs on each side. Four delegates having same views wish to sit on one particular side whereas 2 delegates having views opposite to them wish to sit on the other side of the table. In how many ways can these 16 delegates be seated?
   (a) $^8C_4 \times {}^8C_2 \times 10!$
   (b) $^8P_4 \times {}^8P_2 \times 10!$
   (c) $(8!)^4 \times (10!)^2$
   (d) 48
   (e) None of these

4. In how many ways can 3 children in a family have all different birthdays in a leap year?
   (a) $^{365}C_3$
   (b) $^{365}C_2 - 1$
   (c) $365^2 \times 364 \times 363$
   (d) $364 \times 363 \times 362$
   (e) None of these

5. A box contains 20 tickets of identical appearance, the tickets being numbered 1, 2, 3, ..., 20. In how many ways can 3 tickets be chosen such that the numbers on the drawn tickets are in arithmetic progression?
   (a) 18   (b) 33
   (c) 56   (d) 90
   (e) 84

6. An intelligence agency decide on a code of 2 digits selected from 0, 1, 2, ..., 9. But the slip on which the code is handwritten, allows confusion between the top and the bottom, because these are indistinguishable. Thus, for example, the code 81 could be confused with 18. How many codes are there such that there is no possibility of any confusion?
   (a) 25   (b) 75   (c) 80
   (d) 70   (e) None of these

7. For the BCCl, a selection committee is to be chosen consisting of 5 ex-cricketers. Now there are 10 representatives from various zones. It has further been decided that if Kapil Dev is selected, Sunil Gavaskar will not be selected and vice versa. In how many ways can this be done?
   (a) 140   (b) 112   (c) 196
   (d) 56   (e) 80

8. An executive wrote 5 letters to 5 people A, B, C, D and E and asked his secretary to place them in 5 envelopes also marked A, B, C, D and E. The secretary, however, placed the letters at random into the envelopes such that each envelope received exactly one letter. Then the number of arrangements in which exactly 2 letters are placed in correct envelopes is
   (a) 10   (b) 15   (c) 30
   (d) 25   (e) 20

9. From a pack of 52 playing cards, 4 cards are removed at random. In how many ways can the 1st place and 3rd place cards be drawn out such that both are black?
   (a) 64,974   (b) 62,252   (c) 69,447
   (d) 15,92,500   (e) 64,256

10. If the vowels A, E, I, O and U are given by 0the symbols !, @, #, $ and % respectively, then the message given by the defence code 2$%8!5@ will be
    (a) YOU VASE (b) YOU SAVE (c) YIU SAFE
    (d) YIU SAVE (e) YIU VASE

11. The following diagram shows the road map of a city. The lines through the city indicate roads but there is no road through the park. All the roads are either parallel or perpendicular to each other. Peter wants to

go from X to Y travelling the minimum possible distance. In how many ways can he make his journey?

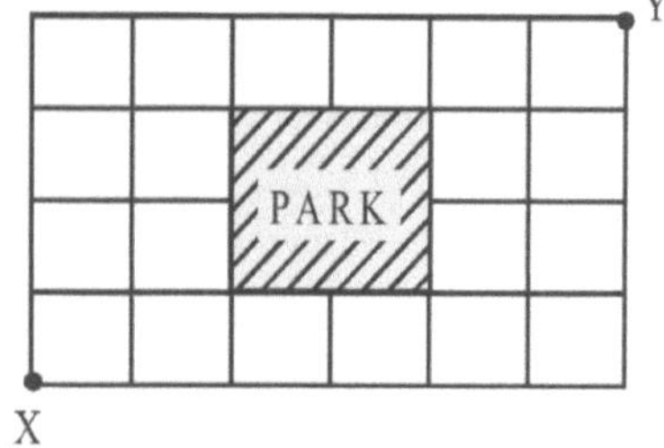

(a) 55   (b) 100   (c) 166
(d) 220   (e) 110

12. How many five-digit numbers can be formed such that it has the following properties:
I. It has at least one zero and at most three zeros.
II. The non-zero digits are non-repeating.

(a) 9962   (b) 17378   (c) 12570
(d) 14398   (e) 15408

13. If two dices are thrown simultaneously, then what is the probability that the product of the numbers appearing on the top faces of the dice is less than 36?

(a) $\dfrac{35}{36}$ (b) $\dfrac{1}{6}$ (c) $\dfrac{23}{36}$

(d) $\dfrac{32}{36}$ (e) $\dfrac{34}{36}$

14. Two urns contain 3 white and 4 black balls, and 2 white and 5 black balls. One ball is transferred to the second urn and then one ball is drawn from the second urn. Find the probability that the first ball transferred is black, given that the ball drawn is black.

(a) $\dfrac{15}{39}$ (b) $\dfrac{39}{56}$ (c) $\dfrac{8}{13}$

(d) $\dfrac{10}{39}$ (e) $\dfrac{5}{13}$

15. In a pack of cards having numbers between 100 and 999 (both inclusive), what is the probability of drawing a multiple of 3, the number should comprises of digits 1, 0, 2, 3, 4?

(a) $\dfrac{24}{900}$ (b) $\dfrac{33}{900}$ (c) $\dfrac{1}{30}$

(d) $\dfrac{20}{900}$ (e) None of these

16. If we pick a number between 1 and 999 s (both inclusive) randomly, what is the probability that the number is an even number with no digit repeated?

(a) $\dfrac{662}{999}$ (b) $\dfrac{631}{999}$ (c) $\dfrac{337}{999}$

(d) $\dfrac{320}{999}$ (e) $\dfrac{373}{999}$

17. Σn is written for $n = 1$ to $n = 99$ on cards. What is the probability of drawing a card with an even number written on it?

(a) $\dfrac{1}{2}$ (b) $\dfrac{49}{100}$ (c) $\dfrac{49}{99}$

(d) $\dfrac{50}{99}$ (e) $\dfrac{2}{3}$

18. In the previous question, what is the probability that the number is more than 100?

(a) $\dfrac{13}{99}$ (b) $\dfrac{86}{99}$ (c) $\dfrac{14}{100}$

(d) $\dfrac{85}{100}$ (e) $\dfrac{73}{99}$

19. There are 1001 red balls and 1001 black balls in a box. Two balls are drawn without replacement one after the other. Let 'P_s' be the probability that two balls drawn at random from the box are of the same colour, and let 'P_d' be the probability that they are of different colours. The difference between P_s and P_d is

(a) 0   (b) $\dfrac{1}{2002}$ (c) $\dfrac{1}{2001}$

(d) $\dfrac{2}{2001}$ (e) $\dfrac{1}{1001}$

20. Sudip thought of a two-digit number and divided the number by the sum of the digits of the number. He found that the remainder is 3. Sonal also thought of a two-digit number and divided the number by the sum of the digits of the number. She also found that the remainder is 3. Find the probability that the two-digit number thought by Sudip and Sonal is same.

(a) $\dfrac{1}{11}$ (b) $\dfrac{1}{12}$ (c) $\dfrac{1}{13}$

(d) $\dfrac{1}{14}$ (e) $\dfrac{1}{15}$

Fundamentals of
Permutations & Combinations

ANSWERS AND EXPLANATIONS

Problems for Practice (Non MCQ)

1. $\dfrac{428}{99}$ **2.** 27   **3.** 1824

4. 5^7 **5.** 12   **6.** 7

7. 4722   **8.** 28   **9.** 0

10. 22   **11.** 9   **12.** 7

13. 3(viz. 2, 3 and 17)   **14.** 27   **15.** 2080

16. 36 lakhs   **17.** 13   **18.** $3^{3^{3^{33}}}$

19. 46; BA   **20.** 51; 43961   **21.** 20A; −365

22. Integer values not possible   **23.** 36

24. 983   **25.** 6912   **26.** $\dfrac{168}{73}$

27. 11   **28.** 0   **29.** 7

30. 2   **31.** 0   **32.** 1

33. 5, 5 and 2 in order   **34.** 48   **35.** 60984; 4

36. 38   **37.** Q = 1   **38.** 111111111

39. $1+\sqrt{5}$ **40.** 11   **41.** 71

42. 499   **43.** 2 or 11   **44.** 24, 120

45. 32   **47.** 7   **48.** 124; 7

49. 15; 15   **50.** 9   **51.** 7 different solutions

52. 60489

53.
```
    2 9 7 8 6
  +     8 5 0
  +     8 5 0
  -----------
    3 1 4 8 6
```

54. 33

55. 7   **56.** 8

57. (a) 15.32743...   (b) 11.533203   (c) 1432   (d) 3A71   **58.** 128; 256

Practice Exercise 1 : Level 1

1	c	2	d	3	a	4	c	5	d	6	c	7	b	8	c	9	d	10	e
11	c	12	c	13	d	14	d	15	b	16	b	17	b	18	a	19	a	20	a
21	b	22	d	23	c	24	d	25	d	26	c	27	b	28	c	29	c		

Practice Exercise 2 : Level 1

1	d	2	e	3	d	4	b	5	c	6	b	7	e	8	b	9	a	10	c
11	d	12	c	13	b	14	c	15	b	16	c	17	a	18	c	19	c	20	b
21	a	22	b	23	d	24	d	25	e	26	c	27	d	28	b	29	b	30	e
31	d	32	d	33	a	34	e	35	a										

Practice Exercise 3 : Level 2

1	b	2	a	3	e	4	d	5	b	6	d	7	d	8	a	9	d	10	d
11	d	12	d	13	b	14	a	15	c	16	d	17	b	18	a	19	d	20	a
21	a	22	b	23	a	24	d	25	b	26	c	27	c	28	a	29	c	30	c

Practice Exercise 4 : Level 2

1	b	2	e	3	a	4	b	5	e	6	a	7	b	8	c	9	d	10	a
11	c	12	a	13	a	14	d	15	c	16	b	17	d	18	a	19	c	20	c
21	c	22	a	23	c	24	c	25	d	26	b										

Practice Exercise 5 : Level 2

1	c	2	a	3	c	4	b	5	a	6	b	7	b	8	b	9	e	10	b
11	c	12	e	13	d	14	b	15	c	16	b	17	b	18	c	19	c	20	e
21	a	22	e	23	b	24	c	25	c	26	b	27	d	28	c	29	a	30	a
31	e	32	b	33	e	34	c												

Practice Exercise 6 : Level 3

1	b	2	a	3	b	4	a	5	b	6	b	7	d	8	a	9	d	10	c
11	c	12	c	13	a	14	e	15	b	16	c	17	e	18	c	19	b	20	a
21	e	22	a	23	b	24	d	25	c										

Practice Exercise 7 : Level 3

1	c	2	a	3	d	4	c	5	d	6	e	7	b	8	c	9	b	10	b
11	a	12	c	13	e	14	a	15	c	16	e	17	c	18	c	19	e	20	c
21	e	22	a	23	c	24	d	25	b	26	b	27	e	28	c	29	d	30	b
31	e	32	a																

Career Launcher MBA

Answers and Explanations

Problems for Practice (Non MCQ)

1.   4

2.   ₹4200, ₹2400

3.   *(a)* 30   *(b)*   20

4.   10%

5.   45%

Practice Exercise

1	b	2	a	3	b	4	c	5	d	6	b	7	e	8	c	9	a	10	b
11	c	12	b	13	d														

Practice Exercise (Non MCQ)

Level – 1

1. *(a)* (i) 3 (ii) 4   *(b)* (i) 8, 4 (ii) 10 and 4 or 7 and 6

2. *(a)* 5 *(b)* 5   **3.** $^{17}P_3$ **4.** $^{6}P_4$ **5.** 9×10^6 **6.** $^{17}P_2$ **7.** 4^7

8. 260   **9.** $\dfrac{1}{2}(5!)$ **10.** *(i)* $4 \times {}^{9}P_3$ *(ii)* $^{9}P_4$ **11.** 242

12. $\dfrac{17!}{7!\ 6!\ 4!}$ **13.** $18! \times 2$ **14.** $^{10}C_6 \times {}^{7}C_3$ **15.** 321

16. *(i)* $^{20}C_3 - {}^{5}C_3$ *(ii)* $^{20}C_2 - {}^{5}C_2 + 1$ **17.** 36   **18.** 5^5 **19.** 1   **20.** $^{5}P_5$

21. $^{5}C_1 \times {}^{5}P_1 + {}^{5}C_2 \times {}^{5}P_2 + {}^{5}C_3 \times {}^{5}P_3 + {}^{5}C_4 \times {}^{5}P_4 + {}^{5}C_5 \times {}^{5}P_5$

22. $\dfrac{5!}{2!}$ **23.** $2 \times 4!$ **24.** $\dfrac{9}{25}$ **25.** 4×5^3 **26.** 5^4 **27.** $^{6}P_5$

28. $5! + \dfrac{5!}{2!} \times {}^{4}C_3$ **29.** $5! + \dfrac{5!}{2!} \times {}^{4}C_3 \times 5$ **30.** 4^3 ways   **31.** $^{m}C_2 \times {}^{n}C_2$ **32.** $^{100}C_{50} \times {}^{50}C_{30} \times {}^{20}C_{20}$

33. 66 ways   **34.** 89   **35.** $\dfrac{3}{4}$ **36.** $\dfrac{3}{4}$ **37.** *(i)* $\dfrac{9}{40}$ *(ii)* $\dfrac{1}{4}$

<u>Level – 2</u>

38. 9400   **39.** $625(2 + 3 + 4 + 5)\,(10000) + 500\,(2 + 3 + 4 + 5)\,(1111) = 95277000$

40. *(i)* $^9C_3$ *(ii)* $^9P_3$ *(iii)* $\left(^9C_3 \times {}^6C_3 \times {}^3C_3 \right)\left(\dfrac{1}{3!} \right)$

41. $\dfrac{11}{144}$ **42.** $\dfrac{25}{56}$ **43.** 0.1296   **44.** $\dfrac{3}{5}$

Practice Exercise 1 : Level 1

1	b	2	d	3	c	4	a	5	d	6	c	7	b	8	c	9	d	10	d
11	d	12	c	13	e	14	d	15	b	16	b	17	b	18	d	19	d	20	c
21	e	22	a	23	b	24	c												

Practice Exercise 2 : Level 2

1	d	2	d	3	a	4	b	5	b	6	d	7	d	8	b	9	e	10	c
11	c	12	d	13	b	14	c	15	b	16	d	17	e	18	c	19	b	20	c
21	c	22	e	23	c	24	d	25	b	26	d	27	b	28	a	29	c		

Practice Exercise 3 : Level 2

1	d	2	e	3	d	4	c	5	c	6	d	7	a	8	a	9	c	10	a
11	b	12	d	13	d	14	c	15	b	16	e	17	c	18	b	19	c	20	c
21	c	22	e																

Practice Exercise 4 : Level 3

1	a	2	d	3	b	4	e	5	d	6	c	7	c	8	e	9	d	10	b
11	e	12	e	13	a	14	c	15	b	16	e	17	c	18	b	19	c	20	d

Problems for Practice (Non MCQ)

Level – 1

1. Let x = 4.323232..
    Then 100 x = 432.323232...

    $99x = 428 \Rightarrow x = \dfrac{428}{99}$

2. The nearest multiple of 84 greater than 8961 is 8988.
    Hence, 27 must be added to 8961 to make it divisible by 84.

3. LCM of 12 and 16 = 48
    Dividing 1834 by 48, quotient = 38, remainder = 10
    Hence, the nearest number is 1834 – 10 = 1824

4. $a^b > b^a$, if a < b and a, b > 3.

5. HCF of 2 numbers is 48 and HCF of the other 2 is 36.
    HCF of all 4 is the HCF of 48 and 36 = 12.

6. Number of steps would be (n – 1), where n is the number of numbers.
    Hence, number of steps = 7.

7. LCM of 21, 25, 27 and 35 = 4725
    Therefore, required number = 4725 – 3 = 4722.

8. The first time they would meet at the starting point is LCM (7, 4) = 28 min

9. 732 is nothing but $(27^2 + 3)^{732}$. The last term of the expansion is 3^{732} which again is completely divisible by 27. Thus, the remainder is 0.

10. N = 5 [7x + 4] + 2 = 35x + 22
    $\therefore$ When divided by 35, remainder = 22.

11. The last digits of
    $9^1 = 9$
    $9^2 = 1$
    $9^3 = 9$
    Thus, 9 exhibits a cyclicity of 2.
    Therefore, the last digit of $(729)^{59} = 9$.

12. The last digits of
    $3^1 = 3$
    $3^2 = 9$
    $3^3 = 27$
    $3^4 = 81$
    $3^5 = 243$
    Thus, cyclicity of powers of 3 is 4.
    Hence, last digit of $123^7 = 7$.

13. Reduce it to factorised form and you will find that there are only three prime bases 2, 3 and 17.

14. Let the number of saplings in each row and column = x.
    Then $x^2 = 729$.
    Therefore, x = 27.

15. If there were n saplings in each row and column, then the number of new saplings planted in the rows = (n – 1)n
    Number of new saplings planted in each column
    = n(n – 1)
    Hence, total number of saplings planted
    = (n – 1)n + n(n – 1)
    = 2n(n – 1)
    Since n = 27
    $\therefore$ Number of saplings along the rows and columns
    = 2 × 27 × 26
    Saplings planted diagonally between any two saplings
    = $(n – 1)^2$
    Hence, total number of saplings will be 2 × 27 × 26 + 26^2
    = 2080

16. The youngest son got 6x

    $= \left(\dfrac{1}{2}\right)\left(\dfrac{2}{3}\right)\left(\dfrac{1}{2}\right) \times$ total amount.

    Hence, total amount = 36x.
    $\because$ x has to be an integer, so minimum wealth the businessman had is 36 lakh.

17. Split the number 36 into 3 factors. Add up all the 3 factors. All the sums are uniquely different except 2 combinations that give 13. They are 6, 6, 1 and 9, 2, 2.

18. The largest number that can be formed is $3^{3^{3^{33}}}$.

19. a. Consecutively dividing 54 by 12, the remainders are 4 and 6 in the reverse order.
        Hence, $(54)_{10} = (46)_{12}$.

    b. Consecutively dividing 142 by 12, the remainders are 11(i.e. B) and 10 (i.e. A) in the reverse order.
        Hence, $(142)_{10} = (BA)_{12}$.

20. a. $(110011)_2 = 2^5 \times 1 + 2^4 \times 1 + 2^3 \times 0 + 2^2 \times 0$
        $+ 2^1 \times 1 + 2^0 \times 1$
        $= 32 + 16 + 2 + 1 = (51)_{10}$
    b. $(ABCD)_{16} = 16^3 \times A + 16^2 \times B + 16^1 \times C + 16^0 \times D$
        $= 40960 + 2816 + 192 + 13 = (43961)_{10}$

21. a. $(20A)_{12}$
    b. $-(365)_8$

Level – 2

22. X + Y = 19
    4X + 6Y = 9
    The two equations do not give an integer as an answer.

23. $\dfrac{10x+y}{x+y}=4$ ... (i)

$x + 3 = y$ ... (ii)

Solving the two equations, we get

$x = 3$ and $y = 6$

Therefore, the number = 36.

24. If N be the required number, then $N = 6x + 5$ and $N = 5y + 3$.

The first such number = 23

The largest number less than 1000 which is a multiple of 30 (LCM of 6 and 5) is 990 and the penultimate number is 960.

Hence, $N = 960 + 23 = 983$.

25. LCM of (15, 20, 21, 23, 35) = 9660

K × 9660 will be divisible by given numbers

From the given information,

K × 9660 − 2748 = 4 digit number

For this to happen the maximum value K can take is 1.

So the four-digit number = 9660 − 2748 = 6912

26. Let the number of units of work be LCM (6, 7, 8) units, i.e 168 units.

Hence, A does 28 units in 1 day; B does 24 units in 1 day and C does 21 units in 1 day.

Working together they finish 73 units in 1 day.

Hence, time taken = $\dfrac{168}{73}$ days

27. If N be the required number, then

$N = 5x + 1$ and $N = 6y + 5$

When $y = 1$, we have 11, which satisfies

$5x + 1$ for $x = 2$.

$\therefore$ N = 11

The next number satisfying this condition would be

$11 + \text{LCM}(6, 5) = 41$.

28. Let the number be x.

Then $x \div 145$ leaves the remainder 58.

$\therefore x = 145y + 58 = 29 (5y) + 29 \times 2$

Hence, x is totally divisible by 29.

$\Rightarrow$ Remainder = 0

29. $86 \times 293 \times 4919$

$= (17 \times 5 + 1)(17 \times 17 + 4)\ (17^3 + 6)$

When we do the multiplication, all the terms except $1 \times 4 \times 6$ will be divisible by 17. Hence, the remainder will be $24 - 17 = 7$.

30. $7^{13} + 1 = (6 + 1)^{13} + 1$

In the binomial expansion of $(6 + 1)^{13}$, all terms except the last one are multiples of 6.

Last term = 1

Hence, remainder = $1 + 1 = 2$.

31. **Method 1:**

10^{200} can be written $(8 + 2)^{200}$. There are in all 201 terms in this expansion. The first 200 terms have a 8 in them. Hence, they can be expressed as a multiple of 8. The last term is 2^{200}, which is $2^3 \times 2^{197}$

This is also a multiple of 8. Hence, 10^{200} is a multiple of 8. Hence, the remainder is 0.

Method 2:

$10^{200} = 2^{200} \times 5^{200} = 2^3 \times 2^{197} \times 5^{200}$. This is obviously divisible by 8. Hence, the remainder will be zero.

32. $(30)^{40}$ can be written $(34 - 4)^{40}$

This in turn can be written $34M + 4^{40}$

$= 34M + 16^{20} = 34M + (17 - 1)^{20} = 34M + 17N + 1^{20}$

(34M is a multiple of 34 and 17N is a multiple of 17)

When this expression is divided by 17, the remainder is 1.

33. $N = 5 [7(8x + 4) + 3] + 2 = 35(8x) + 140 + 17$

$= 280x + 157$

When this is divided by 8, quotient = $35x + 19$ and remainder = 5.

When $(35x + 19)$ is divided by 7, quotient = $5x + 2$ and remainder = 5.

When $(5x + 2)$ is divided by 5, quotient = x and remainder = 2.

34. Let $a = 2^x \times 3^y \times 5^z$

The possible values of x are 0, 1, 2, 3.

The possible values of y are 0, 1, 2.

The possible values of z are 0, 1, 2, 3.

Hence, the number of values of a that is possible is $4 \times 3 \times 4 = 48$. Hence 48 factors.

35. Breaking $6^{10} \times 7^{17} \times 11^{27}$ into prime factors

$= 2^{10} \times 3^{10} \times 7^{17} \times 11^{27}$

$\therefore$ Number of factors

$= (10 + 1) \times (10 + 1) \times (17 + 1) \times (27 + 1)$

$= 11 \times 11 \times 18 \times 28 = 60984$

Number of prime factors = 4 (i.e. 2, 3, 7, 11)

36. Total factors possible are

$(4 + 1) (2 + 1) (4 + 1) = 5 \times 3 \times 5 = 75$.

as $ab = N$

So choosing a out of 75 factors, b will have its value accordingly. But in this (a, b) and (b, a) forms the same set. So we have to divide it by 2. Out of these 75 sets, one set will be of the form $(\sqrt{N}, \sqrt{N})$ which need not to be divided by 2.

$\therefore$ Total sets = $\dfrac{75 - 1}{2} + 1 = 37 + 1 = 38$ sets

37. PQRS can be written as PQR × 10 + S which is equal to PQR × QS

PQR × 10 + S = PQR × QS

PQR(QS − 10) = S

PQR is a three-digit number. So even if it is multiplied by a single non-zero digit it will not give S, a single digit number. So for this to be possible, QS = 10.

Which gives Q = 1

38. This is a property found in integers containing only 1's.

For example, $\sqrt{121} = 11$

$\sqrt{12321} = 111$ and so on

Thus in the given case, there being nine 1's in the number, its square will have the highest number 9, i.e. 12345678987654321

39. $(3+\sqrt{5})^2 = 9 + 5 + 2 \times 3 \times \sqrt{5}$

$= 14 + 6\sqrt{5} = 14 + \sqrt{36 \times 5}$

$= 14 + \sqrt{180}$

$\therefore \sqrt{14 + \sqrt{180}} = \sqrt{(3+\sqrt{5})^2} = 3 + \sqrt{5}$

$3 + \sqrt{5} + 3 + \sqrt{5} = 6 + 2\sqrt{5} = (1+\sqrt{5})^2$

$\Rightarrow 6 + 2\sqrt{5} = \left(1+\sqrt{5}\right)^2$

Now, the original expression $= \sqrt{5 + \sqrt{5} + 1 + \sqrt{5}}$

$= \sqrt{6 + 2\sqrt{5}} = \sqrt{\left(1+\sqrt{5}\right)^2} = 1 + \sqrt{5}$

40. The numbers that can be formed are xy and yx.
Hence, $(10x + y) + (10y + x) = 11(x + y)$. If this is a perfect square, then $x + y = 11$.

Level – 3

41. $x + y = 8$ ... (i)
$10y + x = 10x + y - 54$
$9y - 9x = -54$
$9x - 9y = 54$ ... (ii)
Solving equation (i) and (ii), we get $x = 7$ and $y = 1$
Therefore, the number = 71

42. Number of multiples of 3 less than 3000

$= \dfrac{3000}{3} - 1 = 999$

(–1, since 3000 is also a multiple of 3.)
Number of multiples of 3 less than or equal to 2000

$= \dfrac{2000}{3} \Rightarrow 666.66$

$\Rightarrow$ 666 multiples
Number of multiples of 3 lying between 2000 and 3000 is
$999 - 666 = 333 = X$ ... (i)
Similarly, for number of multiples of 4 less than 3000

$= \dfrac{3000}{4} - 1 = 750 - 1 = 749$

(–1, since 3000 is also a multiple of 4.)
Number of multiples of 4 less than or equal to 2000

$= \dfrac{2000}{4} = 500$

Number of multiples of 4 lying between 2000 and 3000 is
$749 - 500 = 249 = Y$ ... (ii)
Similarly, LCM (3, 4), i.e. 12.
Number of multiples of 12 lying between 2000 and 3000 is
$249 - 166 = 83 = Z$ ... (iii)
Hence, number of multiples of 3 or 4
$= X + Y - Z = 333 + 249 - 83 = 499$

43. The number is divisible by 8 so last three digits should be divisible by 8.
Thus Y = 0 or 8.
The number is also divisible by 9, sum of the digits must be divisible by 9.

43 + x + y is divisible by 9.
When Y = 0, X = 2
When Y = 8, X = 3
X + Y = 2 or X + Y = 11

44. Let two numbers be x , y
$x + y = 144$
HCF of two numbers is 24
Let $x = 24a$, $y = 24b$
Where a, b are co-prime to each other
$24a + 24b = 144$
$a + b = 6$
Possible values are
$a = 1, b = 5$, or $a = 2, b = 4$ or $a = 3, b = 3$
But a, b are co-prime to each other
So $a = 1, b = 5$
$\therefore x = 24$ and $y = 120$

Alternative method:
Sum = 144 = 24 + 120
Hence, the numbers are 24, 120
Other possibilities are 48 + 96, 72 + 72
But for each of them, HCF is not equal to 24.

45. On simplifying $\dfrac{2^{643}}{96}$ is reduced to $\dfrac{2^{643}}{2^5 \times 3} = \dfrac{2^{638}}{3}$. Thus, the remainder will be the last term of the expression $(3 - 1)^{638}$ and then multiply it by 32. It is important to multiply it by 32 because the initial expression is $\dfrac{2^{643}}{96}$ and not $\dfrac{2^{638}}{3}$.
Hence, final remainder is $1 \times 32 = 32$.

46. $244^{1500} - 1$ is divisible by 7 as the remainder when

$\left(\dfrac{244^{1500}}{7}\right) = 1$ and also $\dfrac{244^{1500}}{11} = \dfrac{2^{1500}}{11}$

$= \dfrac{32^{300}}{11} = \dfrac{(33-1)^{300}}{11} = +1$ and

$\dfrac{244^{1500}}{13} = \dfrac{(-3)^{1500}}{13} = \dfrac{(27)^{500}}{13} = 1$

$\therefore 1 - 1 = 0$ (Net remainder is zero)
So it is divisible by 7, 11, 13 and 1001.

47. End digit of a number will depend upon cyclicity of the number. Cyclicity of 7 is 4.

We will have to determine the remainder when $11^{22^{33}}$ is divided by 4.
The power to 11 is an even number therefore the remainder if $11^{22^{33}}$ is divided by 4 will be 1.
$N = 7^{4N+1}$
Its end digit will be 7.

48. a. $10 \times 20 \times 30 \ldots \times 1000$
$= 10^{100}[1 \times 2 \times 3 \ldots \times 100]$
$= 10^{100}(100!)$
Now $2 \times 5 = 10$
Highest power of 5 in 100!

$$= \frac{100}{5} + \frac{20}{5} = 20 + 4 = 24$$

$\therefore$ Number of zeros = 100 + 24 = 124

Hint: Need to check for only 5 since it has the smaller power.

   b. $(5 \times 10 \times 15 \times 20 \times ... \times 45)$

      $= 5^9(1 \times 2 \times 3 \times 4 \times ... \times 9)$

      $= 5^9 \times 9!$

      Highest power of 2 in $5^9 \times 9!$, is 7.

      $\therefore$ Number of zeros = 7

49. a. $6 = 3 \times 2$

      Hence, we have to find the highest power of 3 which divides 34!

      Highest power $= \left(\dfrac{34}{3} + \dfrac{11}{3} + \dfrac{3}{3} \right) = 11 + 3 + 1 = 15$

   b. $12 = 2^2 \times 3$

      We have to check the highest power of 3 and highest power of 2^2.

      Highest power of 3 = 11 + 3 + 1 = 15

      Highest power of 2 = 17 + 8 + 4 + 2 + 1 = 32

      Hence, highest power of 4 = 16

      $\therefore 34! = 3^{15} \times 4^{16} \times N$. (N is not divisible by 2 or 3.)

      Therefore, highest power of 12 in 34! = 15.

50. Find the positive integer solution satisfying

    $4x + 3y = 120$

    $3y = 120 - 4x$

$$y = 40 - \frac{4}{3}x \qquad \qquad ... (i)$$

For positive integer value of y, x can take value from 3 to 27, i.e. 9 values

if x = 3, y = 36

if x = 6, y = 32

....

....

if x = 27, y = 4

Hence, total 9 positive integer solutions satisfy the above equation.

51. $5x + 3y = 100$

    There are more than one solutions.

    All these would be the integer solutions that satisfy the equation.

    There are 7 solutions for (x, y) : (20, 0), (17, 5), (14, 10), ..., (2, 30).

52.

```
        4  2  3
    x   a  b  c
    ─────────────
       4c 2c 3c
    4b 2b 3b  x
    4a 2a 3a  x  x
    ─────────────
    6  --  --  8  9
```

    $3c = 9; \ c = 3$

    $6 + 3b = \_\_ 8; \ 3b = \_\_2$

    $\Rightarrow 3b = 12$

    $b = 4$

    $4a + x = 6$, where x maybe the carry-over from 4b +2a

    Now, $4 \times 1 + 2 = 6$

$4 \times 2 + 0 = 8$ is not possible. Hence, a = 1

$\therefore 423 \times 143 = 60489$.

53.

```
        F O R T Y
  (+)       T E N
  (+)       T E N
  ─────────────
      S I X T Y
```

(1) Y + N + N ends with Y. Hence, N + N must be either 0 or 10.

(2) T + E + E + (1) or T + E + E ends in T. The first case is not possible since no case of T + E + E + 1 can end with the same digit as T because E + E + 1 can neither be 0 nor 10.

(3) So N = 0; E = 5

(4) O must have got a carry-over of 2 and if O = 9, then I = 1. In every other case, I can take only a value = 0 which already N has taken.

So

```
    F 9 R T Y
      T 5 0
      T 5 0
    ─────────
    S 1 X T Y
```

From here T must be at least 7 because the second digit of S1XTY is 1 and that of F9RTY is 9. We get

```
        2 9 7 8 6
          8 5 0
  (+)       8 5 0
  ─────────────
        3 1 4 8 6
```

54. We can write the 32 numbers in the following fashion

1	2	3	4	5	6	7	8	9	10	11	12	13	14	15	16
32	31	30	29	28	27	26	25	24	23	22	21	20	19	18	17

The sum of the two numbers in any column is 33. When we have to select 17 numbers, in any selection we will always have a pair of numbers which appear in a single column in the above table.

Thus for any selection their will be a pair of numbers which add up to 33.

55. Single digit numbers are 9.

    Two-digit numbers are 90.

    Three-digit numbers are 900.

    Four-digit numbers are 9000.

    If we write one after another, 9 + 180 + 2700 = 2889 digits already written till all three-digit numbers.

    Thereafter, 7111 digits are still left and each number after 999 will have 4 digits.

$$\frac{7111}{4} = 1777.75$$

Thus, we can skip 1777 numbers after 999.

(1777 + 999 = 2776). The third digit of the succeeding number will be the answer.

(The third digit of 2777, i.e. 7.)

56. Five numbers are 20, 22, 23, 25 and 27.

    To get distinct sum by taking 2 at a time, take first number and get the sum of taking other numbers.

    e.g.

    $20 + 22 = 42 \qquad \qquad ... (i)$

Answers and Explanations

20 + 23 = 43   ... (ii)

20 + 25 = 45   ... (iii)

20 + 27 = 47   ... (iv)

Here we have 4 distinct sums. Now take the second number, i.e. 22, add with other number and write down only those sums which are not the same as calculated earlier.

i.e. 22 + 27 = 49   ... (v)

concept will remain same for the rest numbers,

23 + 25 = 48   ... (vi)

23 + 27 = 50   ... (vii)

25 + 27 = 52   ... (viii)

Hence, 8 distinct sum can be formed.

57. (a) $(13.421)_{10} = (\ )_8$

        $0.421 \times 8 = 3.368$
        $0.368 \times 8 = 2.944$
        $0.944 \times 8 = 7.552$
        $0.552 \times 8 = 4.416$
        $0.416 \times 8 = 3.328$

$(13)_{10} = (15)_8$ Continue this process till you get zero after the integer part.

$(0.421)_{10} = (0.32743...)_8$

$\therefore (13.421)_{10} = (15.32743...)_8$

(b) $(13.421)_8 = (\ )_{10}$

$(13)_8 = (\ )_{10}$

$1 \times 8^1 + 3 \times 8^0 = 8 + 3 = 11$

$(13)_8 = (11)_{10}$

$(0.421)_8 = (\ )_{10}$

$4 \times 8^{-1} + 2 \times 8^{-2} + 1 \times 8^{-3}$

$= 0.5 + 0.03125 + 0.001953 = 0.533203$

$(0.421)_8 = (0.533203)_{10}$

$(13.421)_8 = (11.533203)_{10}$

(c) $(1100011010)_2 = (\ )_8$

$2^3 = 8$

Make pair of three digits from right hand side of the number and write the decimal equivalent for the pairs. Insert leading zeroes to make a pair of 3

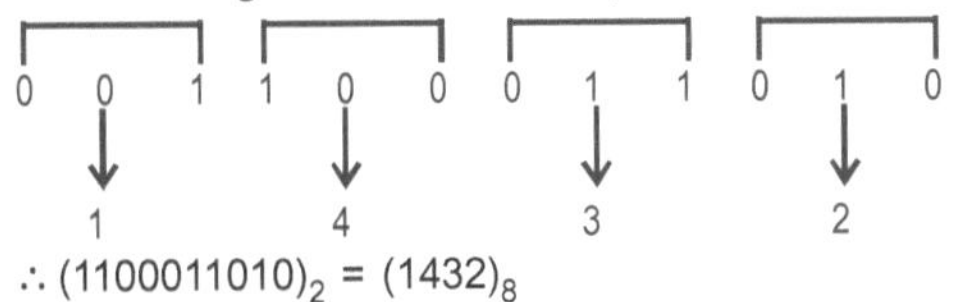

$\therefore (1100011010)_2 = (1432)_8$

(d) $(3221301)_4 = (\ )_{16}$

$4^2 = 16$

Make pair of two digits from the right hand side of the number and write the decimal equivalent for the pairs. Insert leading zeroes to make a pair of two

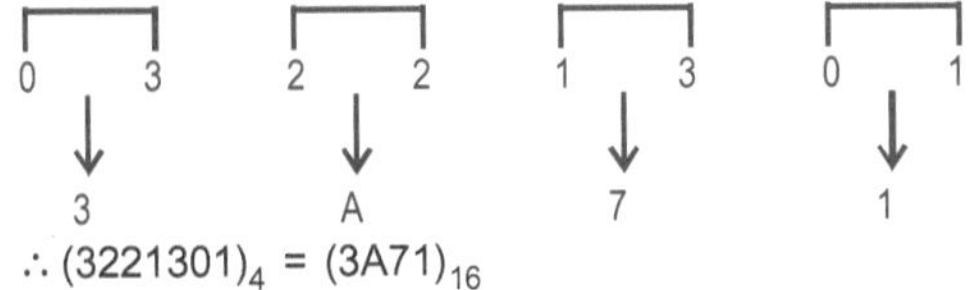

$\therefore (3221301)_4 = (3A71)_{16}$

58. Let Meera have x flowers in the beginning.
Then the number of flowers she had in the end is

$$x \left(\frac{3}{4}\right)\left(\frac{3}{4}\right)\left(\frac{3}{4}\right)\left(\frac{1}{2}\right) = \left(\frac{27}{128}\right) x$$

Since this value is between 20 and 60, the value of x must be either 128 or 256.

a. 128

b. 256

Practice Exercise – 1 : Level 1

1. c   LCM × HCF = Product of Number

$$N_2 = \frac{5200 \times 40}{520} = 400$$

2. d   1

3. a   Whole number starts with zero.

4. c   According to definition, answer is option (c).

5. d   Unit place digit = Unit place digit of $(4 \times 1 \times 9 \times 8)$
Therefore, unit digit of the number = 8.

6. c $\sqrt[3]{32} \times \sqrt[3]{250} = (32)^{1/3} \times (250)^{1/3} = (32 \times 250)^{1/3}$
$= [2^5 \times 2 \times 5^3]^{1/3} = 2^{6 \times 1/3} \times 5^{3 \times 1/3}$
$= 2^2 \times 5 = 20$

7. b $3125 \div 25 \text{ of } 25 - \sqrt[3]{125}$
$= 3125 \div (25 \times 25) - (125)^{1/3}$
$= 3125 \div 625 - 5$
$= 5 - 5 = 0$

8. c $18.18 \div 9 + 2.7 \text{ of } 3 = 18.18 \div 9 + 8.1$
$= 2.02 + 8.1 = 10.12$

9. d   Using BODMAS, we get 3511 as answer.

10. e   Unit's digit is governed by product of individual unit's digit only. Unit's digit of
$(7 \times 8 \times 7 \times 3) = 6$.

11. c $\dfrac{451*603}{9}$.

$\because$ Sum of all digits must be divisible by 9

$\therefore * = 8$

12. c   Number formed by last 3 digits must be divisible by 8.
$\therefore * = 3$

13. d 8756×99999
$= 8756 \times [100000 - 1]$
$= 875600000 - 8756 = 875591244$

14. d $1399 \times 1399 = (1400 - 1)^2$
$= (1400)^2 + (1)^2 - 2(1400)(1)$
$= 1960000 + 1 - 2800 = 1957201$

15. b $397 \times 397 + 104 \times 104 + 2 \times 397 \times 104$
$= (397 + 104)^2 = (501)^2$
$= (500 + 1)^2$
$= (500)^2 + (1)^2 + 2(500)(1)$
$= 250000 + 1 + 1000 = 251001$

16. b   Change the fractions into decimals and then check.

17. b $x = 6 - \sqrt{35}$

$$\therefore \frac{1}{x} = \frac{1}{6-\sqrt{35}} \times \frac{6+\sqrt{35}}{6+\sqrt{35}} = \frac{6+\sqrt{35}}{1} \Rightarrow 6+\sqrt{35}$$

18. a   Number should be divisible by 9 and 11 both.

19. a   Let the numbers be x and 1365 + x.
Then, 1365 + x = 6x + 15 or x = 270

20. a   The best way is to factorize the number,
i.e. 385 = 5 × 7 × 11. Hence, first prime number = 5.

21. b   When 99547 is divided by 687, remainder is 619.
∴ Nearest number = 99547 + 68 = 9961

22. d   99990

23. c   100011

24. d $n = 4 \times Q + 3$ (Q = Quotient)
$2n = 2 \times 4 \times Q + 6$
When 2n is divided by 4, Quotient = 2(Q + 1) and remainder = 2

25. d   Given expression $\dfrac{2^{n-1}\,(2+1)}{2^n\,(2-1)} = \dfrac{3}{2}$

26. c $D = \dfrac{abcd}{9999}$, 49995 = 9999 × 5

Hence, once we multiply D with 9999 we will get a natural number.

27. b $a^3 + b^3 + c^3 = 3\,abc$ if a + b + c = 0

28. c $x \div \dfrac{3}{8} \times \dfrac{5}{6} = x \times \dfrac{8}{3} \times \dfrac{5}{6} = x \times \dfrac{40}{18}$

Equivalent to dividing by $\dfrac{18}{40} = \dfrac{9}{20}$

29. c $72 \times 12 = 24 \times N \Rightarrow N = 36$

Practice Exercise – 2 : Level 1

1. d $P = 2^8 \times 3^4 \times 5^4 \times 7^2 \times 11^2 \times 23^2$
∴ Total number of factors = (8 + 1) (4 + 1) (4 + 1)
(2 + 1) (2 + 1) (2 + 1) = 6075

2. e $\dfrac{(a+b+c)}{3} = 6$, $\dfrac{(b+c+d)}{3} = 7$, $d - a = 3$

Hence, no unique solution can be obtained as the last equation can be derived from the first two.

3. d   Assume the quotient to be x, then divisor = 12x
It is given that 12x = 5 × 48, x = 20.
Dividend = Divisor × Quotient + Remainder
= (12 × 20) × 20 + 48 = 4848

4. b   All the terms in the series except 2! and 4! are divisible by 5,
therefore remainder will be the same as the remainder when
(2! + 4!) is divided by 5 i.e. the remainder will be 1.

5. c   We can have at least two such sets of prime numbers 71,
73, 79 and 67, 73, 83.

6. b   By cross multiplying, we get

$\dfrac{2}{3} \bowtie \dfrac{13}{21}$ 42 > 39

Therefore, $\dfrac{2}{3} > \dfrac{13}{21}$

Similarly by doing for the other fractions we get largest and

smallest fractions are $\dfrac{2}{3}$ and $\dfrac{11}{18}$ respectively. Their sum

$$= \frac{23}{18} = 1\frac{5}{18}$$

7. e $\dfrac{1}{11}(11x + 11y) = x + y$

So, both sides are equal.
Hence, data given is insufficient.

8. b   Since average of 4 even numbers is 27, it shall have
2 numbers on either side.
24, 26, 28 and 30.

You can check this: Average $= \dfrac{108}{4} = 27$

9. a   We divide 1153 by 15 and write the remainders and quotient
at appropriate places.
∴ The number is 51D.

10. c $x = 17^4$
$y = (17 - 3)\,(17 - 1)\,(17 + 1)\,(17 + 3)$
$= (17^2 - 9)\,(17^2 - 1)$; therefore, x > y
$= 17^4 - 10 \times 17^2 + 9$
Therefore, x − y > 1000.

11. d   We just need to check the last digit of 7^{194321}
194321 is of the form 4k + 1, where k is a natural
number, so the last digit will be $7^1 = 7$.

12. c $6084 = 2^2 \times 3^2 \times 13^2$
So the total number of factors of 6084 is
(2 + 1) × (2 + 1) × (2 + 1) = 27

Now these make $\left(\dfrac{27+1}{2}\right) = 14$ pairs, each giving 6084, as

their product.

But the factor $2 \times 3 \times 13 = \sqrt{6084}$ couples with itself hence,
we must subtract 1.
Option (c) is correct.

Career Launcher MBA

13. b $(100)_{10} = (10)_{100}$. Hence, we need two digits.

14. c When $(24 + 1)^{625}$ is divided by 24 the remainder is 1 When 26 is divided by 24 the remainder is 2.
Hence, the required remainder will be 1 + 2 = 3.

15. b The factors that are common must also be the factors of the HCF (N, M).
HCF (N, M) = $2^2 \times 3^4$
Number of factors of $2^2 \times 3^4$
= (2 + 1) × (4 + 1) = 15
So there are 15 factors that are common to both.

16. c $1^2 = 1$, $11^2 = 121$, $111^2 = 12321$ …
$11111111^2 = 123456787654321$
Hence, digit sum = 64

17. a The given expression can be written as

$$\frac{\left(\frac{4}{3}\right)^4+\left(\frac{3}{4}\right)^4+1}{\left(\frac{4}{3}\right)^2+\left(\frac{3}{4}\right)^2+1} ; \quad \frac{\left[\left(\frac{4}{3}\right)^2+\left(\frac{3}{4}\right)^2+1\right]\left[\left(\frac{4}{3}\right)^2+\left(\frac{3}{4}\right)^2-1\right]}{\left(\frac{4}{3}\right)^2+\left(\frac{3}{4}\right)^2+1}$$

$$=\left(\frac{4}{3}\right)^2+\left(\frac{3}{4}\right)^2-1 = \frac{16}{9}+\frac{9}{16}-1=\frac{193}{144}$$

Note: $\dfrac{a^4+b^4+1}{a^2+b^2+1}=a^2+b^2-1$

18. c $$N=\left[\frac{2^4(1^4+2^4+3^4+\cdots \text{ till n terms})}{(1^4+2^4+3^4+\cdots \text{ till n terms})}\right]^{\frac{1}{4}}$$

$$=\left(2^4\right)^{\frac{1}{4}}=2$$

19. c $2 + 7 + 6 + x = 20 \Rightarrow 15 + x = 20$; $25 + x + y = 50$ where $15 + x = 20$;
Hence, $10 + y + 20 = 50 \Rightarrow y = 20$.

20. b $\because$ Sum of odd and even is always odd.
$\therefore$ At least one has to be odd and the rest evens to give an odd number.

21. a $\left(28+10\sqrt{3}\right)^{\frac{1}{2}} - \dfrac{1}{\left(7-4\sqrt{3}\right)^{\frac{1}{2}}}$

$$=\left[5^2+(\sqrt{3})^2+2.5.\sqrt{3}\right]^{\frac{1}{2}} - \frac{1}{\left[2^2+(\sqrt{3})^2-2.2.\sqrt{3}\right]^{\frac{1}{2}}}$$

$$=\left[(5+\sqrt{3})^2\right]^{\frac{1}{2}} - \frac{1}{\left[(2-\sqrt{3})^2\right]^{\frac{1}{2}}}$$

$$=5+\sqrt{3} - \frac{1}{2-\sqrt{3}} = 5+\sqrt{3} - (2+\sqrt{3}) = 3$$

22. b $13^{36} = (13^3)^{12} = (2197)^{12} = (2196+1)^{12}$ So when it is divided by 2196 the remainder will obviously be 1.

23. d $19^n + 1$ can be written in two ways:
(i) $(18 + 1)^n + 1$
(ii) $(20 - 1)^n + 1$
Now check with the options.

24. d We need to find odd multiples of 11 × 3 = 33

$$\therefore \frac{200}{33} \approx 6.06 \text{ and } \frac{400}{33} \approx 12.1$$

$\therefore$ We have 3 such numbers, i.e.
33 × 7 = 231
33 × 9 = 297
33 × 11 = 363

25. e Any prime number greater than 3 is always of the form $6k + 1$ or $6k - 1$.

26. c Number of boxes = 2 × 3 × 4 + (3 × 4) + 4 + 1 = 41

27. d m^3 and n^3 have the same signs as m and n respectively have. So (d) will definitely hold good.

28. b Each of the numbers can be written as a multiple of 111. The factors of 111 are 111, 37, and 3.

29. b Check with the options. Option (b) can be written 2^2, 3^2, 4^2, 5^2 … so on, which is not an arithmetic progression.

30. e The product of any n consecutive numbers would be divisible by the product of the 1st n consecutive natural numbers, i.e. n!

31. d Work with the choices.

$$\frac{24}{6} = 4 \text{ and } 24 \times 2 = 48$$

Digits when reversed, number is 42.
So the difference is (48 − 42) = 6

32. d I. It is divisible by a − b as well.
II. True if n is even.
III. Not a perfect square. If square must end in 25 at least.
IV. True

33. a Every prime number greater than 3 can be written
$6N + 1$ or $6N - 1$. Hence, $P^2 + 17 = (6N)^2 + 1 \pm 12N + 17$.
So when divided by 12, it must leave a remainder 6.

34. e $\because \left[\dfrac{100}{5}\right]+\left[\dfrac{100}{25}\right]$

= 20 + 4 = 24
100! has 24 zeroes.
100! + 200! = 100![1 + 101 × 102 × ... × 200]
which will again give 24 zeroes at the end.

35. a The numbers possible are:
102, 111, 120, 123, 132, 135, 147, 153, 159, 174, 195.

Practice Exercise – 3 : Level 2

1. b Sum of squares of n natural numbers

$$= \frac{n(n+1)(2n+1)}{6} = \frac{10 \times 11 \times 21}{6} = 385$$

2. a (a) evaluates to 216, the maximum.

3. e $(3^5)^{4/5} = 3^4$ is the smallest.

4. d $2 + 4 + +6 + 8 + ... + 100$ (50 even numbers)
$50 \times (50 + 1) = 2550$.
Sum of first n even number is $n(n + 1)$

5. b Using BODMAS, we get 181.5 as answer.

6. d Square root of 1296 = 36 not 34.

7. d $\because 1 + 2 + 3 + ...+ n = \dfrac{n(n+1)}{2}$

$\therefore 1 + 2 + 3 + ... + 45 = \dfrac{45 \times 46}{2} = 1035$

8. a By observing $\dfrac{4}{5} > \dfrac{3}{5} > \dfrac{2}{5} > \dfrac{1}{5}$

Numerator is decreasing and denominator is same.

Now we have to compare $\dfrac{4}{5}$ and $\dfrac{7}{15}$

$\dfrac{4}{5} = \dfrac{4 \times 3}{5 \times 3} = \dfrac{12}{15} > \dfrac{7}{15}$

$\therefore \dfrac{4}{5}$ is the greatest.

9. d LCM of 2, 3, 4, 5, 6, 7 = 420
Smallest 4 digit-number divisible by LCM
= 420 × 3 = 1260

10. d $x + y = 2 (x − y)$; $xy = 27$.
Only option (d) gives $xy = 27$

11. d The largest fraction is $\dfrac{5}{6}$.

12. d Numbers are 8, 9, 10
$\therefore$ Sum = 8 + 9 + 10 = 27

13. b Every such number must be divisible by LCM of 4, 5, 6, i.e., 60.
Such numbers are 240, 300, 360, 420, 480, 540.
There are 6 such numbers.

14. a Put n as 2, 4, 6, etc.

15. c $3 + \dfrac{3}{3 + \dfrac{1 \times 3}{10}} = 3 + \dfrac{3 \times 10}{33} = 3 + \dfrac{10}{11} = \dfrac{43}{11}$

16. d Considering the unit's digit only, in numbers like 509, 519, 529 ... 589, 9 occurs 9 times.
Considering the ten's digit, from 590-598, (590, 591, 592 ... 598) 9 occurs 9 times.
Hence, there are 9 + 9 = 18 numbers between 500 and 600 that contain the digit 9 exactly once.

17. b We know that 2 × 5 = 10 (one zero)
The given product can be written as
$33 \times (5^2 \times 7) \times (2^2 \times 5 \times 9) \times (2^2 \times 3) \times (2^2 \times 11) \times (2^4 \times 5) \times (2 \times 11 \times 3)$
The powers of 2 and 5 are $2^{11} \times 5^4$
Only when one 5 is multiplied with one 2 a zero will be produced.
So there are 4 zeros.

18. a $56^{56} + 56$ can be written as $(57 − 1)^{56} + 56$
All the terms except $(−1)^{56}$ of $(57 − 1)^{56}$ will be divisible by 57, so remainder will be 1.
Once 56 is added to $(57 − 1)^{56}$ the sum will be divisible by 57. So remainder will be 0.

19. d Suppose the numbers are 2n, 2n + 2 and 2n + 4, where n is a whole number.
$2n(2n + 2) (2n + 4) = 2 \times 2 \times 2 (n) (n + 1) (n + 2)$
Now $n(n + 1) (n + 2)$ is product of three consecutive natural numbers and at least one of them will be divisible by 2 and at least one of them will be divisible by three.
$\therefore n(n + 1) (n + 2)$ is divisible by 6.
$\therefore 8(n) (n + 1) (n + 2)$ will always be divisible by 48.

20. a Since LCM = 102 = 2 × 3 × 17
Therefore, 17 has to be a component of at least one of the numbers. Only choice (a) or (e) will fit. By checking we get the answer as option (a).

Alternative method:
The choices (b), (c) and (d) will have a factor of 5 in the LCM {they have multiples of 5 in numbers} so the only logical choice is (a) or (e).

21. a $21600 = 2^3 \times 3^3 \times 10^2$; we need another pair of 2 × 3 so that it becomes a perfect square. Hence, it needs to be multiplied by 2 × 3 = 6.

22. b From 259 to 458 there are two hundred natural numbers and so there will be 2 × 20 = 40 8's. From 459 to 492 we have 13 more 8's and so answer is 40 + 13 = 53

23. a $n^3 + 2n = n(n^2 + 2)$
Any natural number is either of the form 3m or 3m ± 1, where m is a whole number.
If n = 3m, then $n(n^2 + 2)$ is definitely divisible by 3.
If n = 3m ± 1 then,
$n^2 + 2 = (3m ± 1)^2 + 2 = 9m^2 ± 6m + 1 + 2$
$= 9m^2 ± 6m + 3 = 3 (3m^2 ± 2m + 1)$
$\therefore n(n^2 + 2) = (3m ± 1) [3(3m^2 ± 2m + 1)]$, i.e. divisible by 3.

Alternative method:
Try with some natural numbers and get the answer.

Career Launcher MBA

Answers and Explanations

24. d   N = 238a + 79 = 17 × 14a + 17 × 4 + 11
        Hence, on dividing N by 17, the remainder is 11.

        Note: This method would have failed had 17 not been a
        factor of 238.

25. b   All the terms except the last one are multiples of 16 Last
        term = 1
        Hence, remainder when 17^{23} is divided by 16 = 1

26. c $9^6 = (8 + 1)^6$ So remainder is 1.
        So in $9^6 + 1$ the remainder is 2.

27. c $N = 2^{50} × 50!$ The highest power of 5 in 50! is 12, therefore
        there will be 12 zeroes at the end of N.

28. a   If $2^{32} + 1 = a + b$
        Since $a^3 + b^3 = (a + b)^3 - 3ab (a + b)$
        $= (a + b) [(a + b)^2 - 3ab]$
        So $(a^3 + b^3)$ is divisible by same numbers as $(a + b)$.

29. c $4^{61}(1 + 4 + 16 + 64 + 256) = 4^{61}(341)$, 341 is divisible by 11.

30. c   The answer should be a multiple of LCM (8, 9,10)
        $= 360 = 2^2 × 3^2 × 2 × 5$
        In order to make it a perfect square, we need to multiply
        (2 × 5) to it, i.e. 360 × 2 × 5 = 3600

Practice Exercise – 4 : Level 2

1. b   LCM of 7, 10, 15 = 210
        Least multiple of LCM, less than 2024
        = 1890 (210 × 9)
        1890 + 3 = 1893 (3 is remainder)
        Hence, 2024 – 1893 = 131 is the least number.

2. e   The data is inconsistent as the LCM is always a multiple of
        HCF. Here HCF = 75 and LCM = 216 do not show consistency,
        i.e. no such numbers are possible.

3. a   By divisibility rule of 3, 4 + 5 + a + 6 = multiple of 3
        $\Rightarrow$ a = 3 or 6 or 9 [since 'a' is a single-digit number]
        By divisibility rule of 11
        (4 + 5) – (6 + a) = multiple of 11 or zero.
        $\Rightarrow$ a = 3
        $\therefore$ Only a = 3, is the right answer.

4. b   Best way is to check the options, i.e.
        (a) is not possible.

        (b) $\frac{1}{24} × 72 = 3$ cube of 3 = 27 which is the reverse of 72.

        (c) $\frac{1}{24} × 48 = 2$ cube of 2 = 8 which is not a two-digit
            number.

5. e   aaaaaa = aaa × 1000 + aaa
        = aaa (1000 + 1) = 1001 (aaa) = 7 × 11 × 13 (aaa)
        This is obviously divisible by 7, 11 and 13.

6. a   LCM of 2, 3, 4, 5 and 6 = 60
        On dividing 1000 by 60 remainder is 40
        Hence, closest number to 1000 divisible by 2, 3, 4, 5 and 6
        = (60 – 40) + 1000 = 1020

        Note: (1000 – 40) = 960 is also divisible by 60, but 1020 is
        closer to 1000.

        Alternative method:
        Only choice a is divisible by three.

7. b   The greatest number is formed by writing the digits in
        descending order, i.e. 54320
        The least number is reverse of this.
        (Only the first digit has to be non-zero), i.e. 20345
        Now 54320 – 20345 = 33975

8. c   Working backwards,
        C = D + 6
        B = C + 9 = D + 15
        A = B + 13 = D + 28
        Hence, A + B + C + D = 4D + 49 = 417
        D = 92
        So, A = 120

9. d   To convert from base 6 to base 10, multiply each digit in
        base 6 number.

        $(1234)_6 = \left(4 × 6^0 + 3 × 6^1 + 2 × 6^2 + 1 × 6^3\right)_{10}$

        $= (4 + 18 + 72 + 216)_{10} = (310)_{10}$

10. a   N = (29 × 5 + 3) × (29 × 10 + 3) × (29 × 20 + 1) ×
        (29 × 30 + 4)
        In expansion of this only the last term, i.e.
        3 × 3 × 1 × 4 = 36 is not divisible by 29 and will leave a
        remainder of 7.

11. c   The total multiples of 31 in 1000! $= \dfrac{1000}{31} = 32$

        (31, 62, 93, … 992)

        The total number of multiples of $31^2 = 961$

        In (1000)! $= \dfrac{1000}{961} = 1$

        $\therefore$ Total power of 31 in 1000! = 32 + 1 = 33

12. a   If n is even, then even + even + 1 = odd
        If n is odd, then odd + odd + 1 = odd
        Therefore, $n^4 + n^2 + 1$ is always odd

13. a   LCM of powers = 12

        The numbers are equal to $(125)^{\frac{1}{6}}$, $(121)^{\frac{1}{6}}$, $(123)^{\frac{1}{6}}$

        Thus, $\sqrt{5}$ is the greatest amongst these three numbers,

        comparing $\sqrt{5}$ with other numbers, amongst

        $(25)^{\frac{1}{4}}$ and $(36)^{\frac{1}{4}}$, $36^{\frac{1}{4}}$ is greater.

Finally, comparing $(36)^{\frac{1}{4}}$ and $\sqrt[12]{27}=(3)^{\frac{1}{4}}$; $\sqrt[4]{36}$ is the greatest of all the numbers.

14. d $(1556)_{10}=(?)_{16}$

$$\begin{array}{r|l} 16 & 1556 \\ \hline 16 & 97 \quad \longrightarrow 4 \\ \hline & 6 \quad \longrightarrow 1 \end{array}$$

$\therefore (1556)_{10}=(614)_{16}$

15. c Follow the instructions given in question 14 and convert base 7 to base 10

i.e. $(413)_7=(3\times 7^0+1\times 7^1+4\times 7^2)_{10}=(206)_{10}$

Now convert it to base 8

$$\begin{array}{c|c|c} 8 & 206 & \\ \hline 8 & 25 & 6 \\ \hline & 3 & 1 \end{array}$$

$\therefore (206)_{10}=(316)_8$

Hence, $(413)_7=(316)_8$

16. b Squaring the three expressions given, we get

$10+2\sqrt{21},\ 10+2\sqrt{25},\ 10+2\sqrt{24}$, $10+2\times 4=18$

Therefore, (b) is the greatest.

17. d Suppose the number is ab.

We have $(10a+b)+\dfrac{75}{100}(10a+b)=10b+a$

Hence, $\dfrac{b}{a}=\dfrac{2}{1}$

18. a $N=1-\dfrac{1}{2}+\dfrac{1}{2}-\dfrac{1}{3}+\dfrac{1}{3}-\dfrac{1}{4}+\dfrac{1}{4}-\dfrac{1}{5}+\cdots+\dfrac{1}{12}-\dfrac{1}{13}$

$=1-\dfrac{1}{13}=\dfrac{12}{13}$

19. c If ten's digit is 1, we have two such numbers, viz. 10 and 11.
When ten's digit is 2, we have three such numbers, viz. 20, 21 and 22.
…
…
When ten's digits is 9, we have 10 such numbers, viz. 90, 91…99.
$\therefore$ Total number of such numbers is
$2+3+4+\ldots+10=54$

20. c Any power of 5 when divided by 4 gives a remainder of 1.
Here the power of 3 is itself a power of 5 and will give a remainder of 1 when divided by 4.
The last digit of the number will be $3^1=3$.
And hence, last digit of the given number is $3+1=4$.

21. c All even powers of 3 are of the form 4n + 1
$\therefore$ Last digit of first term is 2 also all odd powers of 3 are of the form 4n + 3
$\therefore$ Last digit of the term is 8
{By cyclicity of last digit}
Thus, the last digit of expression is $2-8=4$

22. a The 50th term $=\dfrac{1}{\sqrt{99}+\sqrt{101}}$

$\Rightarrow$ The given series

$$=\dfrac{\sqrt{1}-\sqrt{3}}{\left(\sqrt{1}-\sqrt{3}\right)\left(\sqrt{1}+\sqrt{3}\right)}+\dfrac{\sqrt{3}-\sqrt{5}}{\left(\sqrt{3}-\sqrt{5}\right)\left(\sqrt{3}+\sqrt{5}\right)}+\cdots$$

$$+\dfrac{\sqrt{99}-\sqrt{101}}{\left(\sqrt{99}-\sqrt{101}\right)\left(\sqrt{99}+\sqrt{101}\right)}$$

$$=\dfrac{\sqrt{1}-\sqrt{3}}{-2}+\dfrac{\sqrt{3}-\sqrt{5}}{-2}+\dfrac{\sqrt{5}-\sqrt{7}}{-2}+\cdots+\dfrac{\sqrt{99}-\sqrt{101}}{-2}$$

$$=\dfrac{1}{-2}\left[\sqrt{1}-\sqrt{3}+\sqrt{3}-\sqrt{5}+\cdots+\sqrt{99}-\sqrt{101}\right]$$

$$=\dfrac{1}{-2}\left[\sqrt{1}-\sqrt{101}\right]=\dfrac{\sqrt{101}-\sqrt{1}}{2}$$

23. c $1+2+3+4+5+6+7+8+9+10=100$
We know that LHS = 55 thus by changing '+' to '×' we have to increase the LHS by 45 to make it equal to RHS.
If we replace the last '+' sign we increase the sum by $9\times 10-10-9=71$ which is too high.
Same way for last but 1 increase is of 55 which is again too high.
Same way for last but 2 increase is of $7\times 8-7-8=41$
Thus, by replacing one '+' we cannot get the desired increase.
$\therefore$ We change one more '+'.
We see that by replacing first and third '+' we get the desired increase.

24. c

$$\sqrt{\dfrac{(12.12)^2-(8.12)^2}{(0.25)^2+(0.25)(19.99)}}+\dfrac{\left[\left(8^{-\frac{3}{4}}\right)^{\frac{5}{2}}\right]^{\frac{8}{15}}\times 16^{\frac{3}{4}}}{\sqrt[3]{\left[\left((128)^{-5}\right)^{\frac{3}{7}}\right]^{\frac{-1}{5}}}}$$

$$=\sqrt{\dfrac{(12.12+8.12)(12.12-8.12)}{(0.25)(0.25+19.99)}}+\dfrac{\left[\left((2^3)^{\frac{-3}{4}}\right)^{\frac{5}{2}}\right]^{\frac{8}{15}}\times 16^{\frac{3}{4}}}{\sqrt[3]{\left[\left((2^7)^{-5}\right)^{\frac{3}{7}}\right]^{\frac{-1}{5}}}}$$

$$=\sqrt{\dfrac{(20.24)\,(4)}{\frac{1}{4}\,(20.24)}}+\dfrac{(2)^{\frac{-45}{8}\times\frac{8}{15}}\times 2^3}{\sqrt[3]{(2^{-5})^{\frac{-3}{5}}}}$$

$$=4+\dfrac{1}{2}=4.5=\dfrac{9}{2}$$

25. d   Option (a) becomes false if all are negative integers.
         Option (b) becomes false if e > 0 and rest all are negative.
         Option (c) is not necessarily the middle number or need not
         be the average, e.g. 0, 1, 2, 3, 1000
         Option (d) is always true.

26. b   From 100 to 200 there are 101 numbers. There are 100 1's
         in the hundred's place.
         10 1's in the ten's place
         and 10 1's in the unit's place.

Practice Exercise – 5 : Level 2

For questions 1 and 2:

As the number is divisible by 99 it is divisible by 11 also. Now sum of
digits at odd and even places is $33 + Q$ and $16 + P$ respectively.
Thus, $17 + Q – P$ is either 0 or 11 or 22 … now $Q > P$. Thus, $Q – P$ is
+ve but < 9 as both are single digit numbers since $Q – P > 0$ hence
$17 + Q – P$ cannot be 0 or 11 and can only be 22 as $Q – P < 9$ thus
$Q – P = 5$

Now since it is divisible by 99 it is divisible by 9 too.
$\Rightarrow 49 + P + Q$ is divisible by 9
Thus, $P + Q = 5$ or 14. But as maximum value of Q is 9 and
$Q – P$ is 5.
Thus, maximum value of $P + Q = 13$ $\therefore P + Q = 5$
Thus, we get $P = 0, Q = 5$

1. c   2. a

3. c   The smallest number that is made of 6's only and is divisible
         by 7 is 666666.

         $\therefore M = \dfrac{666666}{7} = 95238$

         $\therefore N = 9 + 5 + 2 + 3 + 8 = 27$
         Last digit of 27^{36} is 1.

4. b $7^{187} = (7^4)^{46} \times 7^3 = (2401)^{46} \times 343$
         Now $2401 = 2400 + 1$
         So when $(2401)^{46}$ is divided by 800, the remainder
         must be 1. So the remainder when 7^{187} is divided by
         800 is $= 1 \times 343 = 343$

5. a $a = 5p; b = 5q + 1; c = 5r + 2$ and thus replace in the
         expression $2a + 3b – 4c$ to get the answer.
         (Hint: Replace only the remainders to get the final remainder
         or put $a = 0, b = 1$ and $c = 2$)

6. b   We see that PP must be less than 22, otherwise the cube
         of PP will have at least 5 digits. Hence, the only possible
         option for $PP = 11 \Rightarrow PP^3 = 1331$
         Since $Q (PP^3) = $ a four-digit number with ten's digit as one,
         hence $Q \times 3$ ends within $1 \Rightarrow Q$ has to be 7.

7. b   Let quotients obtained when this number is divided by 5 and
         6, be x and y respectively.
         Number $= 5x + 2 = 6y + 1$
         given that $= x – y = 3$
         $5x + 2 = 6y + 1$
         or $(6 –1) x + 2 = 6y + 1$
         or $6x + (2 – x) = 6y + 1$
         or $6(x – y) + 1 = x$

or $6 \times 3 + 1 = x$
$\Rightarrow x = 19$
$\Rightarrow$ Number $= 19 \times 5 + 2 = 97$
Hence (b) is the correct option.

[**Note:** that x will be greater than y as 5 is smaller than 6]

8. b   All the bells will be ringing simultaneously after every L min,
         where L = LCM (2, 3, 4, 6, 8, 9, 12) = 72 min. Then from
         6 a.m. till 5 p.m. of the same day, nine times all 7 bells would
         ring simultaneously. (Except the first one at 6 a.m.)

9. e   There are 10 numbers beginning with 6, i.e. 60 to 69. There
         are 9 numbers ending in 6. So total number of sixes is 19.

         Alternative method:
         In first 1 – 99 every digit (1 to 9) appears 20 times.
         So 6 will not there for one time.
         So total number of times when 6 appears = 19

10. b   Whatever be the arrangements of numbers, smallest number
         selected will be 1.

11. c   The largest of the largest numbers in each column is 25.
         Hence, $25 – 1 = 24$.

12. e   (A) $\sqrt{3}$ is not a rational number, therefore, $3\sqrt{3}$ is also
             not a rational number.
         (B) Rational number multiplied by another rational number
             gives a rational number.
         (C) Let, if possible $7 = x^3$, where x is a rational number.
             Therefore, $x = \sqrt[3]{7}$. But $\sqrt[3]{7}$ is not a rational number,
             which is the contradiction.

13. d   The number of students will be of the form:
         $(2 \times 3 \times 5 \times 7 \times 11)N + 1 = 2310N + 1$, where N is a natural
         number. For N = 1, 2, 3 and 4, the number of students will be
         a four-digit number.

14. b   The best way to solve this is by reverse substitution. If you
         look at the answer choices, you will observe that only option
         (b) satisfies the given condition,
         i.e. $24 = 3 \times (2 \times 4)$

15. c   Check with digits A = 1, 2, 3, ... 9.
         Note that for a perfect square number with ten's place odd,
         unit's place of the number must be 6.
         $(AA)^2 = DCBA$, then $66^2 = 4356$
         Then $D = 4$

16. b   Divide 10×10^2, i.e. 1000 by 3×10^2, i.e. 300 remainder is
         100, i.e. 1×10^2 and not 1.
         so when, 798630×10^{24} is divided by 18×10^{24}, the remainder
         is 6×10^{24} (and not 6)

17. b   LCM of 6, 7, 8 and 9 = 504
         $\therefore$ All bells toll after 504 s.
         $\therefore$ In 2 hr, number of times they would toll together

         $= \dfrac{2 \times 60 \times 60}{504} = 14.28$

         $\Rightarrow$ If we start counting just before the moment all of them
         toll together, we would see them tolling 15 times.

18. c   Since all x, y and z are non-zero whole numbers and xy = z, y > x.

So z > x; and $z \geq y$. Since numbers are distinct $y \neq z$.

So z > x, z > y $\Rightarrow$ z > x^3 is correct answer.

19. c $a_3^2 - a_2^2 = 57 = 19 \times 3$ or 1×57

Case I: $(a_3 + a_2)(a_3 - a_2) = 19 \times 3$
$\therefore a_3 + a_2 = 19$ and $a_3 - a_2 = 3$
or $a_3 = 11$, $a_2 = 8$
Hence, $a_1 = 3$

Case II: $(a_3 + a_2)(a_3 - a_2) = 57 \times 1$
$\therefore a_3 + a_2 = 57$ and $a_3 - a_2 = 1$
or $a_3 = 29$, $a_2 = 28$
Hence, $a_1 = 1$

20. e   I.   Square never ends in 8.
II.   e.g. $10^2 = 100$
III. e.g. 729
Hence, none of these.

21. a   Before 4th operation: $\dfrac{4}{4} + 4 = 5$

Before 3rd operation: $\dfrac{5}{4} + 4 = \dfrac{21}{4}$

Before 2nd operation: $\dfrac{21}{16} + 4 = \dfrac{85}{16}$

Before 1st operation: $\dfrac{85}{64} + 4 = \dfrac{341}{64}$

So n = $\dfrac{341}{64}$

22. e   LCM of 4, 5, 6 and 7 = 420
Smallest four-digit number = 1000
So essentially we need the largest three-digit number, which satisfies 420x + 2 = 842. (For x = 2)

Note: Solution can also be done worked out the choices.

23. b $\dfrac{a}{b} = \dfrac{1}{5}$ ... (i)

As difference between two fraction is $\dfrac{1}{10}$, second fraction

has to be $\dfrac{1}{10}$ $\left[\because \dfrac{1}{5} - x = \dfrac{1}{10}, \quad x = \dfrac{1}{10} \right]$

$\dfrac{a-2}{b+5} = \dfrac{1}{10}$
From (i), b = 5a

$\dfrac{a-2}{5a+5} = \dfrac{1}{10}$; $\dfrac{a-2}{a+1} = \dfrac{1}{2}$; a = 5

Alternative method:
Use choices to answer the question.

24. c $(51)^{51} = (51)^{50} \times 51 = [(51)^2]^{25} \times 51 = (2601)^{25} \times 51$
Here if we expand 2601 to any power, the last two digits will remain '01' and hence when multiplied by 51, it will give 51 as last two digits of the expression. Hence, ten's digit = 5

25. c   Clearly, the original number is a multiple of 9. This eliminates option (b), (d) and (e).
Through elimination process, (c) is the correct answer.

$\dfrac{10125}{9} = 1125$ (we can get after erasing zero).

1125 = 9 × 1 + 25 (Multiple of 9)

26. b   Digit erased is 0.

27. d   The number formed by last three digits must be 375. Then for first two places, each place has 5 options. Thus, 5 × 5 = 25 numbers are possible.

28. c   Answer is (c), since there is one duck in-between two ducks both in front and behind, therefore the least number of ducks that could swim is obviously 3.

29. a   The 2 digits at unit & tens place can be only 2 or 3.
$\therefore$ The hundredth digit must be 6. So the no. can be 623 or 632 on reversing the digits the nos. become 326 or 236. But the difference between 623 & 326 is 297 .

30. a   Take 1 coin from bag 1, 2 from bag 2, 3 from bag 3 … 10 from bag 10. By weighing in a spring balance the deviation from the expected weight will help us identify the defective bag.
e.g. Deviation = 6g, implies it is bag 6.

31. e   90 × 80 × … × 10 can be expressed as a power of 5. The exponent of 5 would be 5^{10}.

32. b   Parity of the first page and last page will not be the same. Since the first page number is 123, i.e. odd, the last page can be 132 or 312, i.e. even.

33. e $N_1 = 222x + 35$, $N_2 = 407y + 47$

$N_1 + N_2 = (37 \times 6 \times x + 35) + (37 \times 11 \times y + 47)$

$\Rightarrow$ Remainder when $N_1 + N_2$ is divided by 37

$= \dfrac{(35+47)}{37} = 8$

34. c   All the numbers from 200 to 299 begin with 2, i.e. 100 numbers and 10 numbers between 100 and 200 (102, 112, ..., 192) end with 2.
So number of such numbers = 100 + 10 = 110.

Practice Exercise – 6 : Level 3

1. b   Difference between divisor and remainder
= 35 − 25 = 45 − 35 = 55 − 45 = 10
LCM of 35, 45, 55 = 5 × 7 × 9 × 11 = 3465
Required Number = 3465 − 10 = 3455

Career Launcher MBA

Short cut:
3455 is the only option from which when we subtract 35, we get 3420 which is divisible by 45.

2. a LCM of 2, 3, 5 = 30
$\therefore$ number of coconuts = 30 + 1 = 31

3. b $x = 5 - \sqrt{7}$

$$\therefore \frac{1}{x} = \frac{1}{5 - \sqrt{7}} = \frac{5 + \sqrt{7}}{\left(5 - \sqrt{7}\right)\left(5 + \sqrt{7}\right)} = \frac{5 + \sqrt{7}}{18}$$

$$\therefore x + \frac{1}{x} = \frac{95}{18} - \frac{17\sqrt{7}}{18}$$

4. a $\dfrac{A}{2} = \dfrac{B}{3} = \dfrac{C}{4} = x \Rightarrow A = 2x,\ B = 3x \text{ and } C = 4x$

$\Rightarrow A : B : C = 2 : 3 : 4$

Largest part = $\left(243 \times \dfrac{4}{9}\right) = 108$

5. b Substitute n = 1.

6. b LCM of 3, 6, 9, 12, 15, 18 is 180
So, the bells will toll together after every 180 s, i.e. 3 min.

In 30 min, they will toll together for $\left(\dfrac{30}{3}\right) + 1 = 11$ times.

7. d $n = 5k + 2$

$\Rightarrow n^2 = 25k^2 + 10k + 4$

$$\frac{n^2}{5} = 5k^2 + 2k + \frac{4}{5}$$

Hence the remainder when n^2 is divided by 5 is 4.

8. a Substitute n = 1, 2

9. d $y = \sqrt{2} + 1$

$$\Rightarrow y + \frac{1}{y} = \frac{y^2 + 1}{y} = \frac{\left(\sqrt{2} + 1\right)^2 + 1}{\left(\sqrt{2} + 1\right)}$$

$$= \frac{\left(4 + 2\sqrt{2}\right)}{\sqrt{2} + 1} = \frac{2\sqrt{2}\left(1 + \sqrt{2}\right)}{\left(\sqrt{2} + 1\right)} = 2\sqrt{2}$$

Short cut:

$$\left(\sqrt{2} + 1\right) + \frac{1}{\sqrt{2} + 1} = \left(\sqrt{2} + 1\right) + \left(\sqrt{2} - 1\right) = 2\sqrt{2}$$

10. c Let ten's digit be x. Then, unit's digit = (x + 3)
Sum of the digits = x + (x + 3) = 2x + 3
Number = 10x + (x + 3) = 11x + 3

$$\frac{11x + 3}{2x + 3} = \frac{4}{1} \Leftrightarrow 11x + 3 = 4(2x + 3) \Leftrightarrow x = 3$$

$\therefore$ Number (11x + 3) = 36

Alternative method:
Check the conditions given in the question in the options.

11. c This question is to be done in two steps:
(a) make the bases equal
(b) equate the powers and solve
By equation, we have

$$32^{x-2} = \frac{64}{8^x}$$

$$\Rightarrow \left(2^5\right)^{x-2} = \frac{2^6}{\left(2^3\right)^x} \Rightarrow 2^{5x-10} = 2^{6-3x}$$

$\therefore$ Equate the powers and solve $\Rightarrow 5x - 10 = 6 - 3x$
$\Rightarrow x = 2$

12. c The total number of multiples of 5 in 30!
= 6 (5, 10 … 30)

The total number of multiples of $5^2 = 25$ in 30!
= 1 (25 only)

Further powers of 5 cannot be there as $5^3 = 125 > 30$
$\therefore$ The greatest power of 5 that divides 30! exactly
= 6 + 1 = 7

13. a Suppose numbers are x and y, we have
$x(x + y) = 3666$ … (i)
$y(x + y) = 2418$ … (ii)
Adding (i) and (ii), we get
$(x + y)^2 = 6084$
$\therefore x + y = 78$ … (iii)
Subtracting (ii) from (i), we get
$x^2 - y^2 = 1248$
or $(x + y)(x - y) = 1248$
or $78(x - y) = 1248$ from (iii)
$\therefore x - y = 16$

14. e Perfect square just above 20 = 25 = 5^2
Perfect square just below 2000 = 1936 = 44^2
Hence, there are 44 − 5 + 1 = 40 perfect squares
(20 even and 20 odd).
$\Rightarrow$ Out of 2000 − 20 + 1 = 1981 numbers (990 odd and 991 even), 20 are even perfect squares. The other 971 even numbers are not perfect squares.

15. b Since HCF is 39
$\therefore$ Let numbers be 39a and 39b
(a and b are coprimes)
We have,
39a × 39b = 15210, or ab = 10
There are only two pairs of natural numbers whose product will be 10.
(1, 10) and (2, 5) are the pairs.

16. c We can safely ignore the first 2 digits (as they are lost in subtraction), this gives us {for last 2 digits).
(10c + d) − (10d + c) = 54
$\Rightarrow 9(c - d) = 54$
$\Rightarrow c - d = 6$

17. e If we factorize the number 161 = 23 × 7
Now there are many pairs of x and y.
LCM of which is 161.
(i) 7, 23 (ii) 7,161 (iii) 23,161
Hence, answer is (e).

18. c   AA + BB = CDC
As sum of 2 two-digit numbers cannot be greater than 200 so C = 1
Now, taking different combinations of AA and BB, e.g. (44, 77), (88, 33), (99, 22), (66, 55) etc., so that C = 1, we see that in all such cases D = 2.
Hence, the only value of D is 2.

19. b   Suppose the number is ab.
We have a + b = 5   ... (i) and
$2(10a + b) - (10b + a) = 41$ ... (ii)
Solving (i) and (ii), we get
a = 3 and b = 2
∴ 32 is the number and 40% of this is 12.8.

Alternative method:

We can multiply the options by $\dfrac{100}{40}$ (as it is 40% of the number), and then check for properties.

(a) $11.8 \times \dfrac{100}{40} = 29.5$ (not a whole number)

(b) $12.8 \times \dfrac{100}{40} = 32$ (satisfies the given conditions)

so the answer is (b).

20. a   Let us assume that the numbers are 13x and 13y
∴ Product of the two numbers
= HCF × LCM = 13x × 13y
13x × 13y = 13 × 455
∴ xy = 35
The numbers can be
13 × 1, 13 × 35 or 13 × 5, 13 × 7
Only one number lies within the given limits, 13 × 7= 91.
Hence, the answer is (a).

Alternative method:
Only option (a) is a factor of 455.

21. e   Let us assume the middle number to be x.
Then the three consecutive numbers are
(x − 1), x and (x + 1)
$x^2 = (x - 1)(x + 1) + 1$
$x^2 = x^2 - 1 + 1$ have become equal.
Hence, this condition will hold for every number.

22. a $1^1 \times 2^2 \times 3^3 \times 4^4 \times \ldots 100^{100}$
Zeroes will be formed by multiplication of 2 and 5.
So, we have to calculate the powers of 5 only as 5 is the higher of the two primes.
Now power of 5 = $5^5 \times 10^{10} \times 15^{15} \ldots 25^{25} \ldots 100^{100}$
i.e. 5 +10 + 15 + 20 + 25 × 2 +...+ 75 × 2...+ 100 × 2
Here, 25 × 2, 50 × 2, 75 × 2 and 100 × 2 are there because
$25 = 5^2$
So total power of 5
= (5 + 10 + ... + 100) + (25 + 50 + 75 + 100)
= 1050 + 250 = 1300

23. b   x can have only one value, i.e. 2.
2 is the only even prime number.
The square of an even number is even.
When 3 is added it becomes odd (7 in this case).
For all other prime numbers the square is odd, but on adding 3 to them, the resultant number is a multiple of 2, and hence ceases to be prime.

24. d   In unit's place we will have all the numbers from 0 to 9 ten times each. In ten's place again we will have all the numerals from 0 to 9 ten times each.
In hundred's place we will have 99 one's and 1 two's.
∴ The sum will be
$10(0+1+\ldots+9) + 10(0+1+\ldots+9) + 99 \times 1 + 1 \times 2 = 1001$

25. c   54 = 2 × 27
The highest power of 3 in 31! is 14.
∴ The highest power of 27 will be 4.
⇒ The highest power of 54 will be 4.

Alternative method:
As $54 = 2 \times 27 = 2 \times 3^3$
We count the highest power of 3 (14) in 31! and take one-third of that (14) {only quotient part} to find the highest power of 3^3 in 31!

Practice Exercise – 7 : Level 3

1. c   Convert the part before the decimal.
$(1101)_2 = 1 \times 2^0 + 0 \times 2^1 + 1 \times 2^2 + 1 \times 2^3 = (13)_{10}$
For the part after decimal take negative powers of 2
∴ $(0.011)_2 = \left(0 \times 2^{-1} + 1 \times 2^{-2} + 1 \times 2^{-3}\right)_{10} = (0.375)_{10}$
∴ The answer is 13.375.

2. a $\dfrac{3}{4} + \dfrac{5}{36} + \dfrac{7}{144} + \ldots + \dfrac{19}{8100}$

$1 - \left(\dfrac{1}{2}\right)^2 + \left(\dfrac{1}{2}\right)^2 - \left(\dfrac{1}{3}\right)^2 + \left(\dfrac{1}{3}\right)^2 - \left(\dfrac{1}{4}\right)^2 = +\ldots + \left(\dfrac{1}{9}\right)^2 - \left(\dfrac{1}{10}\right)^2$

$= 1 - \dfrac{1}{100} = \dfrac{99}{100} = 0.99.$

Alternative method:

$\dfrac{3}{4} + \dfrac{5}{36} + \dfrac{7}{144} + \cdots + \dfrac{19}{8100}$

The denominators are of the form

$4 = 2^2 \times 1^2$, i.e. $n^2 \times (n-1)^2$

$36 = 3^2 \times 2^2$

$144 = 4^2 \times 3^2$

⋮

$8100 = 10^2 \times 9^2$

And the numerator is of the form n + (n − 1)
3 = 2 + 1
5 = 3 + 2
7 = 4 + 3

⋮

19 = 10 + 9

∴ $\dfrac{n + (n-1)}{n^2 \times (n-1)^2} = \dfrac{1}{(n-1)^2} - \dfrac{1}{n^2}$

Career Launcher MBA   Answers and Explanations

Thus, the series can be divided as

$$\frac{3}{4}+\frac{5}{36}\cdots\frac{19}{8100}=1-\left(\frac{1}{2}\right)^2+\left(\frac{1}{2}\right)^2-\left(\frac{1}{3}\right)^2\cdots$$

$$=1-\left(\frac{1}{10}\right)^2=0.99$$

3. d $(12630)_x=(3402)_{10}$

$\Rightarrow(3402)_{10}=\left(0\times x^0+3\times x^1+6\times x^2+2\times x^3+1\times x^4\right)_{10}$

$=\left(3x+6x^2+2x^3+x^4\right)_{10}$

Now we have 3 choices for x. We substitute from the given answer choices and check for last digit. We see that 9 gets eliminated.
If we put x = 7, it satisfy Hence correct option will be (d).

4. c Check choices. Working backwards with the smallest choice 9, we get inconsistent data. Working with 12 we get 28 apples in the beginning. Hence, initially there must have been 28 apples. Therefore, taking option (c), we arrive at consistent solution.

5. d $abc = a! + b! + c!$
$\Rightarrow 100a + 10b + c = a! + b! + c!$
Now
6! = 720 and 7! = 5040. If 7 is one of digits, then the sum of the factorials become a four-digit number or more. Hence, the numbers 7, 8, 9 can be neglected.
Consider 6! = 720. But number 7 cannot be there in hundred's place.
Hence, we can neglect 6 also.
Now
5! = 120, 4! = 24, 3! = 6, 2! = 2, 1! = 1 and 0! = 1. To get a three-digit number, 5 has to be present in the number. But 5 cannot be in hundred's place as then the number becomes greater than 500 which cannot be obtained as the sum of factorials. Also, maximum possible number is 5! + 4! + 3!
= 120 + 24 + 6. Also, 'a' cannot be 0 as it is a three-digit number. Hence, a = 1.
Then different possible cases are 154, 153, 152, 125, 135, 145.
From this we find that only 145 satisfies given condition.

$$\therefore(b+c)^a=(4+5)^1=9$$

Alternative method:
$abc = a! + b! + c! \Rightarrow 100a + 10b + c = a! + b! + c!$
Since 6! = 720 and 7! = 5040
None of the numbers is equal to or greater than 6.
Also amongst b and c either one has to be 5 as abc is a three-digit number and 5! = 120 and 4! = 24
Also b + c can have maximum value of 10 (given that none of them is more than 5) and a can at best be 2 as a! + 5! + 5!
= 240 + a! so the only option possible is (d).

6. e Since 300 < abc < 400
$\Rightarrow 100a + 10b + c = a^3 + b^3 + c^3$
Put a = 3 and rearrange, we get
$300 + 10b + c = 27 + b^3 + c^3$
$\Rightarrow (b^3-10b)+(c^3-c)=273$

Now put b = 6 and 7 (as b and c are both less than or equal to 9 and 6^3 and 7^3 are the nearest cubes to 273.) For b = 6,
We get $c^3-c=117$ and no value of c satisfies this.

For b = 7 we get $c^3-c=0$ and two values of c, i.e. c = 0 and c = 1 satisfies this.
Thus, abc = 370 or 371
Hence, abc cannot be uniquely determined.

7. b Pairs are (0, 1), (2, 1), (3, 1), (4, 1), (5, 1), (6, 1), (7, 1), (8, 1) and (9, 1).

8. c Suppose the numbers are M and N and the divisor is D.
We have $M = DQ_1 + 547$
$N = DQ_2 + 349$
$M + N = D(Q_1 + Q_2) + 896$
When M + N is divided by D it leaves a remainder of 211,
i.e. $D(Q_1 + Q_2) + 896 - 211$.
$= D(Q_1 + Q_2) + 685$ is divisible by D. It means 685 is divisible by D. But we know that D > 547, because divisor is always greater than the remainder.
So only possible value of D is 685.

9. b Any perfect square x can always be written as
$x = a^m \times b^n \times c^p \times \ldots$ where a, b, c are prime factors and m, n, p are all even. Now total number of factors of x = (m + 1)(n + 1) (p + 1) …
$= odd \times odd \times odd \times \ldots =$ An odd number.

10. b **Concept:**
We can see that by symmetry n = p and hence all we need to calculate is n and m.
n = 280 and m = 180
$\therefore 2n - m = 380$

11. a A = 185, B = 14 and C = 5
Hence, $C^3 = 125$

12. c If (P − 7) is a multiple of 11, (P + 4) and (P + 15) must be multiple of 11 as well because P + 4 = (P − 7) + 11 and P + 15 = (P − 7) + 22. Since (P + 4) and (P + 15) are consecutive multiples of 11, so one of them must be an even number. Hence, (P + 4) (P + 15) will always be divisible by 11 × 11 × 2 = 242

13. e Surprised! Many of you must have answered (c) but that will be the case if p is a prime number.
Hence, from given information we cannot say anything about q. It may be the case that p = 64 and q = 1.

14. a $83! - 82! = 83.82! - 82!$
$= 82! (83 - 1) = 82.82!$
Now to check highest power of 82 in 82! we just have to check the highest power of 41 in 82!. So, highest power of 82 in 82! is 2. Hence, highest power of 82 in 82. 82! will be 3.

15. c $(1923)^{1924^{1925}}=(1924-1)^{some\ even\ power\ =\ x}$

$\therefore$ Since all but last term are divisible by 1924.

$\Rightarrow$ Remainder = Last term = $^xC_0\times(1924)^0\times(-1)^x=1$

16. e   Suppose the number is abcde, when it is added to edcba the sum will be
$(10001a + 1010b + 200c + 1010d + 10001e)$.
Now whether the sum is divisible by 11 or 11111 or 101 completely depends on the values of a, b, c, d and e.

17. c $ab + ba = 11(a + b)$
$abcd + dcba = 1001(n + d) + 110(b + c)$
$= 11[91 (n + d) + 10(b + c)]$
Similarly, we can check for all even digit numbers as in question 37. So k must be multiple of 11.

18. c $ab \times cd = (10a + b) (10c + d)$
$= [40b + 10a - 39b] [51d - (50d - 10c)]$
$= (13 \times 10 \times k_1 - 39 b) (51 d - 17 \times 10 \times k_2)$
$= 13 \times 17 (10 k_1 - 3b) (3d - 10k_2)$
Hence the largest number will always divide the product of ab and cd is 221.

19. e $A = \{a_1, a_2, a_3, ... a_n\}$, $n \geq 8$
means there will be atleast 8 natural numbers in the set A. But it doesn't mean that $a_1 < a_2 < a_3 ... < a_n$. i.e. It doesn't give any idea about comparision of those numbers.
$\therefore$ (a), (b), (c), (d) could be negative also.
Thinking about option (d) $(a_{n-1} - a_n)^2$, will be always +ve.

20. c   HCF of two distinct natural numbers can never be a multiple of their LCM.

For questions 21 and 22:
As $Y : S = 1 : 4$
So Y = 1 and S = 4 or Y = 2 and S = 8 but Y = 1 and S = 4 is not possible because in that case V = 10, which is not possible.

8	1	6
7/3	5	3/7
4	9	2

21. e   22. a

For questions 23 and 24:
$V_n + V_{n+1} = \quad K \qquad 1 \leq n \leq 999$

$V_1 + V_2 = K = V_2 + V_3 = V_3 + V_4 = ...$

$V_1 + V_2 = V_2 + V_3$ and $V_2 + V_3 = V_3 + V_4$
$\Rightarrow V_1 = V_3$ and $V_2 = V_4$
$\therefore V_1 = V_3 = V_5 = ... = V_{999}$ = Odd subscript terms and
$V_2 = V_4 = V_6 = ... = V_{1000}$ = Even subscript terms
Now $V_{987} = 987 \Rightarrow V_{odd} = 987$
$\therefore V_{236} = K - V_{237}$, i.e. $K - V_{odd} = K - 987$
Again $V_{100} = 100 \Rightarrow V_{even} = 100$
$V_{odd} = K - 100$
$\therefore V_{10} + V_{11} + V_{12} + V_{13} + V_{14} - V_{15} - V_{16} - V_{17} - V_{18} - V_{19}$
$= [V_{10} + V_{12} + V_{14} - V_{16} - V_{18}] + [V_{11} + V_{13} - V_{15} - V_{17} - V_{19}]$
$(V_{even} - V_{odd})$ [After canceling terms]
$= 100 - (K - 100) = 200 - K$
Also $= V_{14} - (K - 100) = V_{14} + 100 - K$

23. c   24. d

25. b $a \neq 0$; $d = odd$
d can be equal to 3, 5 only.
$3! = 1 \times 2 \times 3$
$c(3) = a(1) + b(2)$ or $a(2) + b(1)$
$5! = 3 \times 5 \times 8$
$c(8) = a(5) + b(3)$ or $a(3) + b(5)$
But $c \neq 8$ because for this condition II is violating.
So c cannot take 8.
$5! = 4 \times 5 \times 6$
But in this case $c \neq a + b$
So $c \neq 6$
So c can take only 3.

26. b   (i) for e = 0, then d = ?
Let d = 1, $1 - 1 + 1 = 1 - 0$
$a = 1$ $b = 1$ $c = 1$ $d = 1$
For d = 5 as $5! = 4 \times 5 \times 6$
$4 - 5 + 6 = 5 - 0$
So for e = 0, d can take 1 and 5.
So first condition is not true.
(ii) for d = 5 numbers are

a = 3	a = 4	a = 4	a = 5
b = 8	b = 5	b = 6	b = 6
c = 5	c = 6	c = 5	c = 4
e = 5	e = 0	e = 2	e = 2

In all the numbers a + b + c > d + e. So second condition is true.

27. e   Ten cigarettes give 10 stubs. From 10 stubs 3 more cigarettes can be made (2 stubs would be obtained from 2 cigarattes formed by joining 8 stubs).

28. c   I.   Except for n = 1 and n = 2 for every other term X_n is less than n.
II. If the nth term is X_n then n has to be less than or equal to the sum of the first X_n natural numbers.
e.g. if $X_n = 5$ $n \leq (1 + 2 + 3 + 4 + 5)$ and also greater than $(1 + 2 + 3 + 4)$.
III. The statement is similar to (II). If $X_{n+1} - X_n = 1$, then X_n must be the last number in a set of X_n, i.e. the total number of terms till the last X_n is $1 + 2 + 3 + ... X_n$.

29. d   (a) For any n, the expression is always even.
(b) Sum of the squares of a number of integers
$$= \frac{n(n+1)(2n+1)}{6}$$
So $n(n + 1)(2n + 1)$ is divisible by 6.
So it must also be divisible by 3.
(c) The value of quotient is infact equal to 6.
(d) Since $n(n + 1)(2n + 1)$ can be divisible by 237 when either of n or (n + 1) or (2n + 1) is 237 or multiple of 237.
(e) For n = 2, expression is divisible by 5.
Hence, (d) is incorrect.

30. b $a^2 - 2b^2 = 1$
$\Rightarrow a^2 - 1 = 2b^2$
$\Rightarrow (a - 1)(a + 1) = 2b^2$
$\therefore a$ is odd.

Moreover $(a + 1)(a - 1)$ has to be divisible by 8 as product of two consecutive even numbers is divisible by 8.

$\Rightarrow 2b^2$ is divisible by 8

$\Rightarrow b^2$ is divisible is 4

$\therefore b = 2$

$\therefore (3, 2)$ is required pair

31. e

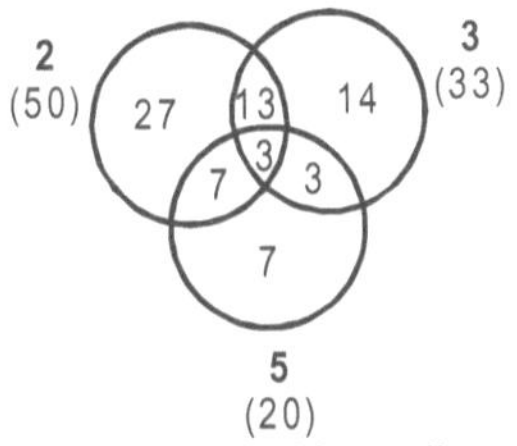

2
(50) 27 13 14 **3** (33)
7 3 3
7

5
(20)

The following Venn diagram shows the distribution on numbers between 1 and 100 that are divisible by 2, 3 or 5 or a combination or two or more of them. So we can see that there are 50 numbers that are divisible by 2, 33 numbers by 3 and 20 numbers by 5. There are 3 numbers divisible by 2,

3 and 5, while 7 are divisible by 2 and 5 (only), 13 are divisible with 2 and 3 (only) and 3 that are divisible by 5 and 3 (only). That leaves with 27 of them divisible by 2 only, 14 by 3 only and 7 by 5 only.

So $(27 + 13 + 14 + 7 + 3 + 3 + 7) = 74$ numbers are divisible by one or more among 2, 3 and 5.

So 26 numbers are not divisible by them.

32. a   Total corn sold = $\dfrac{1}{10} \times$ Time (In seconds)

Time $= 10\dfrac{1}{2}$ hr $= 630$ min

Productive time = 2 min in every 5 min

Number of 5 min periods $= \dfrac{630}{5} = 126$

Productive time $= 126 \times 2$ min $= 252$ min

Corn sold per day $= \dfrac{252 \times 60}{10} = 1512$

Notes

Practice Exercise (Non MCQ)

1. Number of guys wearing at least one of the two
= 70% of 30 = 21
Hence, the number of guys wearing both
= (10 + 15) − 21 = 4

2. The maximum amount would be when all of them have a drink and there are more number who drink whisky.
Hence, maximum would be when there are 15 who drink whisky and 5 who drink rum in the party.
Hence, total cost = 15 × 4 × 60 + 5 × 4 × 30
= ₹4200
The minimum amount would be when there are only 15 who drink, 10 of whom prefer rum in the party.
Hence, minimum amount = 10 × 4 × 30 + 5 × 4 × 60
= ₹2400
Either way it is a costly party!!
So say no to booze!!

3. (a) The maximum number would happen in the case when all those who passed in the first subject also passed in the second subject. Hence, it would be 30.
Note: In this case, the number of people passing in at least one subject would be minimum, i.e. 40.
   (b) The minimum number would happen when the number of people who passed in at least one subject is equal to 50.

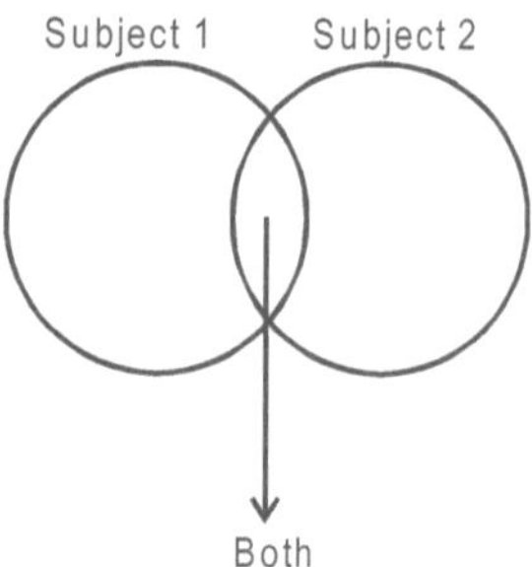

Let S_1 and S_2 denote the number of people passing in Subject 1 and Subject 2 respectively.
The union is 50.
Hence, S1 + S2 − Both (S1, S2) = 50
Both (S1, S2) = 30 + 40 − 50 = 20

4. Only 80% of the vehicles have the problem.
60% of vehicles had a problem with their engines, it means at least 20% had problem with door or tyre or both.
50% had a problem → With tyre → 30% with door or engine or both
60% had a problem → With doors → 20% with tyre or engine
It means if there is no intersection in these three, then at most (20 + 30 + 20) = 70%
Vehicles will have problem in one or two categories.
Hence, at least 10% vehicles will have all three problems.

5.

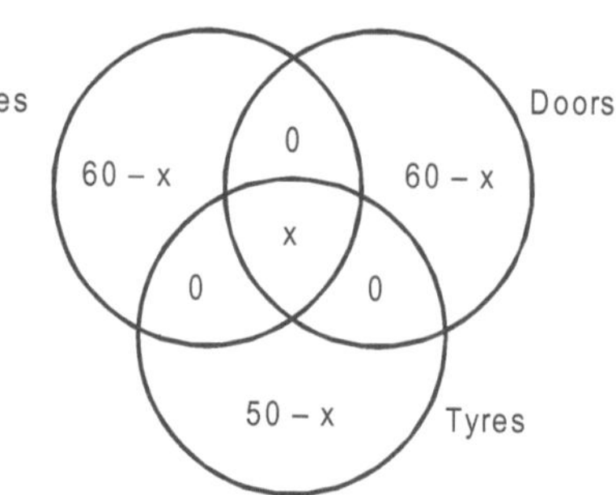

Total vehicles = 60 + 110 − 2x
= 170 − 2x = 80
$\Rightarrow$ x = 45%

Practice Exercise

1. b For finance = 64% of 500 = 320 = n(A)
For operation = 56% of 500 = 280 = n(B)

$$n(A \cup B) = n(A) + n(B) - n(A \cap B)$$

or $500 = 320 + 280 - n(A \cap B)$

or $n(A \cap B) = 100$

where A is for finance and B is for operation.

For questions 2 to 4:
Let x = Number of residents
$\therefore x - 3 = 0.3x + 0.75x - 6$
x = 60
$\therefore$ Venn diagram will look like.

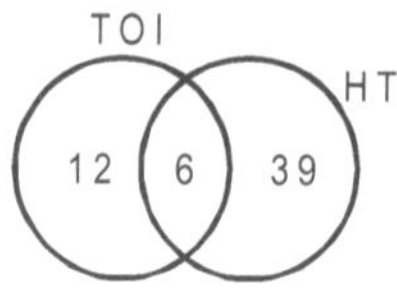

Reading neither = 3

2. a   3. b   4. c

For questions 5 and 6:
Let x = Number of students
$x - 0.05x = 70 + 0.5x - 0.25x$
$\therefore$ x = 100
Hence, Venn diagram will look like

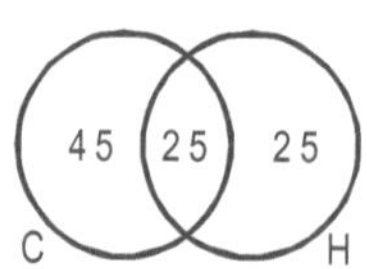

5. d   6. b

Notes

Level – 1

1. (a) (i) $^{10}P_r = 720$

   $$\Rightarrow \frac{10!}{(10-r)!} = 720$$

   We can see $10 \times 9 \times 8 = 720$
   $\Rightarrow (10 - r)!$ must be 7!
   $\Rightarrow r = 3$

   (ii) $^{9}P_r = 3024$

   $$\Rightarrow \frac{9!}{(9-r)!} = 3024$$

   We have $9 \times 8 \times 7 \times 6 = 3024$
   $\Rightarrow (9 - r)!$ must be 5!
   $\Rightarrow r = 4$

   (b) (i) $1680 = 10 \times 12 \times 14 = 8 \times 7 \times 6 \times 5$
   Hence, n = 8 and r = 4
   (ii) Similarly, 5040 can be written as
   $= 10 \times 7 \times 72 = 10 \times 9 \times 8 \times 7$
   or
   $= 7 \times 6 \times 5 \times 4 \times 3 \times 2$
   Therefore, n = 10 and r = 4 or n = 7 and r = 6.

2. (a) $\dfrac{^nP_5}{^nP_3} = \dfrac{2}{1} \Rightarrow \dfrac{(n-3)!}{(n-5)!} = \dfrac{2}{1}$

   $\Rightarrow (n - 3)(n - 4) = 2$
   $\Rightarrow n = 5$

   (b) $^9P_5 + 5 \times ^9P_4 = ^{10}P_r$

   $$\Rightarrow \frac{9!}{4!} + 5 \times \frac{9!}{5!} = ^{10}P_r$$

   $$\Rightarrow \frac{9!}{4!} + \frac{9!}{4!} = ^{10}P_r$$

   $$\Rightarrow \frac{2 \times 9!}{4!} = ^{10}P_r$$

   $$\Rightarrow \frac{10 \times 9!}{5 \times 4!} = ^{10}P_r$$

   $$\Rightarrow \frac{10!}{5!} = ^{10}P_r$$

   $$\Rightarrow ^{10}P_5 = ^{10}P_r$$

   $\Rightarrow r = 5$

3. First let us select 3 candidates out of 17 candidates in $^{17}C_3$ ways. Then 3 scholarships can be awarded to them in 3! ways.

   The answer will be $^{17}C_3 \times 3! = ^{17}P_3$

4. By the same logic as above, the answer is $^6P_4$.

5. '0' cannot take the first place. So there are 9 possibilities for the first place. For the remaining 6 places, the 10 digits can appear in any of the places in 10^6 ways.
   Hence, total number of ways $= 9 \times 10^6$

6. There are a total of 17 stations.
   Any person boarding and getting down would be using any two of the 17 stations.
   $\Rightarrow$ A total of $^{17}P_2$ tickets of different kind must suffice any requirement whatsoever.

7. The first letter can be put in any of the four boxes.
   So there are 4 ways. The second letter can also be put in any of the four boxes and so on.
   The total number of ways $= 4 \times 4 \times 4 \dots$ 7 times

   $$= 4^7$$

8. As the number of digits is not specified, we can make either one digit or 2-digit or 3-digit or 4-digit or 5-digit numbers.

   $\Rightarrow$ Total number of ways $= (4) + (4 \times 4) + (4 \times {}^4P_2) +$

   $(4 \times {}^4P_3) + (4 \times 4!)$
   (As '0' cannot come in the beginning for 2-, 3-, 4-, or 5-digit numbers.)
   $= 4 + 16 + 48 + 96 + 96 = 260$

9. The total number of ways is 5!. Out of these there is equal probability of A speaking before B or B speaking before A.

   Hence, the answer $= \dfrac{1}{2}(5!)$

10. (i) The one thing that must come can take any of the 4 positions. Now out of the 9 remaining, we have to permute 3.

    $\Rightarrow$ Number of ways is $4 \times {}^9P_3$.
    (ii) In this case, we have to arrange 4 out of 9 things.

    $\Rightarrow$ The answer is $^9P_4$.

11. As all letters are distinct, we have the order of letters
    $= A\ B\ L\ O\ R\ U$
    Now with A in the beginning, the remaining letters can be permuted in 5! ways.
    Similarly, with B in the beginning, remaining letters can be permuted in 5! ways. With L in the beginning, the first word will be LABORU, the second will LABOUR. Hence, the answer is 5! + 5! + 2 = 242nd

12. The formula is $\dfrac{n!}{p!\, q!\, r!}$.

    $\Rightarrow$ The answer will be $\dfrac{17!}{7!\, 6!\, 4!}$.

13. Considering two delegates together as one object, $(20 - 2 + 1) = 19$ objects in a circle can be arranged in (18)! ways. Also the two delegates can interchange their positions in 2 ways. Hence, the answer 18! × 2.

14. It is a case of selection, i.e. combination.
So the direct answer is $^{10}C_6 \times {}^7C_3$.

15. The committee can be formed in the following ways.
  (a) 3 ladies   2 gentlemen
or (b) 4 ladies   1 gentlemen
or (c) All 5 ladies
$\Rightarrow$ The number of ways
$= {}^8C_2 \times {}^5C_3 + {}^8C_1 \times {}^5C_4 + {}^8C_0 \times {}^5C_5 = 321$

16. (i) The total number of triangles = $^{20}C_3 - {}^5C_3$
(ii) The total number of straight lines
$= {}^{20}C_2 - {}^5C_2 + 1$

17. The available digits are 0, 1, 2, 3, 4, 5.
Hence, the digits to be used so that the number is divisible by nine are 0, 2, 3, 4, or 0, 1, 3, 5.
Hence, the total number of such numbers is
2 × 3 × 3 × 2 × 1 = 36

18. There are 5 boxes and 5 hats.
Hence, the total number of ways = 5^5

19. If no box has to remain empty and all the hats are identical, then the number of ways = 1.

20. $^5P_5 = 5!$

21. $^5C_1 \times {}^5P_1 + {}^5C_2 \times {}^5P_2 + {}^5C_3 \times {}^5P_3 + {}^5C_4 \times {}^5P_4 + {}^5C_5 \times {}^5P_5$

22. $\dfrac{5!}{2!}$, since 2 hats are similar.

23. 2 × 4!. There are 4! for each of the cases when B1 has H1 and when B1 has H2.

24. Total number of cases = 5^5
Hence, the probability = $\dfrac{2 \times 5^4 - 5^3}{5^5} = \dfrac{9}{25}$

25. Total number of arrangements = 4×5^3

26. In 5^4 arrangements hat H_3 would be in B_3.

27. $^6P_5$

28. There are two cases.
Case (i):
Only one of H_5 or H_6 is among.
The boxes in which case the number of arrangements is $^5P_5$ or 5!.

Case (ii):
When both H_5 and H_6 are in the boxes, the number of arrangements then = $\dfrac{5!}{2!} \times {}^4C_3$

Total number of cases = $5! + \dfrac{5!}{2!} \times {}^4C_3$

29. $5! + \dfrac{5!}{2!} \times {}^4C_3 \times 5$

30. The first prize can be given to any of the four persons. Similarly, the second prize can be given to any of the four persons. Similarly, the third prize can be given to any of the four persons. So the total number of ways = 4 × 4 × 4 = 4^3 ways.

31. Two sets of parallel lines are required for a parallelogram.
Hence, the number of ways is $^mC_2 \times {}^nC_2$.

32. $^{100}C_{50} \times {}^{50}C_{30} \times {}^{20}C_{20} = \dfrac{100!}{50! \times 30! \times 20!}$

33. Since the mangoes are identical and they need to be divided into three groups, introduce two identical partitions to divide them.
The 12 items can now be arranged in $\dfrac{12!}{10! \times 2!}$ ways, i.e. 66 ways.
(You can use the formula $^{n+r-1}C_{r-1}$)

34.

Single step	Double step	Number of ways
10	0	$^{10}C_0 = 1$
8	1	$\dfrac{9!}{8!} = 9$
6	2	$\dfrac{8!}{6! \times 2!} = 28$
4	3	$\dfrac{7!}{4! \times 3!} = 35$
2	4	$\dfrac{6!}{2! \times 4!} = 15$
0	5	$\dfrac{5!}{5!} = 1$

$\therefore$ Total number of ways = 1 + 9 + 28 + 35 + 15 + 1
= 89

35. P (at least one winning) = 1 − P (both loosing)
$= 1 - \left(\dfrac{3}{7} \times \dfrac{7}{12} \right) = \dfrac{3}{4}$

36. 1 − P (None can solve)
$= 1 - \left(\dfrac{1}{2} \times \dfrac{2}{3} \times \dfrac{3}{4} \right) = \dfrac{3}{4}$

37. (i) For both red, we have:
Probability = $\dfrac{3}{8} \times \dfrac{6}{10} = \dfrac{9}{40}$
(ii) For both black, we have:
Probability = $\dfrac{5}{8} \times \dfrac{4}{10} = \dfrac{1}{4}$

38. The total number of 5-digit numbers with two 4s and starting

with a 4 is $1 \times {}^4C_1 \times 1 \times 10 \times 10 \times 10$

$\Rightarrow 4 \times 10^3 = 4000$

The total number of 5-digit numbers with two 4s and not

starting with 4 is $9 \times {}^4C_2 \times 10 \times 10$

$\Rightarrow 6 \times 900 = 5400$

Hence, the total number = 4000 + 5400 = 9400

39. The number of 5 digit number formed using 0, 2, 3, 4, 5 is
$4 \times 5^3 = 2500$

Each of (2, 3, 4, 5) will occur $\dfrac{2500}{4} = 625$ times in ten

thousand's place and each of (0, 2, 3, 4, 5) will occur in

$\dfrac{2500}{5} = 500$ times in other places.

The sum of all 5-digit numbers formed using digits
0, 2, 3, 4, 5 is

$625(2+3+4+5)(10000) + 500(2+3+4+5)(1111)$

$= 9527700$

Note: Repetitions are taken into consideration.

40. (i) The total number of selections of 3 books = ${}^9C_3$

(ii) The total number of ways of arranging 3 of the books =

${}^9P_3$

(iii) The total number of ways of dividing 9 books into 3

groups $= \left({}^9C_3 \times {}^6C_3 \times {}^3C_3\right)\left(\dfrac{1}{3!}\right) = \dfrac{9!}{(3!)^4}$

Note: $\dfrac{1}{3!}$ is a factor that comes because the groups are

not distinguishable as group 1, group 2, or group 3.
Had the groups been distinguishable the answer would be

${}^9C_3 \times {}^6C_3 \times {}^3C_3 = \dfrac{9!}{(3!)^4}$

41. Sum of '9' can be achieved in 4 ways (6, 3), (3, 6), (5, 4),
(4, 5).

Probability of a sum of 9 on the dice $= \dfrac{4}{36} = \dfrac{1}{9}$

Probability of at least 2 coins showing on head

$= {}^4C_2\left(\dfrac{1}{2}\right)^4 + {}^4C_3\left(\dfrac{1}{2}\right)^4 + {}^4C_4\left(\dfrac{1}{2}\right)^4 = \dfrac{11}{16}$

Hence, the required probability $= \dfrac{11 \times 1}{16 \times 9} = \dfrac{11}{144}$

42. Required probability

$P = A\bar{B}\bar{C} + B\bar{A}\bar{C} + C\bar{A}\bar{B}$

$= \dfrac{1}{3} \times \dfrac{5}{7} \times \dfrac{5}{8} + \dfrac{2}{7} \times \dfrac{2}{3} \times \dfrac{5}{8} + \dfrac{3}{8} \times \dfrac{2}{3} \times \dfrac{5}{7} = \dfrac{25}{56}$

43. P (Survival) = P (Not killed by any of the bullets)

$\qquad$ = 1 – P (killed by one or the other)

$1 – [0.4 + 0.6 \times 0.4 + 0.6 \times 0.6 \times 0.4 + 0.6 \times 0.6 \times 0.4]$

$\qquad$ = 1 – 0.8704

$\qquad$ = 0.1296

44. **Method 1:**

This is a problem of conditional probability. Suppose
A → Both odd
B → Sum even

We have to find $P(A\,|\,B)$.

Now $P(A\,|\,B) = \dfrac{P(A \cap B)}{P(B)} = \dfrac{\dfrac{{}^6C_2}{{}^{11}C_2}}{\dfrac{\left({}^6C_2 + {}^5C_2\right)}{{}^{11}C_2}} = \dfrac{3}{5}$

Method 2:

For the sum to be even the combinations are:
(1, 3), (1, 5), (1, 7), (1, 9), (1, 11), (2, 4), (2, 6),
(2, 8), (2, 10), (3, 5), (3, 7), (3, 9), (3, 11), (4, 6),
(4, 8), (4, 10), (5, 7), (5, 9), (5, 11), (6, 8), (6, 10),
(7, 9), (7, 11), (8, 10), (9, 11).
In all there are 25 combinations, of them the combinations
when both are odd, are 15.

Hence, the probability is $\left(\dfrac{15}{25}\right) = \dfrac{3}{5}$

1. b $\quad {}^8P_6 = \dfrac{8!}{(8-6)!}$

$\qquad\quad = \dfrac{8!}{2!} = 20160$

2. d $\quad {}^8C_6 = {}^8C_2 = \dfrac{8 \times 7}{1 \times 2} = 28$

3. c Since there are 5 letters in the word
So the total number of rearrangement is 5! – 1!

or ${}^5P_5 - 1$ that is 119.

4. a In the word AMERICA there are 7 letters and the letter 'A' is
coming twice.
So the total number of rearrangement

$= \dfrac{7!}{2!} - 1 = \dfrac{7 \times 6 \times 5 \times 4 \times 3 \times 2 \times 1}{2 \times 1} - 1 = 2519$

5. d In the word CALCUTTA, there are 8 letters
Letter C is coming twice
Letter A is coming twice
Letter T is coming twice
So the total number of rearrangements

$= \dfrac{8!}{2! \times 2! \times 2!} - 1 = 5039$

Career Launcher MBA

6. c   If any one of the consonant start, next 5 letters can be arranged in $\dfrac{5!}{2} = 60$ ways. And the first consonants itself can be selected in 4 ways.
Hence total number of arrangements = 4 × 60 = 240

7. b   Since both the cards are red, this can be done in $^{26}C_2 = \dfrac{26 \times 25}{2} = 325$ ways as pack of cards contains 26 red cards.

8. c   Since a four-digit number cannot start with 0, the thousand's place can be filled in 3 ways. For each of these ways the other 3 places can be filled in
3! = 6 ways. Total number of four-digit numbers that can be formed is = $^3C_1 \times 6 = 18$

9. d   Total number of matches = $^7C_2 = \dfrac{7 \times 6}{2} = 21$

10. d   Number of ways of exchange
= $^7C_1 \times {}^8C_1 = 7 \times 8 = 56$

11. d   The total number of ways is the number of arrangements of 7 different things taken 3 at a time
= $^7P_3 = \dfrac{7!}{(7-3)!} = 210$

12. c   Surely the number of ways of selection
= $^6C_2 = \dfrac{6 \times 5}{2} = 15$

13. e   The total number of ways of answering the 10 questions
= $^6C_4 \times {}^7C_6 + {}^6C_5 \times {}^7C_5 + {}^6C_6 \times {}^7C_4 = 266$

14. d   The total number of triangles that can be formed
= $^{12}C_1 \times {}^8C_2 + {}^8C_1 \times {}^{12}C_2 = 12 \times 28 + 8 \times 66 = 864$

15. b   The person can pick up one ball of each type in
$^5C_1 \times {}^6C_1 = 5 \times 6 = 30$ ways.

16. b   Let (n + 1), (n + 2), ..., (n + r) be r consecutive positive integers.
∴ Their product = (n + 1) × (n + 2) × (n +3)...(n + r)
$$= \dfrac{n!\{(n+1)\ (n+2)\ (n+3)\cdots(n+r)\}}{n!}$$
$$= \dfrac{(n+r)!}{n!} = \dfrac{(n+r)!}{r!\{(n+r)\ -r\}!} \times r! = {}^{n+r}C_r\ r!$$
Since n and r are integers, $^{(n+r)}C_r$ is also an integer. So the product is divisible by r!.

17. b   There are 13 spades
Two spades out of 13 spades can be taken out in $^{13}C_2$ ways

Total number of sample spaces = $^{52}C_2$

Required probability = $\dfrac{^{13}C_2}{^{52}C_2}$

18. d   There are 4 king
Two kings out 4 kings can be drawn in $^4C_2$ ways.
Required probability = $\dfrac{^4C_2}{^{52}C_2}$

19. d   There are 13 spades and 13 hearts. One spade and one heart can be taken out in $^{13}C_1 \times {}^{13}C_1$ ways.
Required probability = $\dfrac{^{13}C_1 \times {}^{13}C_1}{^{52}C_2}$

20. c   There are 4 king. One king can be taken out in $^4C_1$ ways. Now out of remaining 48 cards, any one card can be taken out in $^{48}C_1$ ways.
∴ Required probability = $\dfrac{^4C_1 \times {}^{48}C_1}{^{52}C_2}$

21. e   An arm can make signal in 4 ways.
∴ Five arms can make signals in $4^5 = 1024$ ways. But this includes the position of all the arms being in rest in which case no signal can be made.
Hence, total number of signals = 1024 − 1 = 1023

22. a   Since the events are independent, the outcome of one will not affect the other.
So the $P(A / B) = P(A) = 0.5$

23. b   Total number of cards = 100 {and not 99}
multiples of three = 33
∴ The required probability = 0.33

24. c   Since there are 6 red balls and all of them are of different sizes, the probability of choosing the smallest among them is $\dfrac{1}{6}$.

Practice Exercise 2 : Level 2

1. d   Letter a can be placed in all 4 positions.
Similarly b can be placed in all 4 positions.
Similarly c can be placed in all 4 positions.
Similarly d can be placed in all 4 positions.
So the total number of arrangement is
4 × 4 × 4 × 4 = 256

2. d   If not mentioned in the question, you have to assume that repetition is allowed. Hence $(4)^4 = 256$

3. a   Thousand's place can be filled only with two digits 4 or 5

Hundred's place can be filled in 3 ways.
Ten's place can be filled in 2 ways.
Unit's place can be filled in 1 way.
So total number of number formed = 2 × 3 × 2 × 1
= 12

4. b Thousands place can be filled in two ways.
Hundred's place can be filled with any of the 4 digits.
Ten's place can be filled with any of the 4 digits.
Unit's place can be filled with any of the 4 digits.
So the total numbers formed = 2 × 4 × 4 × 4 = 128.

5. b In every dice there are six spaces. So in 4 die it is
$6 × 6 × 6 × 6 = 6^4$ and in every coin there are two spaces.
So, in 3 coins it is 2 × 2 × 2.
So the total number of spaces = $6^4 × 2^3$.

6. d

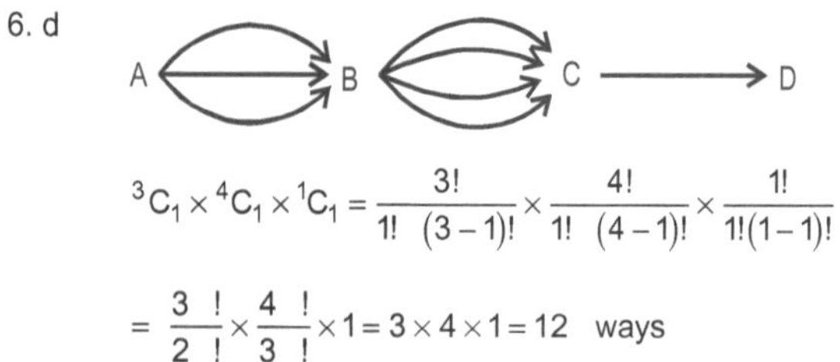

$$^3C_1 × {}^4C_1 × {}^1C_1 = \frac{3!}{1!\ (3-1)!} × \frac{4!}{1!\ (4-1)!} × \frac{1!}{1!(1-1)!}$$

$$= \frac{3\ !}{2\ !} × \frac{4\ !}{3\ !} × 1 = 3 × 4 × 1 = 12 \quad \text{ways}$$

7. d Either a candidate will solve the problem or he would not
solve. So the probability of solving is p = 1 and probability of
not solving is q = 1

$(p+q)^r$ i.e., $(1+1)^5 = 2^5$

The number of ways of solving at least 1 question is
$2^5 - 1 = 32 - 1 = 31$

Alternative method:
Number of ways of solving at least 1 question is candidate
may solve 1 question out of 5.
or he may solve 2 out of 5
or he may solve 3 out of 5
or he may solve 4 out of 5
or he may solve 5 out of 5
i.e. $^5C_1 + {}^5C_2 + {}^5C_3 + {}^5C_4 + {}^5C_5$

$$= \frac{5!}{4!} + \frac{5 × 4}{2} + \frac{5 × 4}{2} + 5 + 1 = 31$$

8. b Placing the 4 Ss in alternate positions can be done in one
way only, i.e
S_S_S_S
Now for this arrangement of the 4 Ss the rest 3 places can
be filled in 3 × 2 × 1 = 6 ways.
∴ Required number of ways = 6

9. e Three men can be selected from 4 men in 4_{C_3} ways.
For each of these ways 2 women can be selected from
4 women in 4_{C_2} ways.
∴ Total number of ways
$$= {}^4C_3 × {}^4C_2 = 4 × \frac{4 × 3}{2} = 24$$

10. c The required numbers of outcomes = 6 × 8 × 10 = 480

11. c The total number of possible arrangements are
$^5C_3 × {}^5C_1 + {}^5C_2 × {}^5C_2 + {}^5C_1 × {}^5C_3$
= 50 + 100 + 50 = 200

12. d Three programmes for first day can be selected in
$^6C_3$ ways. Now 3 programmes can be arranged in
3! ways and for the other day, they can be arranged in
3! ways. So total ways of presenting = $^6C_3 × 3! × 3!$

13. b There are 5 such odd integers, viz. 1, 3, 5, 7 and 9. So the
total numbers that can be formed is 5! = 120

14. c Since the number lies between 3000 and 4000, the digit in
the thousand's place must be 3. Also since the number is
divisible by 5, the digit in the unit's place must be 5. For the
rest 2 places the number of ways they can be filled is
$^4C_1 × {}^3C_1 = 4 × 3 = 12$ ways.

15. b Considering A and B together, they can be arranged in 4! ×
2! = 48 ways.

16. d The specified box may receive any of the 2 balls out of the
given 10 balls in $^{10}C_2$ ways. When 2 such balls have gone
the remaining 8 balls can be distributed in the remaining
3 boxes in 3^8 ways.
∴ Total number of ways = $^{10}C_2 × 3^8$

17. e Taking (A, B) as one member, the total number of ways that
the speakers can be arranged is 4! = 24.

18. c If none of the selected articles is defective, they must be
from the group of 6 non-defective articles. Hence, number
of ways = $^6C_3 = 20$

19. b $P_i = {}^iP_i = 1!$

∴ $1 + 1 · P_1 + 2 · P_2 + 3 · P_3 + \cdots + n · P_n$

$= 1 + 1 + (2 × 2!) + (3 × 3!) + \ldots + (n × n!)$

$$= 1 + \sum_{P=1}^{n} P\ .\ P\ ! = 1 + \sum_{P=1}^{n} \{ (P+1) - 1 \}\ P\ !$$

$$= 1 + \sum_{P=1}^{n} [\ (P+1)\ P\ ! - P\ !] = 1 + \sum_{P=1}^{n} \{(P+1)\ ! - P\ !\}$$

$= 1 + [(2! - 1!) + (3! - 2!) + (4! - 3!) + \ldots + [(n + 1)! - n!]]$
$= 1 + \{\{n + 1)! - 1!\} = (n + 1)!$

20. c **Case I:** Those 3 particular students join the party.
In that case we have to choose 2 more students from
remaining 9 students in $^9C_2 = 36$ ways.

Case II: Those 3 particular students do not join the party.
In that case we have to choose 5 students from remaining
9 students in $^9C_5 = 126$ ways.
∴ Total number of ways = (36 + 126) = 162.

Answers and Explanations

21. c   In the given word there are 5 vowels and 4 different consonants. Considering the 5 vowels as one unit total number of permutations is 5!. For each of these arrangements, the vowels can be arranged among themselves in 5! ways. Therefore, total number of different words = $(5!)^2 = 14400$

22. e   Since numbers between 100 and 1000 have 3 digits and every digit is either 4 or 5, so each of the 3 places in each term can be filled up only in 2 ways.
∴ Total number of such numbers = 2 × 2 × 2 = 8

23. c   Since there are 5 cups of each kind, prepared with milk or tea leaves added first, are identical hence total number of different possible ways of presenting the cups to the expert is $\dfrac{10!}{5! \times 5!} = 252$.

24. d   In a leap year there are 366 days, i.e. 52 weeks + 2 extra days. So to have 53 Sundays one of these two days must be a Sunday. This can occur in only 2 ways, i.e. (Saturday, Sunday) or (Sunday, Monday). Thus, number of ways = 2.

25. b   Choosing 5 sweets out of 10 sweets can be done in $^{10}C_5$ ways. Once he selects 5 sweets for one friend in any of the selections, remaining 5 will always go to the second friend.

Alternative method:

We can divide 10 sweets into 2 equal groups in $\dfrac{10!}{2!(5!)(5!)}$ ways

Now as two family friends can exchange these in 2 ways.

So total ways = $\dfrac{10!}{2!(5!)^2} \times 2! = \dfrac{10!}{(5!)^2}$

26. d   Number of 1-letter word = 4

Number of 2-letter word = $^4C_2 \times 2! = 12$

Number of 3-letter word = $^4C_3 \times 3! = 24$

Number of 4-letter word = $^4C_4 \times 4! = 24$

Therefore, the total number of words
= 24 + 24 + 12 + 4 = 64

27. b   Total number of ways of advertising
= $^4C_2 \times ^3C_1 \times ^2C_1 = 6 \times 3 \times 2 = 36$

28. a   Evidently, the number of numbers = 5!
Sum of the numbers = 24(1 + 3 + 5 + 7 + 9)(11111)
= 600(11111) = 6666600

29. c   We may select fruits of one particular category in 6 ways as none, one, ..., five. Therefore, total number of selections possible = 6^6. But this also includes the case in which we do not select any fruit. Therefore, number of required ways = $6^6 - 1$

1. d   **Case I:**
The person takes one step first. Then possible ways of reaching the top are (1, 1, 1, 1), (1, 1, 2), (1, 2, 1), (1, 3)

Case II:
The person takes 2 steps first. Then possible ways of reaching the top are (2, 1, 1), (2, 2)

Case III:
The person takes 3 steps first.
Then possible ways of reaching the top are (3, 1).

Case IV:
The person takes 4 steps.
This can occur in one way only, i.e. (4, 0).
∴ Total number of ways = 4 + 2 + 1 + 1 = 8

2. e   1 and 5 are odd numbers. Hundred notes of 1 and 5 can only add to give an even number, hence certainly cannot add up to Rs. 255. Hence, the answer is 0.

Alternative method:
Let the number of five-rupee notes = x
Then number of one-rupee notes = 100 − x
Therefore, x × 5 + (100 − x) × 1 = 255
∴ $x = \dfrac{155}{4}$, which does not give a whole number.
Therefore, number of ways = 0

3. d   Three cases: 1W + 6M, 2W + 5M, 3W + 4M,
i.e. $^9C_6 \times ^6C_1 + ^9C_5 \times ^6C_2 + ^9C_4 \times ^6C_3 = 4914$

4. c   Three possibilities: 1W + 6M, 2W + 5M, 3W + 4M
= $^6C_1 \times ^9C_6 + ^6C_2 \times ^9C_5 + ^6C_3 \times ^9C_4 = 4914$

5. c $^{10}C_5 + ^{10}C_4 + ^{10}C_4 = 672$

$^{10}C_5$: When both are not included.

$^{10}C_4$: When one of them is included.

6. d $2000 = 2^4 \times 5^3$
⇒ Three digits are 5 each.
Other two digits can be (2,8) or (4,4)
So, number of integers = $\dfrac{\lfloor 5}{\lfloor 3 \times \lfloor 2} + \dfrac{\lfloor 5}{\lfloor 3} = 30$

7. a   P (of Red ball in first attempt) = $\dfrac{4}{10} = \dfrac{2}{5}$
Here probability will remain same for the next two attempt.
∴ Probability = $\dfrac{2}{5} \times \dfrac{2}{5} \times \dfrac{2}{5} = \dfrac{8}{125}$

8. a   P(white ball) = $\dfrac{6}{10} = \dfrac{3}{5}$ and P(Red ball) = $\dfrac{2}{5}$
Hence probability of 2 white and 1 Red ball is
$\dfrac{3}{5} \times \dfrac{3}{5} \times \dfrac{2}{5} = \dfrac{18}{125}$

This will be multiplied by 3 as red ball can be attain in any of the attempt, i.e. $3 \times \dfrac{18}{125} = \dfrac{54}{125}$

9. c The following combinations are possible. First white, second red, third red, or first red, second white, third red or first red, second red, third white
So the probability

$$= \left(\dfrac{6}{10} \times \dfrac{4}{9} \times \dfrac{3}{8}\right) + \left(\dfrac{4}{10} \times \dfrac{6}{9} \times \dfrac{3}{8}\right) + \left(\dfrac{4}{10} \times \dfrac{3}{9} \times \dfrac{6}{8}\right) = 0.3$$

10. a Probability that A will pass in exam $= \dfrac{1}{3}$

$\therefore$ Probability that A will fail in exam $= \dfrac{2}{3}$

Probability that B will pass in exam $= \dfrac{1}{2}$

Probability that B will fail in exam $= \dfrac{1}{2}$

Probability that both will pass in the exam
= Probability that A will pass and probability that B will pass

$$= \dfrac{1}{3} \times \dfrac{1}{2} = \dfrac{1}{6}$$

11. b Probability that only one person will pass
So the possibility can be either A pass and B fails or A fails and B pass
i.e (A pass and B fail) or (A fail and B pass)

$$= \dfrac{1}{3} \times \dfrac{1}{2} + \dfrac{2}{3} \times \dfrac{1}{2} = \dfrac{1}{6} + \dfrac{1}{3} = \dfrac{1}{2}$$

12. d Probability that at least one person, will pass, so the possibilities can be (A pass and B fails), or
(A fails and B pass) or (Both A and B pass)

i.e. $= \dfrac{1}{3} \times \dfrac{1}{2} + \dfrac{2}{3} \times \dfrac{1}{2} + \dfrac{1}{3} \times \dfrac{1}{2} = \dfrac{1}{6} + \dfrac{1}{3} + \dfrac{1}{6} = \dfrac{2}{3}$

Alternate method: 1 – (None of them pass)

i.e. (A fails and B fails) $= 1 - \dfrac{2}{3} \times \dfrac{1}{2} = \dfrac{2}{3}$

13. d The probability that no one will pass

i.e., both A and B fails $= \dfrac{2}{3} \times \dfrac{1}{2} = \dfrac{1}{3}$

14. c There are only 6 cases, i.e. (1, 1), (2, 2), (3, 3), (4, 4), (5, 5) and (6, 6) out of a total of 36 cases when both the dice show equal values. So in the rest 30 cases one dice shows more value than the other. So the required probability

$$= \dfrac{30}{36} = \dfrac{5}{6}$$

15. b $P(A) = P(\text{get 2 apples}) = \dfrac{^{20}C_2}{^{30}C_2}$

$P(B) = P(\text{get 2 good fruits}) = \dfrac{^{23}C_2}{^{30}C_2}$

$$P(A \cap B) = \dfrac{^{15}C_2}{^{30}C_2}$$

$$P(A \cup B) = P\ (\text{required}) = P(A) + P(B) - P(A \cap B)$$

$$= \dfrac{338}{435}$$

16. e $P(A) = P(\text{getting a two}) = \dfrac{11}{36}$

$P(B) = P(\text{get a sum of seven}) = \dfrac{1}{6}$

$P(A \cap B) = \dfrac{2}{36}$

$\{(A \cap B) \Rightarrow (2, 5)\ \text{and}\ (5, 2)\}$

$\therefore P(A / B) = \dfrac{P(A \cap B)}{P(B)} = \dfrac{\frac{2}{36}}{\frac{1}{6}} = \dfrac{1}{3}$

17. c The required probability $= \dfrac{^{6}C_3 + {}^{4}C_3 + {}^{3}C_3}{^{13}C_3}$

$$= \dfrac{20 + 4 + 1}{286} = \dfrac{25}{286}$$

18. b We can get two tails in $^{3}C_2 = 3$ ways. We can get 3 tails in exactly one way. Thus, the required probability $= \dfrac{3 + 1}{8} = \dfrac{1}{2}$

19. c Probability of a bullet not hitting the target $= \dfrac{2}{3}$
Probability that none of the 3 bullets will hit the target

$$= \left(\dfrac{2}{3}\right)^3 = \dfrac{8}{27}$$

$\therefore$ Probability that the target will hit at least once

$$= 1 - \dfrac{8}{27} = \dfrac{19}{27}$$

20. c Probability that alternative 1 is correct $= \dfrac{1}{4}$

Probability that alternative 1 is wrong $= \dfrac{3}{4}$

$\therefore$ Probable net score $= \dfrac{1}{4} \times 1 \times 200 + \dfrac{3}{4}\left(-\dfrac{1}{4}\right) \times 200$

$= 50 + (-37.5) = 12.5$

21. c Here we can have 4 cases
(i) a is even, b is even.
(ii) a is odd, b is even.
(ii) a is even, b is odd.
(iv) a is odd, b is odd.
Out of these 4 cases, in case (ii) and case (iii), the sum will be odd. So the required probability $= \dfrac{2}{4} = \dfrac{1}{2}$

Career Launcher MBA

Answers and Explanations

22. e	Total number of five-digit numbers = 5! = 120. Now to be a multiple of 4, the last 2 digits of the number has to be divisible by 4, i.e. they must be 12, 24, 32, or 52. Corresponding to each of these ways there are 3!, i.e. 6 ways of filling the remaining 3 places.

∴ The required probability $= \dfrac{4 \times 6}{120} = \dfrac{1}{5}$

Practice Exercise 4 : Level 3

1. a	When 2 particular flowers are next to each other, we consider these 2 as 1 so that the number of permutations is 8! (since permutation is circular). But these 2 flowers can be arranged among themselves in 2! ways without affecting the position of the remaining flowers. Therefore, total number of different arrangements that can be made = 8! 2! Now 2 arrangements are possible in one garland.

Therefore, number of garlands $= \dfrac{1}{2} \times 8! \times 2! = 8!$

2. d	All 6 rings will be worn either in 1 or 2 or 3 or all 4 fingers.
(i)	If all rings are to be worn in one finger, we can use any of the 4 fingers, so 4 ways.
(ii)	If all the rings are to be worn in 2 fingers, first of all we have to select 2 fingers out of 4 in $^4C_2$ = 6 ways. Now in each of these selections we can have following arrangements.
a. 1 ring in first finger, 5 in 2nd finger
b. 2 rings in first finger, 4 in 2nd finger
c. 3 rings in first finger, 3 in 2nd finger
d. 4 rings in first finger, 2 in 2nd finger
e. 5 rings in first finger, 1 in 2nd finger
Therefore, number of ways = 5 × 6 = 30
(iii)	If all the rings are to be worn in three fingers, first of all we will have to select 3 out of 4 fingers in $^4C_3$ = 4 ways. Now in each of the selections, we can have the following arrangements.
(a) 4, 1, 1, in 3 ways
(b) 2, 2, 2 in 1 way
(c) 3, 2, 1 in 6 ways
Therefore, total number of ways = (3 + 1 + 6) × 4 = 40
(iv)	If 6 rings are to be worn in 4 fingers, we can select 4 fingers out of 4 in $^4C_4$ = 1 way.
Now we can have the following arrangements.
(a) 3, 1, 1, 1 in 4 ways
(b) 2, 2, 1, 1 in 6 ways
Total number of ways = 10
Total number of required ways is 4 + 30 + 40 + 10 = 84

3. b	It is given in the question that 4 particular person will sit on one fixed side and 2 particular person will sit on opposite side. Now we have to select 4 other persons who are going to sit with those 4 persons. This can be done in $^{10}C_4$ ways. Now 8 persons on both sides can be arranged in (8!) × (8!) ways.

So total ways $= {}^{10}C_4 \times 8! \times 8!$

Alternative method:
Four persons who wish to sit on one side can be seated in $^8P_4$ ways whereas the two persons who want to sit on the other side can be seated in $^8P_2$ ways.

The rest of the 10 persons can be seated in any of the rest 10 chairs in 10! ways.

∴ Total number of ways $= {}^8P_4 \times {}^8P_2 \times 10!$

4. e	The first child may be born on any of the 366 days in a leap year. (Mind you, you have 366 different days.) For each of these ways the second child can have a birthday on any of the remaining 365 days, and the third child on any of the remaining 364 days.
∴ Total number of ways = 366 × 365 × 364

5. d	If the numbers on the tickets are in AP, they have a common difference of either 1 or 2 or 3 ... or at most 9.
With common difference 1 there are 18 sets, viz.
(1, 2, 3), (2, 3, 4), (3, 4, 5), ..., (18, 19, 20).
With common difference 2 there are 16 sets, viz.
(1, 3, 5), (2, 4, 6), (3, 5, 7), ..., (16, 18, 20) and so on.
Finally, with common difference 9 there are only 2 sets, viz. (1, 10, 19) and (2, 11, 20)
∴ Total number of ways possible
= 18 + 16 + 14 + ... + 2 = 90

6. c	The total number of numbers that can be formed is 10 × 10 = 100. Of the 10 digits, the digits that lead to confusion because of looking at it upside down are 1, 6, 8, 9 and 0. From these 5 digits, number of two-digit numbers that can be formed = 5^2 = 25.
All of these will arise the confusion. But numbers like 00, 88, 11, 69 and 96 will not create confusion.
So the only number that will create confusion will be 25 – 5 = 20 such number.
And numbers that will not create confusion will be 100 – 20 = 80

7. c	Kapil is selected, then Sunil is not. Hence, in this case, there are $^8C_4$ ways of selecting the team, i.e. 70 ways.
Similarly, if Sunil is selected, there are 70 ways. And if both are not selected, there are $^8C_5$ = 56 ways.
Hence, total number of ways = 70 + 70 + 56 = 196

8. e	First choose the two letters that go into two correct envelopes. This occurs in $^5C_2$ = 10 ways. Now of the rest three letters, the first one chosen at random can be put in only 2 ways (i.e. in the two envelopes except its own), the second in 1 way and the 3rd will automatically go into the wrong envelope. This number of ways is 10 × 2 = 20

9. d	There are only two cases:
(1) BRB(B/R) — 26 × 26 × 25 × 49
(2) BBB(B/R) — 26 × 25 × 24 × 49
Total = 26 × 25 × 49(26 + 24) = 26 × 25 × 49 × 50
Just see '0' at the last place. Which is present only in (d).

For question 10:
As Y : S = 1 : 4
So Y = 1 and S = 4 or Y = 2 and S = 8 but Y = 1 and S = 4 is not possible because in that case V = 10, which is not possible.

8	1	6
7/3	5	3/7
4	9	2

10. b

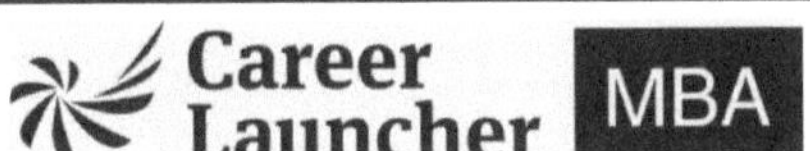

11. e
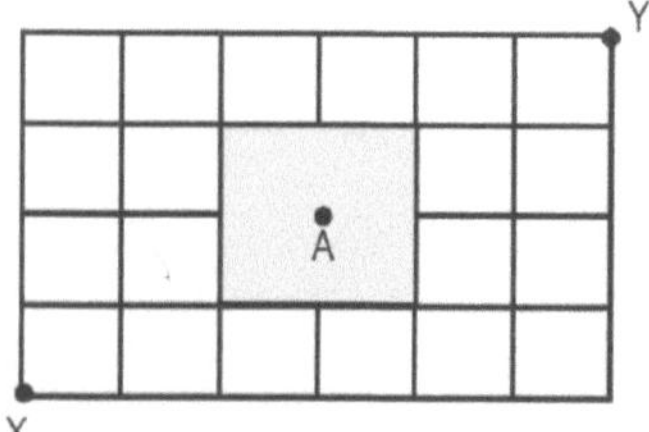

As the person cannot go through the park, only those routes that pass through A must be excluded from the total number of routes from X to Y.

Required number of routes = Total number of routes from X to Y – (Total number of routes from X to A × Total number of routes from A to Y).

Required number of routes

$$= \frac{10!}{6!4!} - \left(\frac{5!}{3!2!} \times \frac{5!}{3!2!} \right) = 110$$

12. e **Case 1:**

Exactly one zero.

The digit at the ten thousands place can be filled in 9 ways.

Zero can be in only one place out of 4 places, so there are 4 ways.

Other three place can be filled in 8, 7 and 6 ways respectively.

So total number of ways = 9 × 4 × 8 × 7 × 6 = 12096

Case 2:

Exactly two zeros

Total number of such numbers = 9 × 8 × 7 × 6 = 3024

Case 3:

Exactly three zeros

Total number of such numbers = 9 × 8 × 4 = 288

The total number of numbers = 12096 + 3024 + 288 = 15408

13. a If two dices are thrown total number of sample spaces = 36

Number of times when product of numbers on their top faces is less than 36.

(1 × 1) (1 × 2) (1 × 3) (1 × 4) (1 × 5) (1 × 6)
(2 × 1) (2 × 2) (2 × 3) (2 × 4) (2 × 5) (2 × 6)
(3 × 1) (3 × 2) (3 × 3) (3 × 4) (3 × 5) (3 × 6)
(4 × 1) (4 × 2) (4 × 3) (4 × 4) (4 × 5) (4 × 6)
(5 × 1) (5 × 2) (5 × 3) (5 × 4) (5 × 5) (5 × 6)
(6 × 1) (6 × 2) (6 × 3) (6 × 4) (6 × 5)

i.e., 35 times

$$\therefore \text{Required probability} = \frac{35}{36}$$

Or 1 – (probability of having product 36.)

$$= 1 - \frac{1}{36} = \frac{35}{36}$$

14. c P(A) = Probability that ball transferred from urn first to second

$$\text{is black} = \frac{4}{7}$$

P(B) = Probability that ball drawn from second urn is black.

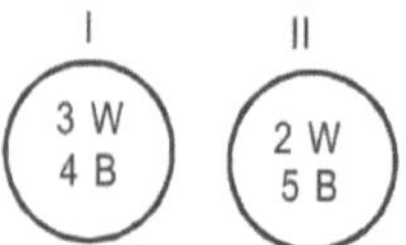

Case I:

If white ball goes to urn II

$$P(B_I) = \frac{3}{7} \times \frac{5}{8}$$

Case II:

If black ball goes to urn II

$$P(B_{II}) = \frac{4}{7} \times \frac{6}{8}$$

$$\therefore P(B) = \frac{3}{7} \times \frac{5}{8} + \frac{4}{7} \times \frac{6}{8} = \frac{39}{56}$$

$$P\left(\frac{A}{B}\right) = \text{Probability of event A when B has occurred}$$

= Probability that ball drawn from Ist urn is black when ball drawn from IInd urn is black

$$= \frac{P(A \cap B)}{P(B)} = \frac{\frac{4}{7} \times \frac{6}{8}}{\frac{39}{56}} = \frac{24}{39} = \frac{8}{13}$$

15. b Assuming all 3 numbers identical, we get 4 such numbers: 111, 222, 333, 444.   … (i)

Assuming 2 numbers are identical, one of which is zero, we get 3 such numbers,

i.e. 303, 300, 330   … (ii)

Now assuming zero is not part, we get 6 numbers, i.e. 411, 141, 114, 414, 441, 144.   … (iii)

Assuming all 3 numbers are different and zero is one of them, we get 8 such numbers, i.e. 102, 201, 120, 210, 204, 402, 420, 240.   … (iv)

Assuming all 3 numbers are different and zero is not a part of it, we get 12 such numbers, i.e. 123, 132, 312, 321, 213, 231, 234, 243, 423, 432, 324, 342   …(v)

Number of favourable cases = (i) + (ii) + (iii) + (iv) + (v) = 33

$$\therefore \text{The required probability} = \frac{33}{900}$$

16. e One-digit even numbers = 4

Two-digit even numbers = 45

Two-digit even numbers with no digit repeated = 45 – 4 = 41 (subtracting case of 22, 44, 66, 88)

Three-digit even numbers with non-repeated digits = Three-digit even number with zero in the last + Three-digit even number without zero

= 9 × 8 × 1 + 8 × 8 × 4 = 72 + 256

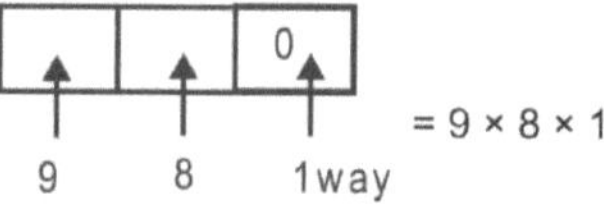

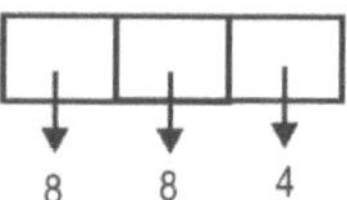

When zero is not there last place has 4 choice (2, 4, 6, 8)

At first place zero cannot come.

∴ 8 choices (repetition not allowed)

∴ Total choices = 9 × 8 × 1 + 8 × 8 × 4 = 72 + 256 ways

$$\text{Required probability} = \frac{4 + 41 + 72 + 256}{999} = \frac{373}{999}$$

Career Launcher MBA

17. c Observing the following table.

n	Σ	Nature
1	1	Odd
2	3	Odd
3	6	Even
4	10	Even
5	15	Odd
6	21	Odd
7	28	Even
8	36	Even

We see that we have 2 odds with 2 evens. This will go on till the card having $\Sigma 96$ giving us 48 even and 48 odd numbers. Now for n = 97 and 98 the Σn will be odd and for n = 99 the card will be even. Thus,

$$P \text{ (required)} = \frac{48+1}{99} = \frac{49}{99}$$

18. b We know that $\Sigma n = 91$ for n = 13

and $\Sigma n = 105$ for n = 14

∴ Out of the 99 cards, 13 cards will have numbers less than 100.

$\Rightarrow$ The required probability $= \dfrac{86}{99}$

19. c
$$P_s = \left(\frac{1001}{2002}\right) \times \left(\frac{1000}{2001}\right) + \left(\frac{1001}{2002}\right) \times \left(\frac{1000}{2001}\right)$$

Black Balls   Red Balls

OR $\boxed{P_s = \dfrac{1000}{2001}}$

and

$$P_d = \left(\frac{1001}{2002}\right) \times \left(\frac{1001}{2001}\right) + \left(\frac{1001}{2002}\right)\left(\frac{1001}{2001}\right)$$

RED – then – Black   Black – then – RED

$$\boxed{P_d = \frac{1001}{2001}}$$

$\Rightarrow$ difference $= \dfrac{1}{2001}$. Hence (c)

20. d Let the two digit number that Sudip thought be 'ab' where 'a' and 'b' are single digit numbers.

Therefore, $10a + b = k(a + b) + 3$, where k is a natural number $\Rightarrow k = \dfrac{10a + b - 3}{a + b}$. Also, a + b > 3

Possible values of a and b for which k is a natural number are tabulated below.

a	b
1	5
2	3
3	1, 3, 5, 9
4	7
5	1, 2, 9
6	No value of b
7	3, 5, 8
8	No value of b
9	4

Therefore, there are 14 such two-digit numbers that give a remainder of 3 when divided by the sum of the digits. Probability that Sonal thought of the same number as

Sudip $= \dfrac{1}{14}$

My Doubts

____

____

____

____

____

____

____

____

Printed by Libri Plureos GmbH in Hamburg,
Germany